Seizing the Word

Seizing the Word

History, Art, and

Self in the Work of

W. E. B. Du Bois

Keith E. Byerman

The University of Georgia Press

ATHENS & LONDON

© 1994 by the University of Georgia Press
Athens, Georgia 30602
All rights reserved
Designed by Kathi L. Dailey
Set in Walbaum and Gill Sans
by Tseng Information Systems, Inc.
Printed and bound by Thomson-Shore, Inc.
The paper in this book meets the guidelines for
permanence and durability of the Committee on
Production Guidelines for Book Longevity of the
Council on Library Resources.

Printed in the United States of America

98　97　96　95　94　C　5　4　3　2　1

Library of Congress Cataloging in Publication Data

Byerman, Keith Eldon, 1948–
　　Seizing the word : history, art, and self in the work of W. E. B.
　　Du Bois / Keith E. Byerman.
　　　　p.　cm.
　　Includes bibliographical references and index.
　　ISBN 0-8203-1624-5 (alk. paper)
　　1. Du Bois, W. E. B. (William Edward Burghardt), 1868–1963.
　　I. Title.
　　E185.97.D73B94　1994
　　305.896′73′092—dc20
　　[B]　　　93-30368

British Library Cataloging in Publication Data available

In memory of my father

Contents

. . . .

Preface

· · · · · · · ·

This book had its origins several years ago in the graduate work I was doing in American studies at Purdue University. W. E. B. Du Bois fit nicely into my interests in American literature, American intellectual history, and Afro-American studies. He was a way to get at the centrality of race in American culture within the principal literary and intellectual movements of his time. The multiplicity of his interests and the controversial character of virtually every stage of his career made it unlikely that my work would ever be boring or mechanical. But more fundamentally, he was essential to my understanding of American culture and the role of blacks in it. In some sense every other project I undertook was shaped implicitly by his definition of the African-American experience, especially in its hyphenated character, which he labeled double consciousness. It was this notion of duality or dialectic that made for me the most sense of the black literature and culture I chose to study. It became necessary finally to return to him to discover the sources of his authority.

None of the existing studies of Du Bois's life and work quite explained what I found so important in his thought, so I had to construct my own answer. What I sought was an explanation that linked the personal and the intellectual, that revealed the intense engagement with moral and ideological issues found even in texts that Du Bois represented as "objective." I have attempted in this study to identify tensions and patterns that cross disciplines and genres, not in order to reduce Du Bois to one thing, but precisely to present some of the complexity and conflict that run through his writing. The studies that have been done over the years have tended to focus on one or another aspect of his career. Francis Broderick in his 1959 study carefully examined Du Bois's training as a scholar and then shifted, as did Elliott Rudwick and August Meier in later works, to an emphasis on social activism. Rudwick, as a sociologist, is most clearly interested in Du Bois's leadership role, while Meier, as a historian, gives much attention to the conflict with Booker T. Washington and to Du Bois's place in historiography. Arnold Rampersad, in his groundbreaking study, writes primarily about Du Bois as a literary figure, although "literary" is used very broadly to cover a range of texts and ideas. More recently, Gerald Horne and Manning Marable have focused on his political radicalism and encouraged a reconsideration of the activities and writings of his later years.

My study attempts a more synthetic approach to Du Bois, primarily by examining him in terms of contemporary literary and cultural theory. My analysis is informed by notions of language as power, discourse as a site of conflict, and "self" and "race" as cultural constructs rather than unitary essences. The ideas of Jacques Lacan, Erik Erikson, and Michel Foucault serve as context for my analysis. In addition, much recent work in minority discourse, feminist theory, and studies in autobiography has been crucial in providing a way to articulate my ideas about Du Bois. The guiding notion is that his writing is always engaged in a confrontation with an existing discourse, which he seeks to deconstruct and then rebuild in his own terms. His challenges to the dominant order make it useful to define his career in terms of Lacan's Law of the Father, the notion that all who would speak must do so in terms of the patriarchal structure. Through this conceptualization, it is possible to see that those against whom Du Bois struggles are symbolic fathers, men (and Du Bois's antagonists are always men) who use their power and authority to impose rules and definitions of reality and the language used to represent it. Du Bois consistently questions such authority, often by labeling it arbitrary and corrupt.

In the process of revising historical, social, or political perceptions, he also subverts the discourse that has been used to express those perceptions. Foucault helps to clarify the nature of the various discourses— literary, social scientific, historical, political, autobiographical—that Du Bois speaks in and against. Thus, for example, he must question the way the historical profession operates in order to tell the story of blacks in Reconstruction; at the same time, he must remain within that discourse so that what he writes can be perceived as "history." What Foucault makes clear is the implicit power confrontation involved in such writing.

Moreover, Du Bois's career shows a clear pattern of the interaction of the personal, the intellectual, and the political. In addition to a number of autobiographical statements, both book- and essay-length, he consistently intertwined his personal and professional experiences; he often, for example, took as personal insults criticisms of his publications or activities. He had a propensity for attacking the integrity of those who questioned his positions on key or even minor issues, as we shall see throughout this study. Those he challenged were consistently men older and/or more powerful than himself, men who positioned themselves or were positioned by public perception as authoritative, patriarchal figures. They serve, metaphorically, as fathers representing Lacan's Law of the Father. Whether they are primarily professional, racial, or political figures, they symbolize in Du Bois's thought and experience the arbitrary authority of a patriarchal order that must be challenged if one's own integrity is to be maintained. In charting this pattern, I have found the work of Erik Erikson on identity to be immensely helpful. Du Bois fits generally into the configuration of the development and psychology of the great man that Erikson has delineated in his studies of Luther and Gandhi.

It is in the father-son trope that I have found a key to Du Bois's work. It allows examination of his principal scholarly contributions through consideration of his maneuverings within academic discourses, which generated by professional authorities, often disallowed the research and publication on racial issues that he wished to pursue. The trope also helps to reveal his manipulation of literary discursive systems, such as the postbellum plantation romance, which in his revision brought the displacement rather than the validation of the white Southern gentleman. Finally, in his writing about himself over many years, he creates an identity shaped by conflict over race, politics, and culture. He casts himself as the aggrieved son who must fight against dishonest or indifferent authorities for the soul of the race or the nation. He becomes the symbol of virtue and integrity, the self-sacrificing and even self-abnegating hero of his personal narratives.

The structure of this study follows this train of thought. The introduction establishes the pattern through analysis of a "program" written by Du Bois on his twenty-fifth birthday, a text which in a sense marks the beginning of his career as a writer. What is significant about this piece is not only that it spells out the goals of his life, but that the underlying assumptions and imagery are the ones that shape all his work. This discussion is followed by a chapter on *The Souls of Black Folk*, which is a kind of master text for Du Bois's oeuvre. Not only does it establish the famous tropes—double consciousness and the veil—for which he is known and which he persistently used, but it also incorporates the various genres—essay, historical-sociological article, fiction, poetry, autobiography—through which he voiced his understanding of the world. In this one short book, in effect, he articulated all the key messages of his career. All of his other works can in a sense be read as an elaboration of this one text.

The rest of the study is divided into three sections: history, art, and self. Within each section, works are discussed in chronological order, allowing for some analysis of the development of his ideas in each area. The divisions are somewhat arbitrary, since the analysis itself assumes that the same "master narrative" applies regardless of genre or discipline. But it is important to see Du Bois operating within and against a variety of discourses, since, I would finally argue, it is his ability to grasp almost intuitively the ideological (and especially racial) underpinnings of language and intellectual constructs that makes him one of the truly important figures in American intellectual history.

I wish to express my appreciation to the University Research Committee of Indiana State University for a grant that made possible two visits to the Du Bois Archive at the University of Massachusetts. Thanks are due also to Linda Seidman and other members of the staff at the Archive, without whose assistance this project could never have been completed, and to Joe Weixlmann, James Payne, Robert Fleming, Darlene Clark Hine, Chester Eisinger, and Lester Cohen, who read parts of this study in various stages of its development. *Contra* Du Bois, in my experience scholarship is at least as often camaraderie as it is conflict.

Seizing the Word

Introduction

. . . .

The Word and the Self

. . . .

        For his twenty-fifth birthday, W. E. B. Du Bois wrote out a program for the occasion and appended to it a statement of his philosophy and goals. Nearly seven decades later, he incorporated this material into his last autobiography. Both the act of inscribing and the content of the writing are significant for the present study. The program is laid out in formal fashion, much as others would be for public celebrations of his birthdays many years later. Even in the privacy of an apartment in Berlin, he represents himself as on a public stage, recording for posterity his performance of a ritual of passing. The program schedules time for music, letter-writing, meals, and a seminar; more significantly, it includes a midnight "sacrifice to the *Zeitgeist*," a short period of reflection about his parents, and the dedication of his library to his mother's memory.

Reinforcing the sense of self-importance implicit in such a program is a thirteen-page statement, which begins with an explanation of how the ritual was executed: "This programme was very pleasantly carried out. I arose at eight and took coffee and oranges[,] read letters[,] thought of my parents[,] sorry, cried, etc."[1] It is noteworthy that the thought about his parents is scripted in the program and thus that his emotion is part of the performance of the ceremony. This performatory quality is reinforced by the "etc.," suggesting a fixed sequence of response. Thus, emotion is contained and controlled in the design of language. It becomes part of the symbolizing and ritualizing of the self that is the pattern of Du Bois's life and writings. So too is the statement, which is, in effect, a kind of instant history of his experience.

The ritual aspect becomes especially clear in the zeitgeist ceremony, library dedication, and extended statement. He calls the ceremony a "curious little sacrific" one, and the element of sacrifice pervades his writings. At this opening moment in his career, he conceives his life in terms of dedication to a cause; he already sees himself at odds with the world. He says in the statement: "I am firmly convinced that my own best developement [sic] is not one and the same with the best developement [sic] of the world and here I am willing to sacrifice. . . . The general proposition of working for the world's good becomes too soon sickly sentimentality" ("Program," 6–7). The ends of the self must be given up for the greater good, but more than this self-surrender is the question of the value of that effort if it becomes mere sentimentality. It will become apparent that the despair implicit in this ceremony is a subtext of much of Du Bois's work.

The dedication of his library to his mother suggests the linkage of the personal and the intellectual. Mary Burghardt Du Bois, who died the year her son graduated from high school, had raised him alone from the time he was an infant. She had supported his early education through domestic labor even though her health was poor. In this sense, her sacrifice created the possibility of his academic career, making the dedication emotionally appropriate.

But he also does not talk about her in his commentary on the program and in fact says little about his feelings anywhere in his work. Her death, for example, is always mentioned only in passing in the autobiographical works. While this may be read simply as characteristic reticence about private matters, it also serves to conceal and suppress a key complexity in their relationship. Several years before marrying Alfred Du Bois, Mary had an illegitimate son by a first cousin. This child, Idelbert, was acknowledged within the Burghardt family, and Du Bois himself maintained at least indirect contact with him for several years. What this information does is problematize the mother as ideal, even though she is highly virtuous.[2] She is always already impure, and the son is always already displaced. Though Du Bois claims her primary attention and affection by all accounts, Idelbert, even in his absence, is always present as the usurper. Apotheosizing the mother through the dedication becomes a way of fictionalizing the past.

Such family history is important in that it helps to explain one of the key patterns in Du Bois's writing. Black women are consistently both praised and seen as impure. Even his fictional heroines are sexually experienced when they meet the heroes. In a chapter in *The Gift of Black Folk* intended as a paean to black women, he states without qualification that under slavery they commonly accepted their roles as "concubines."[3] Moreover, running through much of his work, regardless of genre, is figurative language that metaphorically represents the black race as feminine and also impure. The experience of slavery victimized and corrupted it, and it is generally passive in dealing with the world. In the "Program," Du Bois dedicates himself to "raising" the race, which must be elevated precisely because it has been degraded morally and spiritually. The role of the good racial son, just like that of the biological one, is to uplift the fallen mother.

The presence of the mother draws attention to the absence of the father, who is specifically mentioned in neither the program nor the statement. Alfred Du Bois is an ambiguous figure in his son's various recollections. Very light-skinned, with an uncertain past and no fixed employment, he is said according to the most reliable report to have married Mary Burghardt over her family's strong objections, and then, after two years and the birth of William, left to find work. The Burghardts discouraged their daughter from joining him, and, for all intents and purposes, Alfred Du Bois ceased to exist for his son. Psychologically, of course, the boy would experience his absence as abandonment.[4] This experience offers a valuable interpretive key for the present study. We have, in effect, the inversion of Erik Erikson's description of Martin Luther; here it is the overwhelming absence rather than the presence of the father that is formative for the son.[5] One pattern that is apparent in Du Bois's life and work is the identification of father figures, from at least Booker T. Washington to Joseph Stalin. Moreover, at virtually every stage, there is a sense of betrayal by that father, usually on moral grounds. Similarly, in the historical and fictional works, fathers, whether literal or symbolic, fail to act in ways consistent with the moral order. From the Founding Fathers' compromising on slavery to Harry Truman's facilitating imperialism, powerful men consistently abandon the path of virtue for the sake of self-interest. From Judge Henderson in "The Coming of John" (1903) to Colonel

Breckinridge of *The Black Flame* trilogy (1957–61), fictional patriarchs act in the same way. The absent father in life becomes the corrupt, threatening father in writing.

The family-romance pattern is completed with the necessary self-fathering of the son. If the father cannot be a model, then the son must generate an identity of his own. The "Program" is in fact an effort at self-inscription. At the moment he begins his career, Du Bois seeks to define his philosophy and his future. This moment comes at precisely the age Erikson suggests is typical for great men to articulate such a self-definition.[6] Though raised in genteel poverty and of a race often assumed, even in a tolerant place like Great Barrington, Massachusetts, to have little intellectual capacity, Du Bois not only completes bachelor's degrees from Fisk and Harvard but then does advanced work at Harvard and Berlin, earning a doctorate from the former a year after his self-dedication. His university training becomes the equivalent of Luther's days in a monastery. Having no paternal model for black male adulthood and experiencing himself as different and special, he defers commitment to the world until he can find a role and a discourse that structures that difference. He finds that structure, as is evident already in the "Program," in academic, literary, and moral (often moralistic) expression. He seeks to develop a trope that is his own of the trinity of Goodness, Truth, and Beauty:

> What is life but life, after all? Its end is its greatest and fullest self—this end is the Good. The Beautiful its attribute—its soul, and Truth is its being. Not three commensurable things are these, they [are] three dimensions of the cube—mayhap God is the fourth, but for that very reason incomprehensible. The greatest and fullest Life is by definition beautiful, beautiful,—beautiful as a dark passionate woman, beautiful as a golden hearted school girl, beautiful as a grey haired hero. That is the dimension of *breadth*. Then comes Truth—what is, cold and indisputable: What is *heighth*. Now I will, so help my soul, multiply breadth by height, Beauty by Truth & then Goodness, strength, shall bind them together into a solid Whole. Wherefore? I know not now. Perhaps Infinite other dimensions do. This is a wretched figure and yet it roughly represents my attitude toward the world. ("Program," 5–6)

This passage reflects what Erikson calls the need at such a moment to find one's own language—the voice and the word.[7] Though admitting that the trope he generates is inadequate, Du Bois still finds it an expression of himself and his beliefs, so much so that he copies it verbatim into his last autobiography sixty-seven years later. He has taken the philosophical conventions of his time and made them his own. And it is not surprising that in it he links science (the cube itself and "cold, indisputable Truth"), morality, and narrative (the "dark passionate woman" and the "grey haired hero"). It is precisely this complex that will shape the thought and writing of his career, though, as we will see, it will more often be problematic than his geometric trope implies.

Having created for himself a meaningful structure of values, he then proceeds to identify the specific means by which he can realize these values: "I therefore take the work that the Unknown lay in my hands [and] work for the rise of the Negro people, taking for granted that their best developement [sic] means the best developement [sic] of the world" (7). Since he has shortly before stated that his own development is not identical to that of the world, his dedication becomes self-sacrifice. He articulates here one of the fundamental principles of his lifelong "ideology."[8] Underlying the political shifts in his career from accommodationism to integrationism to black nationalism to Stalinist Marxism is a belief that true self-fulfillment comes only through self-effacement. Virtue is found in those willing to give up personal advantage for the sake of a transcendent moral order. All of his major works are in some sense the drama of the testing of character. Regardless of genre, discipline, or overt ideology, his master narrative remains the same. Opportunities for self-sacrifice or temptations for self-aggrandizement are presented; some (John Brown, the talented tenth,[9] the Soviet Union, himself) become heroic in their insistence on principle, while most (the Founding Fathers,[10] Booker T. Washington, the black bourgeoisie, white Southerners, contemporary America) fail the test and are thereby self-condemned.

This essentially religious view, the idea that those who would find themselves must lose themselves, helps to explain one aspect of his career. He persistently takes more and more radical positions, putting himself at odds not only with the dominant order but also with his allies. The identification with marginalized groups (blacks and political radicals) in part guarantees that the self will not gain personal advantage. But when these groups achieve some success, then it becomes necessary to move further to maintain one's sacrificial status. The irony of Du Bois's life is that the very success of his work for social justice necessitated a repudiation of the means of success. Having struggled through the NAACP, for example, for integration, he would assume a position that he deliberately labeled "self-segregation," a position that required him to resign from the organization. He joined the American Communist Party at a time (1961) when it had been decimated and thoroughly discredited even among radicals and at the very moment when the mainstream civil rights movement was reaching its high point.

This pattern of self-marginalization can partially be explained psycho-biographically. Because the fatherless Du Bois with the always already corrupted mother cannot experience the primal conflict of resistance and desire through which the self is shaped, he must find outside himself, in what Jacques Lacan calls the Law of the Father, the source of selfhood. The notion of transcendent values to which one must submit fits closely Du Bois's statement and the master narrative that informs all his writing. Moreover, the conflict denied him in childhood must repeatedly be enacted in his life and work. He identifies father figures, for himself or the race or the nation, and then attacks them for their betrayal of the moral order. But his attacks lead to some loss on his part (a kind of castration), which paradoxically demonstrates the virtue of his gesture. The last sentence of his program establishes this view: "I will go in to the king—which is not according to the law and if I perish—*I perish*" ("Program," 13). By quoting the Old Testament Esther, Du Bois focuses his ideological (again in Erikson's sense) position. In support of moral principle and in defense of a despised people, Esther is willing to risk her life. Her action is a deliberate violation of civil law in the name of a higher law. The self here chooses its sacrificial destiny and is thereby heroic.

But the self is not thereby rendered invisible. After all, Esther's (and Du Bois's) line uses the pronoun "I" three times. Self-sacrifice in fact becomes the vehicle for self-assertion and self-empowerment. The self armed with the Law of the Father becomes a force that cannot be ignored. Near the end of his statement, Du Bois envisions his future: "These are my plans: to make a name in science, to make a name in literature and thus to raise my race. Or perhaps to raise a visible empire in Africa thro' England, France or Germany" (12–13). The making of a name for the self becomes the means of racial service. The enhancement of the self equals the enhancement of the race. The profound egotism of the statement reflects the views of such literary mentors as Carlyle and Emerson, in that Du Bois casts himself in the role of great man with a purpose that extends far beyond the self. The particular means by which he would enact this destiny are in fact the ones he undertook: science, through *The Suppression of the Slave-Trade* (1896), the *Atlanta Studies* (1896–1913), and *The Philadelphia Negro* (1899); literature, through *The Souls of Black Folk* (1903) and novels, poetry, and pageants; and "empire," through the Niagara movement, the NAACP, the Pan-African movement, and the peace movement.

Moreover, he kept focus on his name through numerous autobiographical works in which he placed himself at the moral and often ideological center of the race's development. These works, such as *Darkwater* (1921) and *Dusk of Dawn* (1940), were themselves mixtures of social science, literature, and ideological manifesto. Through them all runs the centrality of the "I," naming itself, the race, and the world in which they must live. Approximately every twenty years, Du Bois reinscribed that self and its place in a major work, in effect introducing himself to each new generation so that his name would not be forgotten or his voice lost. To maintain his status as uplifter of the race, he had also to reveal the new place at which he had arrived so that the race could follow.

What empowers him to assume this role is his confidence in his grasp of truth. In none of the autobiographies does he admit error, even though his positions change drastically over the years. They are consistently narratives of education, in which he knows more than he did and thus has a fuller view of truth. This certainty leads to what is probably the most controversial claim of the present study: that "race" is at least in part a metaphor in Du Bois's work for his family romance, in which the virtuous son, armed with the Law of the Father, challenges the corrupt father in order to claim for virtue the always already violated mother. By supplanting the father, the son can install an "empire" of reason, morality, and beauty to replace arbitrary power and self-interest. This narrative holds in Du Bois's fiction, his historical and sociological works, and his life stories. Whether he is writing about race, economics, peace, or the self, he is essentially telling the same story. It is the need to tell this tale that is the impelling force in his *écriture*.

It also suggests why he undertakes so many approaches. Everywhere the father is empowered and so everywhere his word must be challenged. Racist distortions and ideology pervade literature, social science, popular culture, and all the other discourses of modern society. These discourses must be subverted and replaced with ones in which the black sons (and daughters) can speak and be spoken of in affirmative ways. Similarly, an economic order based on greed is validated through various means and must be questioned wherever found, even within the race. Fiction, political and social commentary, biography, and historiography can be made to deconstruct the dominant ideology of self-interest. The central drama remains the same across subject, genre, discipline, and time.

The approach of the present work is not to interpret Du Bois's writing primarily in psychoanalytical terms. Rather, it is to identify a pattern in his thought that takes a wide variety of forms and that often generates tensions and conflicts with the usually overtly expressed intentions of his works. Du Bois repeatedly tells us how to read his texts. This study seeks to indicate the ambiguities, complexities, and even subversions of these reading instructions that can be found. The effect of the analysis is not to reject overt meanings, but to show how his language carries far more possibilities than are readily apparent. Du Bois presents to us subtextually an endless struggle of power and oppression, father and son, black and white in both the racial and moral senses. It is a struggle not only for social justice, but for control over language, which for Du Bois is the greatest power. He would seize the word, so as to name the world:

> I rejoice as a strong man to run a race. And I am strong—is it egotism, is it assurance—or is [it] the silent call of the world spirit that makes me feel that I am royal and that beneath my sceptre a world of kings shall bow. The hot dark blood of that black forefather—born king of men—is beating at my heart, and I know that I am either a genius or a fool. O I wonder what

I am—I wonder what the world is—I wonder if life is worth the *Sturm*. I do not know—perhaps I never shall know: But this I do know: be the Truth what it may I will seek it on the pure assumption that it is worth seeking—and Heaven nor Hell, God nor Devil shall turn me from my purpose till I die. ("Program," 2–3)

Master and Man

The Souls of Black Folk as Mastering Narrative

The Souls of Black Folk has been seen by many as Du Bois's most important work. For decades, he received letters from readers about its effects on them, either as blacks struggling to come to terms with experiences of racism or whites trying to comprehend the reality of black life. It has been the most commented on of his writings from a variety of perspectives. But its significance for the present analysis is in its status as a master text in the senses of its incorporation of the principal ideas and methods of Du Bois's thinking, of its thematic concern with masters and men, and of its attempts to displace, in one work, the various discourses of domination operating among his contemporaries.

Many aspects of the book suggest Du Bois's relationship with the dominant culture. The epigraphs for each chapter join a few lines of poetry, usually from a nineteenth-century canonical source, with a few measures from a spiritual. The poetry, in addition to setting the theme and tone of the particular essay, helps to demonstrate Du Bois's own status as a man of culture in the Western tradition.[1] The juxtaposition of this literature with folk melodies implies that blacks have articulated similar feelings and thoughts through their own expressive forms. Thus, the pairing symbolizes common humanity despite racial difference, a claim not taken for granted at the beginning of the twentieth century.

What is also worth noting about the chapter headings is that it is Du Bois who makes the pairings. He is the one able to see the connection between two distinct cultural traditions and to make their similarities apparent to his audience. His is the third voice, the one that binds black and white, that finds identity in difference, the one that can speak across the racial divide. He plays the anomalous role, in the context of American racial ideology, of cultured black man. And though within the book he frequently adopts the position of outsider, whether by choice or compulsion, the discourse of his text is consistently that of a man who has thoroughly absorbed the dominant culture. Many of its fundamental values and ideals are his own.

What is crucial for him is the distinction between these principles and others, such as racism and greed, that he considers to be significant errors of the society. It is this position—the dominant culture is essentially good and true but burdened with mistakes and distortions—that he maintains throughout his career. His lifelong critique of America, then, is aimed at deconstructing those falsehoods, including those asserting that racial and economic domination are natural and basic to the culture. Thus, in *Souls* and throughout his work, he seeks to shape a true discourse out of the distortions that history and human folly have created. He stakes his position at the center of the culture rather than on its margins and then challenges those who would displace and control him. In this sense, he seeks not to supplant patriarchal culture but to denounce its false fathers.

His place within the culture is established not only by the epigraphs but also by the wealth of literary, philosophical, religious, and historical allusions in his text. Also, its language is often self-consciously poetic or witty; the style places its producer squarely within the genteel tradition of late-nineteenth-century writers. Moreover, the discursive forms of elegy, personal essay, exposition, and polemic are used with deep regard for their traditions.[2] The form and style imply a profoundly conservative author who respects the values of the culture that has trained him.

This traditionalist manner is strategically useful, since the matter of the text is often subversive. Du Bois employs conventional forms to assert the spiritual equality of blacks with whites and to undermine the nation's justifications for racial oppression. From his perspective, both of these related but distinct efforts are necessary. Neither showing the possibilities and problems of black life nor attacking racism alone would have an adequate effect, since in Du Bois's view the problem is dialectical. Both black and white aspects must be addressed; both blacks and whites must face their responsibilities. In this sense, he is attempting, through *Souls*, to redefine the entire question. The approach is encyclopedic: the essays are personal, sociological, aesthetic, historical, biographical, and polemical, with a short story added. On most of the discursive grounds on which blacks have been subordinated he seeks to generate new patterns of meaning.

The first few lines of the Forethought indicate the complexity of his approach. On the surface, they are an old-fashioned appeal to the readers' forebearance:

> Herein lie buried many things which if read with patience may show the strange meaning of being black here at the dawning of the Twentieth Century. This meaning is not without interest to you, Gentle Reader; for the problem of the Twentieth Century is the problem of the color line. I pray you, then, receive my little book in all charity, studying my words with me, forgiving mistake and foible for sake of the faith and passion that is in me, and seeking the grain of truth hidden there. I have sought here to sketch, in vague, uncertain outline, the spiritual world in which ten thousand thousand Americans live and strive.[3]

The black writer humbles himself before his white "Gentle Reader," but the posture is parodic in that the whole purpose of the book is to provide a massive dose of the racial truth whites have refused to accept. What has been "buried" is the black reality whites have suppressed, not the multiple meanings of that reality Du Bois clearly offers. Those meanings are "strange" not because blacks are truly alien, but because whites have defined them as other and thus denied them a common humanity. Moreover, this "little book" takes as its large subject what it labels as *the* problem of the new century. In addition, there is nothing "vague" or "uncertain" about the history and experience of blacks detailed in *Souls'* fourteen chapters; they are filled with concrete, precise information and carefully structured arguments and narratives. Finally, the appeal for charity and forgiveness comes from an author who opens his first chapter with an attack on just such people as his "gentle readers" for their racial insensitivity. Thus, the Forethought is an act of "signifying"[4] in which the meaning is the very opposite of its appearance. Du Bois invokes a literary convention to create a mask of submissiveness which he then rips apart throughout his text. He manipulates the language of the dominant culture in order to achieve mastery over the cultural masters.

"Of Our Spiritual Strivings" opens, not with a picture of those struggles, but with an assault on those who consider themselves sympathetic to blacks. The narrator speaks in the first person about being defined as a "problem" and about those responsible for such a designation. They are not violent Southern racists, but Northern liberals who see blacks not as persons but as a political difficulty. They seek to make contact, not with the individual, but with a certain ideological value. They can speak of good blacks they have known or their opposition to Southern atrocities. But, as Du Bois points out (*Souls*, 7), these are only tropes for the real question: "How does it feel to be a problem?"

Crucial to comprehending Du Bois's strategy is understanding why he makes sympathetic whites—those who, in fact, are most likely to read his book—the initial target for attack. One answer is that they are the ones who most fully control the national culture; they, as the economic, political, and cultural establishment, have the patriarchal prerogative of defining and shaping not only black life but also the experiences of the entire South. If Du Bois is to achieve his purpose of making blacks a part of American culture, he must deconstruct and defamiliarize the assumptions of those who exercise cultural hegemony. He goes at this by creating his own version of white speech acts; by pointing out what whites *really* mean when they speak to him, he reverses the act of racial definition.

Another aspect of strategy in these early pages is the use of the first-person perspective. It is to the narrator directly that Northern whites direct their false sympathy; it is he who experiences being a "problem." And the first instance of overt racism is recounted from Du Bois's Massachusetts childhood:

> In a wee wooden schoolhouse, something put it into the boys' and girls' heads to buy gorgeous visiting-cards—ten cents a package—and exchange. The exchange was merry, till one girl, a tall newcomer, refused my card,—

refused it peremptorily, with a glance. Then it dawned on me with a certain suddenness that I was different from the others; or like, mayhap, in heart and life and longing, but shut out from their world by a vast veil. (7–8)

The girl rejects Du Bois's participation in a social ritual and, more specifically, his literal word by refusing his card. And though she is the "newcomer" and he the native son, her affront has the effect of revealing to him his marginal status in his own world.[5] His immediate response is a violent one: "That sky was bluest when I could beat my mates at examination-time, or beat them at a foot-race, or even beat their stringy heads" (*Souls*, 8). But he soon realizes that it is language that is the key: "Alas, with the years all this fine contempt began to fade; for the worlds I longed for, and all their dazzling opportunities, were theirs, not mine. But they should not keep these prizes, I said; some, all, I would wrest from them. Just how I would do it I could never decide: by reading law, by healing the sick, by telling the wonderful tales that swam in my head" (8).

Wresting the word from white control, in this and other texts, means both invalidating white claims to it and generating his own meanings. The trope for this dialectical effort that runs through *Souls* is mastery. The book comprises an American history of racial domination, an exposition of the psychological, social, political, and moral effects of that domination, an exposé of false masters, both black and white, and paeans to black mastery of language.

He begins the process by generating a psychocultural definition of blackness in America:

After the Egyptian and Indian, the Greek and Roman, the Teuton and Mongolian, the Negro is a sort of seventh son, born with a veil and gifted with second-sight in this American world,—a world which yields him no true self-consciousness, but only lets him see himself through the revelation of the other world. It is a peculiar sensation, this double-consciousness, this sense of always looking at one's self through the eyes of others, of measuring one's soul by the tape of a world that looks on in amused contempt and pity. One ever feels his twoness,—an American, a Negro; two souls, two thoughts, two unreconciled strivings; two warring ideals in one dark body, whose dogged strength alone keeps it from being torn asunder. The history of the American Negro is the history of this strife,—this longing to attain self-conscious manhood, to merge his double self into a better and truer self. In this merging he wishes neither of the older selves to be lost. He would not Africanize America, for America has too much to teach the world and Africa. He would not bleach his Negro soul in a flood of white Americanism, for he knows that Negro blood has a message for the world. He simply wishes to make it possible for a man to be both a Negro and an American, without being cursed and spit upon by his fellows, without having the doors of Opportunity closed roughly in his face. This, then, is the end of his striving: to be a co-worker in the kingdom of culture, to escape both death and isolation, to husband and use his best powers and his latent genius. (8–9)

This long passage defines the position Du Bois holds throughout his career. He places blacks in the context of cultures, not races or nations, and gives them equal status in this context.[6] But he immediately problematizes his own characterization. While blacks have special, magical gifts, in the context of white American cultural hegemony they are denied control over their identity. They are compelled to accept white definitions of their being. The much-commented-on term Du Bois uses for this mental state, double consciousness, is richly ambiguous. In psychological theory of the time, including that of Du Bois's mentor William James, "double consciousness" was a form of mental illness in which the victim experienced self-alienation, an inability to maintain a coherent self-image.[7] It is unclear whether Du Bois intends the term to carry the full connotation of a pathological state or intends it metaphorically as a cultural condition. On the one hand, "this sense of always looking at one's self through the eyes of others" implies a lack of self-definition, a dependence on others for one's image. On the other hand, to say "one ever feels his twoness,—an American, a Negro" suggests a cultural and political situation of marginality in which the problem is not lack but excess of self. Blacks in this case are not nothing, but two things, both of which are coherent and meaningful; the difficulty is in successfully joining them for a greater self and, by implication, a greater culture. Both "white Americanism" and "Africanized America" are misguided ideas in this view; each is a form of hegemony that denies the society its full pluralistic, multicultural potential. Thus, psychological health for blacks provides cultural health for America.

But this is only *in potentia*. The ambiguity about the present meaning of being black remains and, even if not deliberate, is certainly useful to

Du Bois's thinking. On the one hand, he has to explain black economic, political, and, as he often points out, moral failures. Racial intolerance and discrimination could not be the only explanation to a society that held to a Protestant ethic of individual responsibility and a belief in the interrelationship of biology and morality. As shall be seen, Du Bois himself partially accepted these beliefs. In this situation, it was useful to be able to explain black failure at least in part as a function of pathology. Slavery and racism had deprived many blacks of a sense of self, and so they lacked the psychological resources to compete in the modern world. This would help explain Du Bois's repeated use of phrases like "the childhood of the race."

But too much reliance on such a position could itself be used to justify racial domination. After all, it would not be necessary to claim belief in inherent black inferiority in order to assume a paternalistic stance in relation to a damaged, incapacitated group.[8] Du Bois himself tended to take this position toward the black masses. But he needed to distinguish people like himself from those others. To do so, he creates a heroic version of the race in whom "dogged strength alone keeps it from being torn asunder" by the "two warring ideals" of Americanness and blackness. Those who have the capacity to be fully integrated into the dominant culture, who, as in Du Bois's case, can easily demonstrate their acquisition of culture, feel anguished that they are not permitted to realize all their possibilities:

> The double-aimed struggle of the black artisan—on the one hand to escape white contempt for a nation of mere hewers of wood and drawers of water, and on the other hand to plough and nail and dig for a poverty-stricken horde—could only result in making him a poor craftsman, for he had but half a heart in either cause. By the poverty and ignorance of his people, the Negro minister or doctor was tempted toward quackery and demagogery; and by the criticism of the other world, toward ideals that made him ashamed of his lowly tasks. The would-be black *savant* was confronted by the paradox that the knowledge his people needed was a twice-told tale to his white neighbors, while the knowledge which would teach the white world was Greek to his own flesh and blood. (*Souls*, 9–10)

Those who succeed under such circumstances are unrecognized great ones, for they do more than others, including whites, are capable of.

The point is to eliminate the waste and frustration in their struggle so as to benefit the entire society.

For Du Bois, the distinction between these two effects of racism is crucial, for it enables him to break down the assumption that race is a fixed biological category. It creates difference within the term "blackness" and in fact makes it a cultural and historical rather than a "scientific" and moral term. To make the term multivalent weakens the linguistic and rhetorical support for racial domination.

The remainder of the initial chapter of *Souls* is devoted to precisely such historical and cultural contextualizing. The trope of human development is used to show how blacks moved from the "child of Emancipation" to the "youth with dawning self-consciousness" (12). Childhood, the postbellum quest for political power, gives way to the race's adolescent desire for education, for the power that comes through knowledge. The metaphor clearly implies the "natural" movement of blacks into "manhood," a term Du Bois uses throughout the book. Manhood in this case means full integration into the social and cultural order; it means becoming a "co-worker in the kingdom of culture." By implication, the frustration of this development through prejudice is unnatural.

The imagery changes to pick up on the notion of perversion. Poverty and ignorance are not sufficient explanations for black limitations: "The red stain of bastardy, which two centuries of systematic legal defilement of Negro women had stamped upon his race, meant not only the loss of ancient African chastity, but also the hereditary weight of a mass of corruption from white adulterers, threatening almost the obliteration of the Negro home" (12). Thus, a crucial source of black problems is a white patriarchal order, since Du Bois's accusation is directed, not against aberrant individuals, but against the Southern social structure itself. White men used their power, not merely to victimize black women, but, more importantly, to construct a legal system that validated such victimization. Discursive power in the form of law sanctions coercive physical power. In addition, Du Bois inverts the racist conventional wisdom of the time by insisting that the infusion of "white blood" into blacks was not a blessing but a catastrophe. The argument had been made from the time of slavery that whatever intelligence and civilized qualities blacks had resulted from the "white" part of their ancestry.[9] Here such virtue is supplanted by "the hereditary weight of a mass of corruption." In the moral drama that is Du Bois's narrative of the history of blacks in America, it is the white fathers who play the villains.

The remainder of *The Souls of Black Folk* develops variations on the dynamic relationships of the dual inner world of blacks and the outer world of white fathers. Thus, the chapters "The Dawn of Freedom," "The Wings of Atalanta," and "The Sons of Master and Man" treat the economic and social aspects of interracial contact, with the consistent demonstration of white failure to bring about a more equitable society. The first of these chapters examines the Freedmen's Bureau, which emerges in this telling as a largely ad hoc institution because of the inability of those in power to take responsibility for the effects of black emancipation. In this version, the black masses, portrayed variously as "that dark human cloud" and "a form hovering dark and mother-like," play the role of supplicant, asking succor and protection from the new white patriarch, the military and federal government. The imaging of the masses as female, a consistent pattern in Du Bois's writing, allows him to justify his tendency to present the race as largely passive and yet a source of virtue and culture. In his narrative, the race can thus be violated, betrayed, and exploited without being held ultimately responsible for its condition. Just as "woman," in nineteenth-century discourse on gender, conflated morality, desire, and culture and meant corruption as well as virtue,[10] so in Du Bois's characterization the black masses could be corrupted because they lacked the resources for moral self-assertion. They had to be taken care of, just as women did, and if this happened, they could rise to the highest moral levels. As shall be seen later, this feminizing of the race also is part of Du Bois's family romance, in which he himself and those like him play the strong son preserving the racial mother from the depredations of the father.

At this point, however, this third element is missing, and he concentrates on showing the tragedy of the failed white fathers. The nation had its opportunity to make right the historical wrong of slavery: "All this vast expenditure of money and brains might have formed a great school of prospective citizenship, and solved in a way we have not yet solved the most perplexing and persistent of the Negro problems"

(*Souls*, 34). But Southern white hostility combined with Northern naïveté, opportunism, indifference, and incompetence to doom the Freedmen's Bureau. Thus, blacks were victimized by the moral failures of
the nation's political and social leaders.

"The Wings of Atalanta" is designed to show another aspect of such
failure. Atlanta, as emblem of the new South, is shown in pursuit of
material wealth rather than moral and cultural ideals. Again, as in the
discussion of the Freedmen's Bureau, Du Bois historicizes the change,
but his use of the Atalanta myth allows him to turn that history into a
cautionary tale. He attributes the change in values to slavery and war:
"A fearful wilderness lay about the feet of that city after the War,—
feudalism, poverty, the rise of the Third Estate, serfdom, the re-birth of
Law and Order, and above and between all, the Veil of Race. . . . Work
and wealth are the mighty levers to lift this old new land; thrift and toil
and saving are the highways to new hopes and new possibilities" (60).
If the South intended to be more than a war-ravaged wasteland, it had
to display some of the energy of the North, whose god, according to Du
Bois, was Pluto. But such a commitment required an acceptance of the
culture of materialism:

> Atalanta is not the first or the last maiden whom greed of gold has led to
> defile the temple of Love; and not maidens alone, but men in the race of
> life, sink from the high and generous ideals of youth to the gambler's code
> of the Bourse; and in all our Nation's striving is not the Gospel of Work
> befouled by the Gospel of Pay? So common is this that one-half think
> it normal; so unquestioned, that we almost fear to question if the end of
> racing is not gold, if the aim of man is not rightly to be rich. And if this is
> the fault of America, how dire a danger lies before a new land and a new
> city, lest Atlanta, stooping for mere gold, shall find that gold accursed! (60)

In his rendering of the process, Du Bois reveals an aspect that is crucial to his reading of history. The "normalizing" of the corruption of
ideals means that the hegemony of the Gospel of Pay becomes deeply
embedded within the culture and thus much more difficult to expose
and eradicate. And it is precisely eradication that is Du Bois's aim; for
even though he is hinting here at an economic reading of history and
culture, he still insists on the moral consequences of such development.
The South sacrifices its best qualities in its pursuit of wealth:

She forgot the old ideal of the Southern gentleman,—that new-world heir of the grace and courtliness of patrician, knight, and noble; forgot his honor with his foibles, his kindliness with his carelessness, and stooped to apples of gold,—to men busier and sharper, thriftier and more unscrupulous. . . . Atlanta must not lead the South to dream of material prosperity as the touchstone of all success; already the fatal might of this idea is beginning to spread; it is replacing the finer type of Southerner with vulgar money-getters; it is burying the sweeter beauties of Southern life beneath pretence and ostentation. For every social ill the panacea of Wealth has been urged,—wealth to overthrow the remains of the slave feudalism; wealth to raise the "cracker" Third Estate; wealth to employ the black serfs, and the prospect of wealth to keep them working; wealth as the end and aim of politics, and as the legal tender for law and order; and finally, instead of Truth, Beauty, and Goodness, wealth as the ideal of the Public School. (61)

Du Bois's stand here is that of the Old Testament prophet as cultured gentleman. The path of wealth is the path of corruption, but it is also, perhaps more importantly, the path of vulgarity. The ideals he espouses and sees as threatened are not those of righteous asceticism, but rather those of high culture. There is, of course, more than a little unintended irony in his portrayal of the Southern gentleman as the model here, especially since a central aim of the essay is to warn Southern blacks against pursuing the chimera of wealth and to urge them to seek instead cultural ideals. But what is crucial here is the set of values—grace and courtliness, honor, kindliness—that the Southern patriarch embodied at the same time that he was flawed by slaveholding and moral irresponsibility. The values are themselves seen as universals, as is suggested by the list of traits to be pursued as an alternative to the Gospel of Wealth: "Patience, Humility, Manners, and Taste" (66). Thus, the modern ideal for the sons of Southern fathers is the gentleman purified of the flaws of history.

The means of attaining the ideal is the university. In fact, Atlanta University is represented as a utopian space:

The hundred hills of Atlanta are not all crowned with factories. On one, toward the west, the setting sun throws three buildings in bold relief against the sky. The beauty of the group lies in its simple unity: a broad lawn of green rising from the red street and mingled roses and peaches;

north and south, two plain and stately halls; and in the midst, half hidden in ivy, a larger building, boldly graceful, sparingly decorated, and with one low spire. It is a restful group,—one never looks for more; it is all here, all intelligible. . . . In a half-dozen class-rooms they [black students] gather then,—here to follow the love-song of Dido, here to listen to the tale of Troy divine; there to wander among the stars, there to wander among men and nations,—and elsewhere other well-worn ways of knowing this queer world. Nothing new, no time-saving devices,—simply old time-glorified methods of delving for Truth, and searching out the hidden beauties of life, and earning the good of living. The riddle of existence is the college curriculum that was laid before the Pharoahs, that was taught in the groves by Plato, that formed the *trivium* and *quadrivium*, and is today laid before the freedmen's sons by Atlanta University. And this course of study will not change; its methods will grow more deft and effectual, its content richer by toil of scholar and sight of seer; but the true college will ever have one goal,—not to earn meat, but to know the end and aim of that life which meat nourishes. (63–64)

In the midst of the profane city is the sacred campus, a version of the Puritan city on a hill. Its value is precisely its difference from its context; its pace has nothing to do with efficiency, its buildings have nothing to do with production. It is also a different discursive universe. It speaks the language of the classics and organizes its discourse according to the trivium and the quadrivium, a method that is itself classical rather than modern. "Usefulness" has been emptied of its economic connotations and reclaimed as knowing the "end and aim" of life. Such a space lies outside of history, not subject to the flaws of other human activity. It provides the sons the opportunity for that purification of ideals not available to the fathers.

The choice of Atlanta University as this symbol is important. Du Bois seeks for it, as a place for the inculcation of values, a status equal to the great traditional and modern universities. This comparison validates his claim for the cultural possibilities of blacks. It offers access to the discursive universe of the dominant society and specifically of its cultural elites. To whites it means that the "kingdom of culture" must be seen as a limited democracy in which all those willing and able to learn the discourse must be allowed their voices. In addition, the representation of the university as utopian space is an implied critique of the world around it. Its nobility, sense of tradition, peacefulness, and moral order contrast sharply with the vulgarity, impermanence, anxiety, and amorality of the acquisitive city, region, and nation. The outside world, because it is so busily and narrowly focused on accumulation, ironically lacks substance and vitality: Du Bois describes the "pall" of industrial wastes that falls over Atlanta each evening.

The moral element of this critique is ancient, and the cultural aspect is common in nineteenth- and early twentieth-century thinking.[11] What is distinct in Du Bois is the application of the critique to black life. Because blacks are like other people, they can be easily tempted by dreams of wealth; and because they are, as he repeatedly observes, just emergent as a civilized group, they are especially susceptible to the Gospel of Pay: "What if the Negro people be wooed from a strife for righteousness, from a love of knowing, to regard dollars as the be-all and end-all of life?" (*Souls*, 63). Here he appeals to origins by asserting that the race has traditionally been concerned with righteousness. These origins in morality and knowledge are consonant with the values of high culture. The classic triad of goodness, truth, and beauty is apparent in both. Again the duality of black and American is foregrounded. The ancient ideals of Afro-American and Western traditions are the same. The university can be the means by which all blacks— some directly and most through the efforts of an educated elite—can bring the traditions together. While blacks must struggle to learn the signifiers of Western culture, which the experience of slavery has denied them, they can be confident, in Du Bois's view, that the signified is identical with that found in their own discursive universe. The problem, then, is not inherent difference but historical oppression and the allurements of false ideals.

"The Sons of Master and Man" develops this idea by examining racial interaction. Du Bois here contends that the South has failed to solve its racial problems because it has not brought together its "best" elements. More clearly here than in most of his writing, he states the validity of class distinctions and his preference for elites. Racial tensions could be greatly eased, if not eliminated, if the "best" of both races were to have the authority to shape Southern society. The "best" are, in essence, educated gentlemen, both black and white. They are the ones with the training described above. Du Bois assumes that such men[12] would be broad-minded, tolerant, generous, and sophisticated. They would be willing to recognize the flaws and limitations of each race and to endeavor to make changes. What the South needs, then, is a biracial meritocracy, a notion that suggests that Du Bois does not dislike hierarchies so much as he does "arbitrary" patriarchies, that is, those based on power, wealth, or violence rather than intellectual or moral ability.

The reasons such an authoritative elite has not emerged are again historical rather than genetic. Southern housing patterns have tended to segregate most thoroughly precisely those who have most in common. Cultured whites are most often in contact with black menials, while educated blacks deal with other blacks and uneducated whites. Each, then, is exposed to less than the best of the other race and therefore develops negative images. Moreover, political and economic power are generally in the hands of the sons of poor whites and "avaricious Yankees." They are the ones least likely to demonstrate the tolerance and patience necessary to bring real change to the South. This situation developed in large part because Southern white "quality" ignored its responsibilities to the region and to blacks. Again, it is the failures of Southern fathers that created current problems.

Du Bois suggests that such failure creates vicious circles in racial matters. The abdication of the Southern white elite leads to racial domination by the forces of "exploitation and debauchment." The effects on blacks are frustration, lack of respect for the legal system, criminality, ignorance, and "listlessness," all of which are then used to justify further racial oppression. The development of black leadership is "left to chance and accident, and not to any intelligent culling or reasonable methods of selection" (124–25). The negligent white patriarchs, who could use Enlightenment principles to solve the problems of race, have chosen not to do so. Two points are significant here. One is Du Bois's view that history can be influenced by a rational morality; issues of moral and social order can be examined through reason and actions carried out through the compulsion of moral duty. This linkage of morality and reason remains strong in Du Bois's thinking even when his ideological perspective changes. The second point is that a white Southern elite is capable of such an enlightened approach. Such a group has the same potential as all the "talented tenths" in Du Bois's life, from the Founding Fathers to the Communist Party. They are intelligent, cultured, capable of transcending narrow self-interest, sympathetic to those less fortunate, and driven by a sense of duty. Ironically, of course, they are the direct descendants of the slaveholders responsible for the racial problem.

But Du Bois is so committed to a culturally conservative position that he can project such an important role for them. Of course, it may well be that their absence is what enables him to view them so positively. His cultural ideal thereby remains untested by historical reality, a patriarchal principle untainted by the vulgarity, selfishness, and irrationality of the contemporary Southern world. And because the ideal remains valid, the sons, both black and white, can both attack the fathers' failures and strive for that ideal. Du Bois's optimism, then, is generated specifically by the absences in the world he is describing. As a son, he devises a patriarchal value system that then authorizes him to reject the fathers in the name of the father.[13] He will be the true father in imagining a new world in which old patriarchal practices are eradicated.

But in this text of black and white, fathers and sons, it is not only whites who take the patriarchal role. "Of Mr. Booker T. Washington and Others" has consistently been seen as the historically and politically most significant chapter in the book. In a sense, every other chapter can be read in terms of this one. The discussions of education, political and social restriction, the psychology of racism, and personal and historical experiences of oppression can be viewed as implicit critiques of Washington's optimistic accommodationist position. It is in this chapter, however, that the battle is directly joined. The essay originally appeared as a review of *Up from Slavery*,[14] Washington's 1901 autobiography, and, for the purposes of the present analysis, it is useful to think of it not merely as a political statement but as an examination of that life.

While Du Bois adopts the style of polite argumentation, his characterization of his subject reveals the nature of his polemic. Each positive attribute assigned to Washington is carefully subverted in line with the moral and cultural principles described in the other essays. In explaining the effect of the Atlanta Exposition address, with its advocacy of compromise on issues of civil rights, Du Bois notes that all white

Southerners, radical or conservative, found in it something to applaud. "So both approved it, and to-day its author is certainly the most distinguished Southerner since Jefferson Davis" (*Souls*, 37). This linking of Washington with the political leader of the slave South suggests Du Bois's true subtext: the compromising of black humanity in order to gain power, both personal and political.[15] In the context of approval of Southern whites, the comparison must be based on shared appeals to racist politics.

Similarly, Washington's economic emphasis is premised on the values of Northern industrialism. He is praised for being able to join Southern and Northern perspectives; the former he grew up with, but the latter he had to study. The result is revealing: "And so thoroughly did he learn the speech and thought of triumphant commercialism, and the ideals of material prosperity, that the picture of a lone black boy poring over a French grammar amid the weeds and dirt of a neglected home soon seemed to him the acme of Absurdities. One wonders what Socrates and St. Francis of Assisi would say to this" (37). Unlike those diligent students of Atlanta University pursuing the mysteries of traditional culture, Washington only sees the immediate and the material. His is the discredited Gospel of Pay rather than the kingdom of culture. The juxtaposition of comparisons here is strategically effective; the distance, morally and culturally speaking, between Davis and Socrates is the measure of Washington's character. Though granting that a great deal has been accomplished, Du Bois implicitly questions the worth of that gain.

Given this characterization, the meaning of Washington for black life becomes highly problematic. The specific areas of policy contention— education, civil rights, voting rights—are precisely issues of value and culture. Du Bois sees an accommodationist position as not only illogical but also devastating for the race. Acceptance of limited training, segregation and discrimination, and restricted franchise would produce an ignorant, emasculated, defenseless mass rather than a cultured, proud, self-reliant people. In particular, he asserts the paradoxical nature of Washington's position:

> 1. He is striving nobly to make Negro artisans business men and
> property-owners; but it is utterly impossible, under modern competitive

methods, for workingmen and property-owners to defend their rights and exist without the right of suffrage.

2. He insists on thrift and self-respect, but at the same time counsels a silent submission to civic inferiority such as is bound to sap the manhood of any race in the long run.

3. He advocates common-school and industrial training, and depreciates institutions of higher learning; but neither the Negro common-schools, nor Tuskegee itself, could remain open a day were it not for teachers trained in Negro colleges, or trained by their graduates. (43)

The joining of culture and manhood in these statements is not accidental. For Du Bois, knowledge is a key to power and self-respect. Only through higher education can come an awareness of the "higher aims" of life, and only through these can come a sense of the ideals of the race. By denigrating the value of such training, Washington in effect accepts the uncivilized condition of the race and, by implication, its status as a child among the family of races.

Such a position would not be so problematic for Du Bois if Washington had not positioned himself as the patriarch of the race. He describes him as the leader of a "cult" with "unquestioning followers." He is the race's Joshua "called of God and of man to lead the headless host" (48). But his position is essentially a false one: he leads blacks not because they have chosen him, but because whites, both Northern and Southern, have crowned him: "While, then, criticism has not failed to follow Mr. Washington, yet the prevailing public opinion of the land has been but too willing to deliver the solution of a wearisome problem into his hands, and say, 'If that is all you and your race ask, take it' " (38). Thus, blacks have been denied an opportunity for exercising a fundamental democratic right, self-determination.

If the patriarch has neglected his responsibilities, it becomes the role of the sons to undertake them:

The black men of America have a duty to perform, a duty stern and delicate,—a forward movement to oppose a part of the work of their greatest leader. So far as Mr. Washington preaches Thrift, Patience, and Industrial Training for the masses, we must hold up his hands and strive with him, rejoicing in his honors and glorying in the strength of this Joshua called of God and of man to lead the headless host. But so far as Mr. Washington apologizes for injustice, North or South, does not rightly value the privilege and duty of voting, belittles the emasculating effects of caste distinctions, and opposes the higher training and ambition of our brighter minds,—so far as he, the South, or the Nation, does this,—we must unceasingly and firmly oppose them. (48)

The sons must bring the father into the moral order; if he refuses, then they must resist him. If they do not do so, he will continue to "emasculate" them. But the rules of the moral order are defined by the son here, and they are the rules that the entire essay is dedicated to showing Washington rejects. Thus, struggle is inevitable. Recognizing this, Du Bois carefully places himself in the tradition of even greater fathers:

> By every civilized and peaceful method we must strive for the rights which the world accords to men, clinging unwaveringly to those great words which the sons of the Fathers would fain forget: "We hold these truths to be self-evident: That all men are created equal; that they are endowed by their Creator with certain unalienable rights; that among these are life, liberty, and the pursuit of happiness." (48)

The rebellion of the black sons is legitimized and authorized by the word of the fathers; if the black father does not embrace that word, then he is the one outside the law. The commentary on Washington thus not only deconstructs his political position but reconstructs the patriarchal order to recognize the true sons.

The narrative of Alexander Crummell, the nineteenth-century cleric and intellectual, represents an alternative life and vision. In his tireless pursuit of truth and excellence, he symbolizes for Du Bois everything that Washington disdains. Moreover, he becomes a model for Du Bois himself:

> I spoke to him politely, then curiously, then eagerly, as I began to feel the fineness of his character,—his calm courtesy, the sweetness of his strength, and his fair blending of the hope and truth of life. Instinctively I bowed before this man, as one bows before the prophets of the world. Some seer he seemed, that came not from the crimson Past or the gray To-come, but from the pulsing Now,—that mocking world which seemed to me at once so light and dark, so splendid and sordid. Four-score years had he wandered in this same world of mine, within the Veil. (156–57)

Crummell in this passage and throughout the chapter is Du Bois's ideal black man—cultured, communicative, intense, and sensitive to the moral significance of race. He is not one who gains his authority from outside, through the machinations of commercial and racist interests, but one who has earned it through decades of struggle.

The life is allegorized by presenting it in terms of three great temptations: hate, despair, and doubt. All are based on race: the bitterness of a father who encourages young Alexander to distrust and hate everything white; the disheartening refusal of a white church hierarchy to provide him with the education and endorsement to follow his calling; and the uncertainty about that calling when black parishioners fail to follow him and white bishops try to impose segregationist conditions on his work. This narrative structure, with the added elements of a wandering in the wilderness and a lack of recognition by the larger world all serve to project a Christ-like image that is simultaneously a racially specific one.

Crummell stands for all those things Du Bois values: education, integrity, hard work, sacrifice, perseverance. He is the hero of double consciousness, asserting his racial identity but seeking to raise his race through the faith of the Episcopal church. To do this, he must resist the antiwhite feeling of his biological father and the racism of the church patriarchs. He must find his own way, become his own father, because of the failures of these sires. But he does so precisely to further the ideals of both. He studies for a long period in England and then spends more years working in Africa. Having thus experienced for and in himself the origins of the "twoness" of black and white, he returns to America:

> Out of the temptation of Hate, and burned by the fire of Despair, triumphant over Doubt, and steeled by Sacrifice against Humiliation, he turned at last home across the waters, humble and strong, gentle and determined. He bent to all the gibes and prejudices, to all hatred and discrimination, with that rare courtesy which is the armor of pure souls. He fought among his own, the low, the grasping, and the wicked, with that unbending righteousness which is the sword of the just. He never faltered, he seldom complained; he simply worked, inspiring the young, rebuking the old, helping the weak, guiding the strong. (163)

The true patriarch is the one who understands the cultural essence of patriarchy, who gains authority through experience and suffering, who rejects the false authority of established father figures, and who sacrifices personal and immediate benefit for the long-term general good. This heroic image is repeated with variations in the biography of John Brown and in Du Bois's own autobiographies. In each case, a dialectic of patriarchal resistance and affirmation is followed. Crummell must fight bitterness, prejudice, and self-aggrandizement to help create a culture that values moral order, justice, authentic democracy, and intellectual development. This fight, in Du Bois's thought, is the eternal struggle of law against anarchy, of reason against ignorance and prejudice, of sons against fathers.

In this context, it is important to look at Du Bois as a father, as he portrays himself in "Of the Passing of the First-Born." What is immediately striking about this representation is his deep ambivalence about the role. In the essay, he repeatedly creates distance between himself and his son. He notes that he is away in Georgia when the child is born in Massachusetts. When he finally arrives, his initial reaction is curiosity bordering on repulsion: "What is this tiny formless thing, this newborn wail from an unknown world,—all head and voice? I handle it curiously, and watch perplexed its winking, breathing, and sneezing. I did not love it then; it seemed a ludicrous thing to love" (150). This immediate response is changed, but not by the baby itself: "[B]ut her I loved, my girl-mother, she whom now I saw unfolding like the glory of the morning—the transfigured woman. Through her I came to love the wee thing, as it grew strong; as its little soul unfolded itself in twitter and cry and half-formed word, and as its eyes caught the gleam and flash of life" (150–51). Even as he comes to recognize its value, as "it" becomes "he," the child is turned into an ambiguous symbol of race: "Why was his hair tinted with gold? An evil omen was golden hair in my life. Why had not the brown of his eyes crushed out and killed the blue?—for brown were his father's eyes and his father's father's. And thus in the Land of the Color-line I saw, as it fell across my baby, the shadow of the Veil" (151).

The child becomes the literal sign of the racial history of America. His eyes and hair are the imprint of that ancestral white father who violated the black mother. He is a text of racism that Du Bois the black father must read. To do so is to return to the site of the primal American crime. It is also to recognize the power of that master-father, who can signify himself through the generations.

But having made that reading, Du Bois reinscribes the meaning of his son. The very marks of the white father reveal the importance of the black father: "Within the Veil was he born; and there within shall he live,—a Negro and a Negro's son. Holding in that little head—ah, bitterly!—the unbowed pride of a hunted race, clinging with that tiny dimpled hand—ah, wearily!—to a hope not hopeless but unhopeful, and seeing with those bright wondering eyes that peer into my soul a land whose freedom is to us a mockery and whose liberty a lie" (151). Only in the eyes of black fathers can the truth be read, for they have experienced the world controled by the white father. They have seen the mockery and lie; they have been denied their manhood through the physical and psychological violence of these arbitrary and inhuman patriarchs; and yet they retain their unhopeful hope and seek to pass it to their marked sons. Both the potential for unmanning and the belief in manhood must be the testament and patrimony of black fathers.

The very complexity of this heritage makes the death of the child from dysentery a complex emotional experience. On the one hand, the response is that of any parent to the loss of a child:

> Is not this my life hard enough,—is not that dull land that stretches its sneering web about me cold enough,—is not all the world beyond these four little walls pitiless enough, but that thou must needs enter here,— thou, O Death? About my head the thundering storm beat like a heartless voice, and the crazy forest pulsed with the curses of the weak; but what cared I, within my home beside my wife and baby boy? Wast thou so jealous of one little coign of happiness that thou must needs enter there,— thou, O Death? (153)

The language, though in the formal, genteel style deemed appropriate for elegies, nonetheless communicates the sense of anguish and loss felt by the speaker. In fact, its formality strengthens the emotion by discursively linking the dead son to the great dead for whom such language is usually reserved.

At the same time, the son retains his role in the text as racial symbol: "No bitter meanness now shall sicken his baby heart till it die a living death, no taunt shall madden his happy boyhood. Fool that I was to think that this little soul should grow choked and deformed within the Veil!" (154) He is the emblem of black fate in a racist society. Du Bois shows us a fundamental social displacement when the funeral march is disrupted by "those pale-faced hurrying men and women" who yell "Niggers" at the marchers. Thus, the narrator reveals a violation of human ritual and by implication the dehumanization inherent in white social order. What is also apparent is the violation of the "natural" patriarchal relationship of father and son. Du Bois recognizes that what is best for his son is not necessarily growth and integration into the existing order. Given the character of that order, it will "deform" rather than form the child; it will deny him legitimacy as a son and power as a father. The best hope, perhaps the only hope, is death: "Sleep, then, child,—sleep till I sleep and waken to a baby voice and the ceaseless patter of little feet—above the Veil" (155).

The elegy, a form that has affirmed cultural values in part by being the traditional expression of mourning, here is itself deformed to become cultural critique. Despite the presence of certain standard features—apostrophe, formal diction, anthropomorphized nature, narrator as friend, and consolation—the text is persistently disrupted by racial and patriarchal elements. The distancing of father and son, the marks of miscegenation, the insulting violations of ritual, the "consolation" that is in fact life-denying resignation, all point to the failure of traditional Eurocentric expression to incorporate black American experience.[16]

This problematizing of artistic form is also apparent in the last two pieces to be examined here. Both "Of the Coming of John" and "Of the Sorrow Songs" are premised on the Du Boisian idea that art expresses social, political, and historical realities.[17] His elegy is as much a commentary on racism as a tribute to his son; in fact, to make such a distinction is pointless for him: his son's blackness meant that even his brief life and painful death were embedded in American history. For Du Bois, the making and evaluation of art always carried ideological weight. This is apparent in the one short story and one essay on aesthetics contained in *The Souls of Black Folk*.

"The Coming of John" is on one level a parable of the arguments made throughout the book. John rises from the Southern masses to go to college, where he learns that education is serious, hard work. After considerable struggle and effort, he becomes not only trained but cultured. Consistent with the model of the talented tenth, he returns home to educate the masses he left behind. But he is frustrated by black provincialism and white resistance to black advancement. When his sister is accosted by the spoiled, bored son of the community patriarch, John's anger explodes in an attack that kills the young white man. At the end, John stands facing the sea, awaiting the lynch mob that approaches him. Thus, we are made to see the difficulties of making blacks "coworkers in the kingdom of culture," when whites claim that territory exclusively for themselves. Du Bois develops some of the irony of the situation in the attack on white John (the identity of names is essential, as we will see); black John acts as he does to protect his sister's honor in the tradition of Southern chivalry. But of course chivalry is secondary to racial domination. John presumes to claim his seignorial rights as a white man dealing with a black woman; black John's response is seen as an attack on a superior rather than a gesture of honor.

A further irony emerges in the doubling of character. Both Johns grow up as the hopes of their respective racial communities. White John would seem to have the advantage because he comes from a privileged home and attends an Ivy League school. But the very wealth of opportunity makes him indifferent to it. He gains nothing from his schooling except dissatisfaction with life in the small-town South. In contrast, black John attends a black institution that requires intellectual diligence, a quality he lacks. After initial failure, he becomes soberminded and studious. He returns home a changed man, committed to improving the black community. Black education, then, produces the better man.

But these means of establishing Du Bois's theme of black uplift and white resistance are disrupted by other elements of the narrative. For example, John's education, while it gives him a larger sense of humanity, appears to do so at the cost of his ability to function within his particular social and historical community. He cannot relate to the blacks for whom his education was a dream. His return is typical:

> John rose gloomily as the train stopped, for he was thinking of the "Jim Crow" car; he stepped to the platform, and paused: a little dingy station, a black crowd gaudy and dirty, a half-mile of dilapidated shanties along a straggling ditch of mud. An overwhelming sense of the sordidness and narrowness of it all seized him; he looked in vain for his mother, kissed coldly the tall, strange girl who called him brother, spoke a short, dry word

here and there; then, lingering neither for hand-shaking nor gossip, started silently up the street, raising his hat merely to the last eager old aunty, to her open-mouthed astonishment. (*Souls*, 172–73)

At a later gathering, John talks of his ideas, but the people fail to understand him, "for he spoke an unknown tongue"; shortly after, his comments on religious provincialism are repudiated "and he realized with amazement that *all unknowingly* he had put rough, rude hands on something this little world held sacred" (174; emphasis added). Similarly, he is reported almost immediately to be teaching the children about the French Revolution and the Rights of Man, again apparently "unknowing" that this will offend local whites, despite his promise to the Judge (white John's father) that he would "accept the situation" of black racial subordination. Not surprisingly, the school is abruptly shut down, leaving the black children without a source of education.

Du Bois's theme of the value of black education in Eurocentric culture seems to carry with it the corollary of deracination. John's thorough training in Western civilization (he goes to his death humming Wagner's "Song of the Bride") requires the erasure of black culture from his identity. He lacks not only the mother-wit that enabled the community to survive but also respect for the traditions it developed over generations. While it could be argued that the vision of progress represented requires a radical shift in perspective, the narrative is structured such that the new ideas are never tested. Every act of John's upon his return is self-defeating: his refusal to find a common language with the black community, his deliberate defiance of white authority, his violence against white John, and finally, his calm, almost suicidal wait for the lynch mob. What the story validates more than black uplift or white oppression is sacrifice. More than John's value as a model of black achievement or racial progress or resistance to white domination is his worth as an offering on the altar of culture. As in the stories of Alexander Crummell and Du Bois's son, life in its harsh historical and racial reality is hopeless. Noble sacrifice becomes the best choice.

All of this suggests that underlying Du Bois's progressive and energetic struggle against injustice is a deep despair, a view shared with many other fin de siècle writers that the kingdom of culture was moribund. A variant interpretation would be a Lacanian one: Castration by the powerful father was inevitable, and so one mutilated oneself as the only possible autonomous gesture. John thus creates the conditions for his own defeat and death and by doing so turns himself into a scapegoat; thereby his principles can remain intact because they have not been tested. As we shall see repeatedly in Du Bois's fictive narratives and elsewhere, the need to create a story disrupts the seamless pattern of ideology and exposes tensions, lacunae, and contradictions that typify his thought.

His analysis of the spirituals attempts to overcome such latent problems through an act of what Robert Stepto calls "immersion."[18] This operates in a variety of ways: he identifies the songs as part of himself; he historicizes them both as slave expression and as American art; and he places his own text within their context. But what he reveals through all these connections is a basic cultural critique. In contradistinction to the sentimental versions of the old South so popular in Du Bois's time, the songs reveal a harsh truth about racial oppression: "They are the music of an unhappy people, of the children of disappointment; they tell of death and suffering and unvoiced longing toward a truer world, of misty wanderings and hidden ways" (*Souls*, 182). They tell, in other words, the same story as *The Souls of Black Folk*.

Du Bois identifies their artistry not in their technique, about which he claims to know little, but in their message of sorrow and transcendent hope. The songs encode a counter-history to the past defined by the dominant culture. They inscribe a narrative of fatherlessness, separation, unrealizable love, endless labor, and exile. They are the voicings of a people whose faith is not in human kindness or white civilization, but in the ultimate justice of the universe, "that sometime, somewhere, men will judge men by their souls and not by their skins" (188).

This distinction between body and spirit is crucial for Du Bois, since he largely accepts the cultural immaturity of blacks. He uses "weird," "quaint," and "primitive," among other terms, to describe both the music and its creators. In the process of repudiating Eurocentric notions of progress, he accepts a key argument: "The silently growing assumption of this age is that the probation of races is past, and that the backward races of today are of proven inefficiency and not worth the saving. Such an assumption is the arrogance of peoples irreverent toward Time and ignorant of the deeds of men. A thousand years ago such an assumption, easily possible, would have made it difficult for the Teuton to prove his right to life" (188). What is rejected here is the contention that history has completed its testing of human groups; what is accepted is that there is a clearly definable measure of such groups that can be used to establish their advancement or backwardness. Even though he historicizes this scale, Du Bois's acceptance of it means that he must find some category other than conventional cultural advancement by which to valorize black expression.

He therefore must define a black aesthetic not in formal or technical terms, but in transcendentally human terms. Thus, it is the message of suffering humanity that defines the quality of the sorrow songs. It is the belief in justice and fundamental equality that makes them great. It is not their expression of life within the veil so much as their imagining of a world above it that makes them the black gift to civilization. And it is this quality that makes them valuable as cultural critique, since their invocation of spiritual values calls into question the materialism and power-hunger of the dominant culture that is one of the themes of *Souls*. Even the spirituals themselves have been bastardized and commodified by that culture. That is why Du Bois is so careful to identify "master songs," those that retain the purity of the slave experience. The phrase works richly as word-play: in addition to claiming their *authenticity*, it suggests their *authority* as counter-narratives to white versions of black history and to their *authoring* of a master narrative that one day will define the transcendently human experience.

Such a reading brings *The Souls of Black Folk* full circle. From the initial attempt to make his text a master work through its revision of genres, disciplines, and experiences, Du Bois has come at the end to recreating traditional black expression—the spirituals—as a tradition that validates and authorizes his project. The claim of a spiritual base that transcends history allows him to engage critically both history and the culture of his present. He speaks, as it were, to his moment in time from outside of it. In this way, because other ways are so problematic, he can master the masters.

2

. . . .

"Cold-Blooded Science"

. . . .

The Suppression of the Slave-Trade
and The Philadelphia Negro

. . . .

The sole aim of any society is to settle its problems
in accordance with its highest ideals, and the only
rational method of accomplishing this is to study
those problems in the light of the best scientific
research.—*"The Study of the Negro Problem," 1897*

Du Bois was the first truly professional black
historian. He and Carter G. Woodson share distinction as the true
fathers of African-American history as an academic field. Prior to
their time, the experiences of blacks in America had been written by
authors with little or no training in research methods and with the primary purpose of generating positive images of black life to counteract
racist assumptions and assertions.[1] Though their methods were different from earlier writers, Du Bois and Woodson shared with them the
sense of black history offered by Earl Thorpe in his study of African-
American historians: "American history with the accent and emphasis
on the point of view, attitude, and spirit of Afro-Americans, as well
as the events in which they have been either actors or the objects of
action" (3). Such a perspective holds true for Du Bois in virtually all of
his historical and sociological projects, whether he is being "objective"
or "propagandistic" and whether he is praising or criticizing the race.

Social science for him is always engaged and thus always within the tradition of black historiography. He consistently resists, challenges, and subverts the conventional social and historical wisdom of the dominant order, including those scholars who have analyzed it.

This engagement means that he often presents different attitudes toward the race because history can serve a variety of purposes; it does not exist purely, for its own sake. Thus, *The Supression of the Slave-Trade* (1896) largely ignores the experiences of blacks in its effort to focus on the tragic failure of the Founding Fathers to end the evil of slavery. *The Philadelphia Negro* (1899) can be critical of the race in many ways, because its strategy of rational urban reform involves black action as well as assistance from the larger community. *Black Reconstruction* (1935) seeks to de-emphasize black responsibility for an era in which corruption was rampant and for which white historians largely blamed blacks. The versions of *The Negro* that were published at various times were designed as popular works intended to improve the white public's attitude toward the race. In all of this, clearly Du Bois is mindful of a kind of "double consciousness" that has pervaded black historiography. On the one hand is the need to inspire the race, both by demonstrating what has been achieved in the past and by urging improvement in the present. On the other hand, it is necessary to insist to whites that blacks in fact have a place in history, that the racial policies of the past have helped to generate the racial problem of the present, and that white efforts for change can be meaningful because blacks have the same needs, desires, and ambitions as whites. Du Bois's special contribution to a large extent was his understanding of how deeply embedded cultural assumptions about race have been in American history and thus how far one must go to deconstruct those assumptions.

Du Bois's perceptions about history and historiography suggest how his social science works can be read in the terms offered by Hayden White. White argues that historical writing is essentially narration in that historians contruct stories so as to make sense of the welter of information they have gathered.[2] History, regardless of the methods and assumptions of the author, is, in this sense, a literary construct. Du Bois's writing lends itself readily to such an interpretation; as the following chapters show, he conceptualizes both the past and the present largely in terms of moral dramas in which conflicts of good and evil, race (literal black and white), and freedom and oppression are developed complete with villains and heroes. The particular narrative pattern he uses, as has already been suggested, is one in which strong father figures abuse their power and must be challenged by virtuous sons and daughters. It should not be surprising in this context that the last work of "history" he produced was the fictional trilogy *The Black Flame* (1957–61). Nor, as we will see, is it unexpected that he believed that literature ought to be functional within history (see chapter 5). All writing is socially purposeful for him. Moreover, the story was always the same; disciplines, genres, and methods, though important, were subordinate to the moral vision.

The earliest books published by Du Bois follow shortly after his long years as a student. Given his training in the social sciences, it is not surprising that these works should be historical and sociological in nature. He felt a strong commitment to the scientific method, but this did not prevent his making large moral claims within a scientific context. Francis Broderick and Arnold Rampersad have effectively shown how the new social science in late nineteenth-century Germany made such a conjunction possible, but they have not developed the full implications of Du Bois's approach.[3] The moral claims often conflict with the context, but more important, they underlie the essential moral drama that shapes these texts.

The works under consideration here—*The Suppression of the Slave-Trade* (1896) and *The Philadelphia Negro* (1899)—take race as their subject and attempt to treat that emotional and controversial issue with objectivity. In each case, however, the nature of the study and of Du Bois's perspective required that he take a moral stance. This stance led him not only into a key tension of his career—science and morality—but also produced texts that implicitly subvert the existing discourse on race in American history and society. In the process, he defines his lifelong thesis: the need for a moral order in an immoral nation.

The Suppression of the African Slave-Trade to the United States, 1638–1870 was originally Du Bois's doctoral dissertation and was published as the first volume of the Harvard Historical Studies in 1896. In method it followed German historiography: Du Bois expected his readers to "test the conclusions of this study by the general principles laid down in German universities."[4] Those principles were taught to him by Albert Bushnell Hart at Harvard and Gustav Schmoller and Adolf Wagner at Berlin. A monograph, the work was built on the new social-scientific principle that the gradual accumulation of specialized studies would provide the basis for responsible, rational generalizations and social-policy decisions. The information gathered was to be documentary or statistical in nature. The documents were drawn from governmental records, from other public and private archives, or from personal or written accounts. Moreover, economic factors were assumed to play a key role in both society and studies of it. The idea was to make history and sociology, as professions, as scientific as possible by using concrete, verifiable data. The materials of history were to be used in much the same way as the materials of the physical sciences.[5]

Such a commitment to empirical study meant that there was a distinct bias in favor of analysis of institutions, especially political institutions. Identifying the sources and tracing the development of law and political organization was a major concern for Hart: "The historians of the generation of Hart and Herbert Baxter Adams sought to understand the present through a study of the development of institutions; Hart's course . . . was devoted almost exclusively to this type of history, and little else was included in Harvard's history offerings."[6] It was under Hart's influence that *Suppression* was written, and it reflects his concerns. But if institutions were examined, the task was to be done critically and not with a presumption of glory. The historian was to be "tough-minded," to use a popular expression of the time, and capable of undercutting popular generalizations if the evidence led in that direction.

Certainly Du Bois had these principles in mind in describing the method and objectives of *Suppression of the Slave-Trade*. It is "based mainly upon a study of the sources, i.e., national, state, and colonial statutes, Congressional documents, reports of societies, personal narratives, etc." (*Suppression*, ix) It deals primarily with the making and enforcement of laws regarding the trade; Du Bois shows little interest in the dynamics of the trade itself or its impact on the Africans who were its victims. Nor does he concern himself with slavery per se. His study is strictly limited and descriptive in nature: "This monograph proposes to set forth the efforts made in the United States of America, from early colonial times until the present, to limit and suppress the trade in slaves between Africa and these shores" (1).

To a large extent, these goals are realized. Du Bois meticulously traces the legal history of trade restrictions down to the Civil War. He covers state, national, and international laws and their enforcement and contextual matters such as the history of European slave trading and international economic changes. He goes through the legislative and diplomatic histories of bills and treaties, identifying proponents and opponents and suggesting reasons for success or failure. He studies enforcement of the laws that did exist by examining communications between law officers and the letters and narratives of those who actually engaged in legal and illegal trading.

But the study is not pure chronological description; Du Bois has a clear thesis in mind. A certain irony is built in from the title page forward. The slave trade was never effectively suppressed; the book is a history of a legal failure. Although the laws were passed, they were only sporadically enforced; moreover, little sentiment existed for enforcement among government officials and Northerners as well as slave-holding Southerners. The laws that were passed were deliberately weak, and only meager appropriations were allotted for enforcement. "On the whole these acts were poorly conceived, loosely drawn and wretchedly enforced. The systematic violations of the provisions of many of them led to a widespread belief that enforcement was, in the nature of the case, impossible" (196).

The reasons for such failure were in part poorly constructed laws and smuggling, but Du Bois also points to official corruption, deception, and indifference. At the local level, he finds that port officials were bribed to ignore violations. He also discovers strong evidence of collusion among judges, smugglers, and prominent citizens. Cases were dismissed despite conclusive evidence, those convicted were given minimal fines, and slaves taken from the ships mysteriously disappeared before decisions were made on their fate. Presidents and diplomats made patently absurd statements about the extent of the trade and resisted international pressure to control the traffic effectively. Du Bois is clearly not afraid to challenge the myths of sacrosanct law, the genius of the Founding Fathers, and the purity of the Southern aristocracy. His history is critical in this sense.

But the institutional element is only one part and perhaps not even the main part of Du Bois's work. He discusses law, but it is most often in the context of economics and morality. The relationship of these two is complex: on occasion they operate in harmony but more often in opposition. The economic theme is the conflict of the free-labor industrial North and the slave-labor agricultural South that results in the Civil War. The moral theme is in the form of a classic tragedy, with the failure of moral decisiveness by the Founding Fathers leading inexorably to that same Civil War.

These themes repeatedly interact in this narrative. It is not clear which is the controlling motif, and this lack of clarity creates certain contradictions within the text. On the one hand, economic analysis encourages the author to explain "what happened" by examining where the financial interests lay and thus why individuals acted in the way they did. On the other, the moral impulse probes beyond such an explanation; the author feels compelled to make judgments about what he considers to be a morally repugnant activity. These contrary tendencies shape the tensions of *Suppression*.

Du Bois is fully aware of the significance of economics in any adequate interpretation of slavery and the slave trade. In his discussions of the colonies, he points out that geographic conditions made slavery and trading either profitable or unprofitable and that the colonies consistently responded according to economic necessity. For example, South Carolina had extensive slave trading "owing to the character of her settlers, her nearness to the West Indian slave marts, and the early development of certain staple crops" (9). In contrast, New York's climate did not lend itself to large slave imports; therefore, "the chief element of restriction in this colony appears to have been the shrewd business sense of the traders, who never flooded the slave market, but kept a supply sufficient for the slowly growing demand" (19). In both cases, laws regarding the slave trade were directly related to the economic self-interest of the colony. Du Bois even suggests that there was a direct correlation between the economics of slavery and the number of laws regarding the trade. In the middle colonies, slavery was not financially important; "for this reason, and because they held a smaller number of slaves, most of these colonies have fewer actual statutes than the Southern colonies" (25).

In the New England colonies, the situation was more complex. Many of the colonists were morally opposed to slavery, and slaves were not economically necessary. But New England was a major supplier of the ships and merchants that carried on the highly profitable trade. The result was that while abolitionism developed early in New England, few laws were passed restricting the slave trade.

This recognition of the impact of self-interest on law has momentous implications for Du Bois's interpretation. He accepts the view that very little could be done about the trade as long as it remained so profitable. The revolutionary period then becomes crucial for his narrative. One of the provisions of the nonintercourse acts was a ban on the slave trade. He sees a combination of economic and political reasons for this action. The colonies needed to act with solidarity even though it might hurt them temporarily. Moreover, there was an oversupply of slaves at the time and thus little profit for traders. It was a period when both slavery and the trade seemed doomed. Little slavery existed in the North, and it appeared to have reached its natural limits in the South.

But this situation did not last, again for economic reasons. The restrictions of the war created a backlog of demand that began to be filled. Du Bois is aware of the irony of strong antitrade legislation's creating a resurgence of the trade: "On the whole, the conclusion is inevitably forced on the student of this first national movement against the slave-trade, that its influence on the trade was but temporary and insignificant, and that at the end of the experiment the outlook for the final suppression of the trade was little brighter than before" (47).

This change in the economic situation, however, was not as important as the assumptions about the economic prospects for slavery. Du Bois sees these assumptions as the source of the tragic drama: "Probably the whole country still regarded both slavery and the slave-trade as temporary; but the Middle States expected to see the abolition of both within a generation, while the South scarcely thought it probable to prohibit even the slave-trade in that short time" (50). The depletion of the land, limited possibilities for expansion, and a fear of slave insurrections made it obvious to everyone that unfree labor must end in due time. Economics would take its own course. Not even the differing timetables created insurmountable problems: "Such a difference might in all probability, have been satisfactorily adjusted, if both parties had recognized the real gravity of the matter. As it was, both regarded it as a problem of secondary importance, to be solved after many other more pressing ones had been disposed of" (50). The failure to act promptly and effectively was the result not of economic factors, but of moral blindness. Regardless of the economic circumstances, slavery had always been, according to Du Bois, a morally "grave" issue. Even if they could not see the economic future, he claims, the Founding Fathers knew that both slavery and the trade were evil. For this reason alone they should have dealt decisively with it. Instead, they treated it as a minor economic problem. This moral indifference is what Du Bois condemns most strongly and what he constantly returns to, as we shall see. Such neglect, he already indicates, had dire consequences: "Here, then, began that *fatal* policy toward slavery and the slave-trade that characterized the nation for three-quarters of a century, the policy of *laissez-faire, laissez-passer*" (50, emphasis added).

Du Bois's belief in a moral absolute is readily apparent. He assumes that an eternal truth exists outside time, geography, culture, or economic circumstance. This truth, he believes, is not merely one he reads back into history; it is available to all people at all times. Therefore, he claims the right to judge those national fathers who fail to act according to it. The applicable aspect of that truth at work here is that it is evil to treat human beings as objects to advance one's self-interest. The failure to take this principle seriously, even if it requires self-sacrifice, has "grave" consequences, in this case national apocalypse.

We find Du Bois relating this moral sensibility to economics very early in the book. In the chapters discussing colonial law, he introduces a moral geography: the farther south one goes, the greater the immorality. Thus, "the settlers of Georgia were of even worse moral fibre than their slave-trading and whiskey-using neighbors in Carolina and Virginia" (7).[7] In contrast, in the middle colonies we find that "the settlers of many of these colonies were of sterner moral fibre than the Southern cavaliers and adventurers, and, in the absence of great counteracting motives, were more easily led to oppose the institution and the trade" (*Suppression*, 16). New England created something of a problem for the typology: these colonists were of the "sternest moral fibre" but they nonetheless engaged in slave trading. Du Bois therefore makes a distinction between internal slavery and the trade. New

England morality favored abolition, but New England business sense recognized the profit to be made in shipping slaves to the Southern colonies:

> The opposition to the importation was therefore from the first based solely on moral grounds, with some social arguments. As to the carrying trade, however, the case was different. Here, too, a feeble moral opposition was early aroused, but it was swept away by the immense economic advantages of the slave traffic to a thrifty seafaring community of traders. This trade no moral suasion, not even the strong "Liberty" cry of the Revolution, was wholly able to suppress, until the closing of the West Indian and Southern markets cut off the demand for slaves. (38)

What is at work here is a dramatic tension between economics and morality. As long as economic pressures are not too great, then the good will be realized. But the greater the demands of self-interest, the less likely are a people or an individual to act morally. Du Bois clearly prejudices the case by stereotyping through "moral fibre," but he does not see this apparently innate characteristic as a mitigating factor. A kind of ethico-economic Calvinism seems to be at work: the South, for example, lacks the moral quality to resist the evils of self-interest, but it is nonetheless guilty of the sin of slavery.[8]

The drama of morality and economics played out here would lead one to believe that economics is the basic fact of history. After all, morality functions effectively only when self-interest is not involved or when it leads to the same end. Not even "moral fibre" seems an effective countervailing force. But Du Bois is not willing to accept this implication, since to do so would be, theoretically at least, to accept the legitimacy of slavery as an economic necessity. He can only get out of this quandary by insisting upon universal moral truth.

The complexity of his perspective becomes clear in his discussion of the Constitutional Convention. Du Bois uses the debate on slavery as well as the trade to exemplify the various attitudes of the participants. The convention generally tried to avoid the issue altogether, but when it was raised, very different arguments were put forth. Members from the border and Northern states tended to argue on moral grounds, claiming that slavery and the trade in slaves were great evils, " 'inconsistent with the principles of the revolution and dishonorable to the American character'" (54). Those from the deep South asserted that the issue was purely one of "interests," that morality had nothing to do with it.

Despite this clear statement of the position of South Carolina and Georgia, Du Bois holds the representatives of those states responsible for the failure of a strong moral stance by the convention: "The difficulty of the whole argument, from the moral standpoint, lay in the fact that it was completely checkmated by the obstinate attitude of South Carolina and Georgia" (55). Obstinacy has moral connotations here; the Southern representatives are deliberately refusing to see the question as it "really" is, that is, as a moral issue.

But the South is not the only culprit. Its obstinance is to be expected, given its low "moral fibre" and the resulting susceptibility to self-interest. The North has no such excuse, at least on the slavery issue. It is guilty of not pressing the issue and of a willingness to compromise, which is always morally questionable in Du Bois's work:

> With the spirit of compromise in the air, it was not long before the general terms were clear. The slavery side was strongly intrenched, and had a clear and definite demand. The forces of freedom were, on the contrary, divided by important conflicts of interest, and animated by no very strong and decided anti-slavery spirit with settled aims. Under such circumstances, it was easy for the Convention to miss the opportunity for a really great compromise, and to descend to a scheme that savored unpleasantly of "log-rolling." The student of the situation will always have good cause to believe that a more sturdy and definite anti-slavery stand at this point might have changed history for the better. (57–58)

The North's real sin is indifference. Having greater moral strength than the South, it had a responsibility to combat evil. Instead, it was willing to accede to many Southern demands. Du Bois does not clarify the meaning of "really great compromise." He seems to have serious doubts about the whole principle of compromise; his implicit argument is that the only adequate resolution would have been immediate banning of the trade and some form of abolition of slavery. Such an argument is consistent with his moral principles but at odds with a descriptive, "scientific" history.

The "log-rolling" compromise, of course, was to delay federal action on the slave trade for twenty years. But this procrastination did more than simply put off the matter: "The Federal Convention lulled the nation to sleep by a 'bargain,' and left to the vacillating and unripe judgments of the States one of the most threatening of the social and political ills which they were so courageously seeking to remedy" (62). The convention made it appear that slavery was a matter of little concern, and this created a sense of indifference on the part of the nation, an indifference that allowed the problem time to grow and become more complex. From this point, history moved inevitably toward conflict. The Founding Fathers, by not fighting economic self-interest with moral weapons, were responsible for the Civil War.

Most of the rest of *Suppression* narrates the ramifications of constitutional failure in the nineteenth century. Slavery did not die out, but rather, through the Louisiana Purchase, the Industrial Revolution, and the invention of the cotton gin, became deeply entrenched in the nation's economy and political structure. Ever more slaves were demanded, a need that was met by any means necessary. Federal legislation was passed beginning in 1808 to suppress the trade, but the apathy encouraged by the convention worked against effective enforcement. As the self-interest of the South grew, there was no parallel growth of moral opposition in the North. The result was complex: the North had an important and vocal minority that continually decried the moral evil of slavery and the trade. The government, however, showed little concern. Notwithstanding abolitionist arguments, every time the issue was raised, a compromise favoring the South was reached. Nonetheless, the North and South drifted further apart economically. Northern labor feared competition from slaves, while Southern agriculturalists resented Northern financial control. The main thrust of Du Bois's argument in this section is that moral indifference and self-interest combined to perpetuate the trade. Furthermore, he argues, contrary to conventional historiographical wisdom, the trade waxed rather than waned during the period between the Constitutional Convention and the Civil War.

The apathy and compromise that facilitated this growth were not even practical in the long run:

Here it was that the fatal mistake of compromising with slavery in the beginning, and of the policy of *laissez-faire* pursued thereafter, became painfully manifest; for, instead now of a healthy, normal economic development along proper industrial lines, we have the abnormal and fatal rise of a slave-labor large-farming system, which, before it was realized, had so intertwined itself with and braced itself upon the economic forces of an industrial age, that a vast and terrible civil war was necessary to displace it. (152)

Here we have the link between economics and morality. Even though self-interest may have dictated constitutional compromise, it could not guarantee that the result would be the best possible; Du Bois recognized no invisible hand that orders economic reality for the general good. Morality, on the other hand, does provide such order and is therefore the higher practicality. Pursuing the truth, even at the cost of immediate self-interest, will eventually lead to a greater economic good. One ought, then, to consider not merely the present but also the future in calculating self-interest. Since morality is based on truth, it is the most rational and practical guide to behavior. To deny morality its due is to end in irrationality and even violence. In the work under discussion, the North is again most culpable because it did not have so strong a self-interest as to blind it to moral understanding. The Founding Fathers, in constructing the law of the nation, serve themselves and expediency but do great harm to the sons of that nation, who must suffer for their failures.

Such a position substitutes Enlightenment ethics for Smithian economics; the reasoning invisible hand is supplanted by the reasoning moral absolute. Morality is to be practiced not merely as an end in itself, but also because it rewards its practitioners. But this ethical capitalism, with its deferred gratification, is used against economic capitalism, since the pursuit of narrow self-interest is moral anarchy and results in chaos in all aspects of life, including the economic.

The moral drama and the economic one come together in the cataclysm known as the Civil War. Of course, they have never been truly separate plot lines, since self-interest has moral consequences and morality has economic ones. Distinctions are made in emphasis, not in substance. Even when Du Bois argues on purely economic grounds, as he does when he contends that the Civil War was caused by irresolvable conflicts in labor theory, he premises those assertions on the moral failure that initiated the differences.

As though the point had not been made sufficiently already, Du Bois adds a final chapter, "The Essentials in the Struggle," which reiterates the moral-economic linkages. "Every experiment of such a kind [as America], however, where the moral standard of a people is lowered for the sake of a material advantage, is dangerous in just such proportion as that advantage is great" (194). A formula has been derived, indicating that the morality of the book is not arbitrarily imposed but is an intrinsic part of the historical period being described. To arrive at such a conclusion requires the acceptance of certain moral axioms: groups of people have moral characters; morality is constant and universally recognized; morality is ultimately rational; and morality directly influences economics and history. Du Bois here constructs his own rules of history, combining Enlightenment and Puritan principles; he then uses these to deconstruct the order of those fathers and to read their narrative as a cautionary tale for the sons.

Armed with these rules, Du Bois becomes a historical "realist": "There is always a certain glamour about the idea of a nation rising up to crush an evil simply because it is wrong. Unfortunately, this can seldom be realized in real life; for the very real existence of the evil usually argues a moral weakness in the very place where extraordinary moral strength is called for" (195).

The language here is carefully chosen. The writer balances his position between inevitability and free will; history moves insistently onward, but that movement is directed by the choices people make. People have a destiny, but it is a destiny they themselves create. Du Bois's penchant for the prophetic voice is evident here. The warning given by the past will be taken seriously only if a clear cause-and-effect relationship is shown between moral choices and historical events. On the other hand, too much emphasis on fate would mitigate against actions that must be taken in the present. He must be tough-minded in refusing to make the meaning of his parable either the passivity of determinism or the anarchy of free will.

Being tough-minded means contradicting the conventional wisdom when necessary and avoiding sentimentality:

One cannot, to be sure, demand of whole nations exceptional moral fore-sight and heroism; but a certain hard common-sense in facing the complicated phenomena of political life must be expected in every progressive people. In some respects we as a nation seem to lack this; we have the somewhat inchoate idea that we are not destined to be harassed with great social questions, and that even if we are, and fail to answer them, the fault is with the question and not with us. (198–99)

The historian-prophet decries the sins of his people. He clearly incorporates an element of irony into this criticism, since it calls on a people who pride themselves on practicality to stop being impractical, attacks a nation built on the work ethic to stop being lazy, and insists that a frontier-bred society stop being cowardly. It is one role of the prophet to tell people what they prefer not to hear, and Du Bois thrives on this role.

But the prophet must also offer a course of action if he is to bring his people within the realm of righteousness. So, he continues, "It behooves the United States, therefore, in the interest both of scientific truth and of future social reform, carefully to study such chapters of her history as that of the suppression of the slave-trade" (199). Historiography is political even when it is scientific. It not only serves to further "scientific truth" but also to provide the groundwork for change. The nation must know the truth if it is to act responsibly. This of course makes Du Bois's work self-justifying; he is serving the greater good by telling the historical truth as he has come to know it. That that truth is not as comforting as some would like is perfectly appropriate and even reassuring; history is supposed to be inspiring and honest, not necessarily beautiful. Its "ugliness" is even a kind of guarantee of its accuracy. But, if nothing else, this narrative of national failure has a definite moral: "From this we may conclude that it behooves nations as well as men to do things at the very moment when they ought to be done" (199). This conclusion seems almost trite; it appears to beg as many questions as it answers. But given the full implications of the narrative, it may merely be understatement. It assumes a morally rational universe that is tenuously maintained by humanity's willingness to act intelligently. The historical narrative preceding this statement is a dramatization of the apocalyptic consequences of not acting in such a way.

To bring the study to such a conclusion appears to move it far beyond the realm of German historical principles. This movement, however, does not simply involve the obvious point that moral assertions seem out of place in a "scientific" study. Rather, the difficulty is that Du Bois bases those assertions on an a priori moral law, an action inconsistent with an empirical ideology. But the German historians themselves assumed a moral stance, one that saw social science as a means of rational social change. Du Bois, in his selection of subject and his narrative design, revises the discipline to fit his moral and ideological purposes. His work is written and published at what has often been referred to as the nadir of the black American experience, referring to widespread racial violence and political and economic oppression. At the moment when Booker T. Washington is encouraging black accommodation to the situation, Du Bois demythologizes the American past to expose a tradition of moral, economic, and political irresponsibility. His parable of the slave trade serves to challenge the sons to do better than the Founding Fathers or, by implication, face similar consequences. Thus, in this most "objective" of his historical works, Du Bois offers one version of his own master narrative.

The Philadelphia Negro applies the scientific principles of Suppression of the Slave-Trade to a study of contemporary black life. "The Philadelphia Negro was the first systematic attempt to analyze scientifically and understand a black community." [9] This comment by Julius Lester reflects Du Bois's own attitude toward his 1899 sociological study. The text is replete with graphs, charts, and maps illustrating virtually every ascertainable fact about black life in the seventh ward of the city. The method is carefully set forward in the first chapter and then followed diligently. Moreover, this work expressly defines the relationship between research and social reform. Built into the study are reformist objectives; having announced the end, Du Bois presumes that his work is disinterested science.

This link between social science and social change is derived from principles established in Berlin: "Schmoller believed that institutions were shaped by ethical ideals, and rejected the view that economic forces were solely the product of natural forces. . . . Above all, such scholarship was to make sure that its ethical pronouncements had a truly scientific basis." [10] This relationship was a major influence in turn-of-the-century American social science and especially affected Du Bois's thinking: "Reflecting this faith of an important segment of America's social scientists that knowledge would lead to the solution of social problems, Du Bois during his early career, passionately believed that research could supply the basis for achieving a racially equalitarian society. He contended that race prejudice was caused by ignorance and that social science would provide the knowledge to defeat injustice." [11]

The knowledge to overcome ignorance must be empirically founded. Du Bois is careful to point out the limits of his own method, a strategy similar to that of the self-effacing novelist in the prefaces to his fiction, but which in this case serves to validate his empiricist commitment:

> The best available methods of sociological research are at present so liable to inaccuracies that the careful student discloses the results of individual research with diffidence; he knows that they are liable to error from the seemingly ineradicable faults of the statistical method, to even greater error from the methods of general observation, and, above all, he must ever tremble lest some personal bias, some moral conviction or some unconscious trend of thought due to previous training, has to a degree distorted the picture in his view. Convictions on all great matters of human interest one must have to a greater or lesser degree, and they will enter to some extent into the most cold-blooded scientific research as a disturbing factor. [12]

The ideal is a science totally removed from the humanity of the scientist. The procedural faults of this young science can be worked out, but the human factor will always complicate matters. The language here, as everywhere in Du Bois, is very important. He fears "moral conviction" in a work designed to facilitate reform. This fear, along with the trope of "cold-blooded" science, suggests a profound need to appear to separate reason from ideology and belief. Again, as is so often the case in his work, Du Bois imagines a realm of truth outside of human desire and value that validates his own sense of universal order. By claiming such a realm, he can disarm those who would question his own status as an unbiased observer. Though black and committed to social justice, he can nonetheless function as a disinterested scientist in examining black life. Moreover, the very "imperfections" that qualify the ideal—personal bias, moral conviction, acculturation—are the factors that give the work its discursive power. One must value black experience in order to study it so carefully, and one must assume that the existing racial discourse is inadequate and that solid research will expose its flaws.

Du Bois's problematizing of objectivity makes it possible for him to define the essential issues for his discipline. The paradigm of the physical sciences cannot be made to apply absolutely to studies such as his. Realizing this, though expressly regretting it, Du Bois sets up a more reasonable standard. Given the nature of the work, "the utmost that the world can demand is, not lack of human interest and moral conviction, but rather the heart-quality of fairness, and an earnest desire for the truth despite its possible unpleasantness. Vice in an ideal world becomes virtue in a real, fallible one" (*Philadelphia Negro*, 3). Du Bois redefines social science so as to validate his own values. The heart becomes an integral part of the method, thus warming that cold-blooded science with human belief. Hard work combines with fairness to produce the truth. Simultaneously, Du Bois places himself again in the category of tough-minded realists, those not afraid to face the ugly facts of life. This stance by implication ought to make his work attractive to those tough-minded men of affairs who make the major political and economic decisions.

Rhetorical strategies are further evident when, having admitted all the limitations on his objectivity, Du Bois fills his chapters with tables and graphs to demonstrate that his study is in fact wonderfully objective. He also converts his weaknesses into strengths. For example, the fact that he is the only field worker could be seen as a defect; however, "whatever personal equation is to be allowed for in the whole study is one unvarying quantity, since the work was done by one investigator, and the varying judgments of a score of census-takers was thus avoided" (3). The mathematical tropes serve to reinforce the reliability of the statement. The first chapter closes with another statement in which the mask of scholarly humility conceals rhetorical control. Given all the qualifications, the results of the research are "presented to the public, not as complete and without error, but as possessing on the whole enough reliable matter to serve as the scientific basis of further study, and of practical reform" (4). Despite its limitations, the work accomplishes its purposes of futhering knowledge and aiding social change; in other words, the end results are the same as they would be if the study were scientifically "perfect."

The study itself is environmentalist, institutionalist, and statistical. Du Bois follows Adolf Wagner in assuming that demographics and other statistics reveal the truth of a subject. He also follows Schmoller in believing that context is of central importance in studying a phenomenon; it is only comprehensible within the framework of its history, environment, and relationships: "The student must clearly recognize that a complete study must not confine itself to the group, but must specially notice the environment; the physical environment of city, sections and houses, the far mightier social environment—the surrounding world of custom, wish, whim, and thought which envelops this group and powerfully influences its social development" (5).

Perspective here is crucial. By asserting the central role of environment, Du Bois begins an attack on racism. Prejudice is premised on the idea that certain characteristics are innate. If Du Bois can show that at least some of the traits assigned to blacks—criminality, laziness, sexual promiscuity—are either false or the result of social influence, he will have built a strong case for reform, since such influence can be changed. He will have forced the hand of those criticizing blacks by showing them how the situation can be improved and placing the burden for doing so on their shoulders. As in *The Suppression of the Slave-Trade,* decisions must be made and action must be taken. Once the truth is clear, then a moral obligation exists to act upon it.

Blacks in Philadelphia represent a distinct group, "a city within a city," with their own history, institutions, and "ideals." He uses interchangeably "people," "race," "nation," and "class" to refer to them. He compares their demographic statistics with those of European nations. He divides them into classes, noting the relationship and responsibility of each to the others. During the course of the book, two things become clear: Du Bois is certain that blacks constitute a separate group, and he is not certain how that group relates to the rest of American society.

The use of the term "class" is ambiguous in the text. At times, as above, it refers to all blacks. More often, however, it refers to specific groups within the black community, divided according to housing, income, and employment (or the lack thereof). These distinctions are part of Du Bois's rejection of the categorizations of blacks by the dominant culture. Blacks do not constitute a homogeneous mass and, in this sense, the title of the book is misleading or perhaps ironic. Du Bois was among the first to recognize the complexity of black social organization. One result of this recognition is that it immediately changes the status of blacks as a group. To be capable of such complexity invalidates the image of the nearly savage black. Another result is that simplistic solutions to the "Negro problem" no longer make sense. Different classes have different needs and ambitions, even if they do belong to an "inferior" race. Possible reform, then, must be based on careful study and thought.

Du Bois rejects an exact correlation between black and white socioeconomic classes. As a group blacks have a much lower status. Their wealthy class approximates the white middle class; their poor are in much worse condition than most white poor. This situation is reflected in employment. The black upper class consists of teachers, doctors, lawyers, clerical workers, and small businessmen. Their middle class comprises manual laborers with regular employment. The lowest classes are the chronically unemployed and criminals.

One major objective of this class analysis is to gain recognition for what E. Franklin Frazier later called the black bourgeoisie.[13] Du Bois sees the future of the race as dependent on the advancement of this professional class. For one thing, he argues, the true reputation of the race ought to be based on an understanding of this group. "In many respects it is right and proper to judge a people by its best classes rather than by its worst classes or middle ranks. The highest class of any group represents its possibilities rather than exceptions, as is so often assumed in regard to the Negro" (*Philadelphia Negro*, 316). Of course, if such a judgment could be obtained, most of the grounds for prejudice would be immediately eliminated, since blacks would be seen as individuals capable of acculturation and achievement rather than as an incompetent, semibarbaric, semicriminal mass.

This upper class is a partial realization of the group ideal Du Bois argues for in such essays as "The Conservation of Races" and "The Talented Tenth." [14] For this reason, the class ought to serve as the model for the lower classes as well as the image of the race for the outside world. Interestingly, this model follows a rather conventional middle-class pattern. It is stable, provincial, educated, and "proper," much like the citizenry of white Philadelphia. Unlike other blacks, this group has a strong belief in the family: "In the upper class alone has the home begun to be the centre of recreation and amusement" (*Philadelphia Negro*, 320). They are ambitious and concerned mainly about money and status; they also tend to isolate themselves from the other classes as they begin to have some success. On this point, in line with his idealization of elites, Du Bois finds them blameworthy: "They make their mistake in failing to recognize that, however laudable an ambition to rise may be, the first duty of an upper class is to serve the lowest classes" (317).

To interpret class relations this way, Du Bois must rely on a paradigm that joins feudal and progressivist values. He makes the feudal aspect explicit later in the book when he says, "His [the black's] social evolution in cities like Philadelphia is approaching a mediaeval stage when the centrifugal forces of repulsion between social classes are becoming more powerful than those of attraction" (392). The same problem of law and will that arose in *Suppression* is apparent here. The language of physics and biology suggests that history and society follow certain scientific laws. But this thrust contradicts the duty that the class has to those below it. The duty has to be freely accepted if it is to be effective, according to the rules of the moral system Du Bois applies. Social evolution then cannot refer to a deterministic model, such as that suggested by the social Darwinists, but rather to an overall pattern of progress that can be affected by conscious action.

Such a reading helps to clarify repeated references in *The Philadelphia Negro* to the "low level of civilization" at which blacks live. From this perspective, all races and nations are judged by an absolute standard of civilization. Blacks are making progress, but compared to others, primarily Western Europeans and white Americans, they have barely begun. The standard is essentially Eurocentric, since European history appears to be the model of cultural evolution, leaving Africa, for example, the traditional "dark continent" of Western thought. Black Americans are out of that stage of barbarism, but they have not yet achieved the sophistication and complexity of modern society. Du Bois clearly indicates his assumptions when he says of the black upper class that "they can hardly fulfill their duty as the leaders of the Negroes until they are captains of industry over their people as well as richer and wiser" (318). In his later works, Du Bois returns again and again to the role of an elite necessary to human progress. As he grows more suspicious of capitalism, education and ideology more than money serve as the criteria for membership, but the expectations for such a group remain the same.

The necessity of moral leadership becomes apparent when Du Bois offers what amounts to a pathological interpretation of the black community. This reading is related to but goes beyond his model of social evolution. The situation of the black family, economic conditions, crime, immorality, lack of social organization, the state of health, and the geographic backgrounds of the population are all symptomatic of a diseased community. He finds causes for this condition in the slave origins of many residents, in discrimination, and in a degree of innate lassitude. Du Bois uses the biological metaphor as a description of reality and in the process argues that victims are to some extent responsible for their victimization.

The black family, according to Du Bois, suffered severe damage during slavery and has yet to recover. "The home was destroyed by slavery, struggled up after emancipation, and is again not exactly threatened, but neglected in the life of city Negroes" (196). The causes of this neglect are largely economic; the low level of income inhibits marriage and the establishment of families. The consequences are great: "As has been before intimated, the difficulty of earning income enough to afford to marry, has had its ill effects on the sexual morality of city Negroes, especially, too, since their hereditary training in this respect has been lax" (116). This means a large number of single men and women and a resultant high level of illegitimacy and social disease. As in *The Suppression of the Slave-Trade*, economics strongly influence morality. As Du Bois puts it, "The Negro urban home has commenced a revolution which will either purify and raise it or more thoroughly debauch it than now; and the determining factor is economic opportunity" (168). Economic stability is necessary to familial stability and thus to morality, since Du Bois sees the family as the major moral institution. "The mass of the Negro people must be taught sacredly to guard the home, to make it the centre of social life and moral guardianship" (195–96). The patriarchal social structure of late nineteenth-century America becomes the standard by which black social organization and morality are to be tested and serves as the basis for reform of the race.

The economic condition of blacks affects virtually every aspect of their lives. Social as well as moral development is possible only when the black community is financially secure. A strong middle class is not possible as long as blacks are limited to menial labor and marginal professional positions. And a strong middle class is seen by Du Bois as the basis of black progress. Without such a model to provide hope, the race is susceptible to political corruption, criminality, and intense social frustration. As a result, Du Bois is careful to point out, the race will become a burden to the city.

But such a middle class is not likely to develop under the conditions in which black Philadelphians find themselves. They are kept out of craft unions, hired by industries only as strikebreakers, and often supplanted by European immigrants in many of the jobs they have traditionally held. Moreover, they enter the scene at an unfortunate moment in economic history: "In another age of industrial development they would have already constituted themselves a growing class of small tradesmen; but to-day the department store and stock company make the competition too great for people with so little commercial training and instinct" (117).

The forces of history could be counteracted if it were not for the added impact of prejudice. Economic advancement is a struggle and "in every such battle, when a Negro is fighting for an economic advantage, there is ever a wide-spread feeling among all his neighbors that it is inexpedient to all this class to become wealthy or even well-to-do" (121). And what is true for the middle class is even more true for laborers. In this case, Du Bois puts the major blame on the white working class, which has a history of prejudice, but more importantly, fears the black threat to wage levels. He balances this accusation somewhat by indicting blacks for being willing to accept lower pay. Interestingly, the group that escapes almost unscathed in his analysis is employers; they are mainly seen as the passive abettors of workers' prejudice. In his argument, no strict cause-and-effect relationship is established between prejudice and economic competition, except to the extent that adverse economic conditions tend to exacerbate racial tensions. This essentially conservative position changes as Du Bois's ideology shifts.

One effect of the economic situation is crime, although the discussion makes clear that there are other causes, especially the process of urbanization. Careful examination of criminal activity is necessary since it is a part of the stereotype of blacks. By showing environmental sources for criminality, Du Bois seeks to undermine the grounds for prejudice. "This phenomenon would seem to have sufficient cause in the increased complexity of life, in industrial competition, and the rush of great numbers to the large cities" (246). The emancipation of an illiterate, ill-trained, and ill-prepared group of people was bound to create social disruption, he contends. Few social institutions existed through which blacks could be prepared for the transition from slavery to industrial labor. The move to Northern cities in search of economic opportunities and the frequent disappointment of expectations naturally aggravated the situation. The resultant crime is therefore to have been expected. But Du Bois is careful to note that this activity is carried on by a small illiterate "class"; the large majority of blacks are as law-abiding as their white fellow citizens. Therefore, the labeling of the race as a criminal mass is wholly irrational.

But that stereotyping exists despite reason and because of racism. The question of prejudice pervades *The Philadelphia Negro*. Even the black church is shown to be a product of racism. The trouble with prejudice, from Du Bois's perspective, is that it cannot easily be reduced to graphs or demographic tables. He does try to define it by offering examples of discrimination, especially in employment, but he willingly admits that it is also deeper and more obscure; it is "a certain manifestation of a real or assumed aversion, a spirit of ridicule or patronage, a vindictive hatred in some, absolute indifference in others" (350). If its nature is difficult to clarify, its effects are quite obvious: "It is certain that Negro prejudice in cities like Philadelphia has been a vast factor in aiding and abetting all other causes which impel a half-developed race to recklessness and excess" (351). Economic conditions, urbanization, illiteracy, and class hostilities interact with and are reinforced by prejudice. If blacks were free to develop according to their abilities, then they would make the same progress as other groups. Instead, however, racism creates cruel ironies. Belief in the basic criminality of the race leads charitable institutions to aid the criminal but not to provide jobs to keep ambitious young blacks out of criminal activity. Prejudice thereby creates its own evidence. A city in the midst of commercial growth refuses to train blacks for industry and commerce and then decries black ineptitude and laziness. "The same Philadelphian who would not let a Negro work in his store or mill will contribute handsomely to relieve Negroes in poverty and distress" (355). White workers exclude blacks from unions and then vilify them when they take jobs as strikebreakers.

Of course, in a sense these are not ironies at all but deliberate acts to keep blacks in a subordinate position. With the flood of immigrants, native white workers have to have some means of controlling wage levels and do so in part by excluding blacks from the job competition. Similarly, employers use the threat of black workers to keep down labor costs. The white benefactor is carefully ineffectual in his philanthropy because practical, long-term assistance such as employment and promotion would threaten the state of dependence in which blacks are kept. A successful black middle class conceivably could undermine the economic power of whites.

Du Bois sees much but not all of this in *The Philadelphia Negro*; to him prejudice is largely a matter of ignorance and unenlightened self-interest. The importance of economic and historical factors in his analysis indicates a complex perspective on this subject; however, his recommendations for reform reflect a belief in good will and rationality as primary human motives: "Social reforms move slowly and yet when Right is reinforced by calm but persistent Progress we somehow all feel that in the end it must triumph" (393). Moreover, "the little decencies of daily intercourse can go on, the courtesies of life be exchanged even across the color line without any danger to the supremacy of the Anglo-Saxon or the social ambition of the Negro" (397). These assertions are grounded more in his moral convictions and belief in the legitimacy of Eurocentric culture than in his empirical evidence, which would logically lead him to more pessimistic conclusions about prejudice, human nature, and reform.

He largely ignores the irrational basis of prejudice. But this neglect is inherent in the nature of the project. To affirm that prejudice has psychological depths too deep to plumb scientifically would be to deny the possibility of intelligent and "practical" reform. His book's raison d'être would be destroyed. He in fact continually returned to this problem, always refusing to believe that it was outside the discourse of reason and yet also displaying an apocalyptic sensibility that suggested despair if reason could not name and resolve the problem. He constantly sought a system of rules by which to structure the issue. His later shifts in ideology can be seen both as efforts at accurate naming and as strategies for resolution. *The Philadelphia Negro* was his attempt to apply the scientific methodology of sociology to what at some level he knew to be an inherently unscientific problem.

In these early works Du Bois uses the techniques of current social science to study what he knew from the beginning to be a complex subject. Though he held up the image of the objective, disinterested scientist as a model, his topic did not allow for total objectivity, and the methods he had been taught permitted the kind of moral engagement he needed. Thus, he could shape the historical drama of *Suppression of the Slave-Trade* and the social gospel sermon of *The Philadelphia Negro* without compromising the principles of his German training. In both cases he questions the motivations and behavior of the dominant order in terms of the declared values of that order and demands a reformation of the society in line with the Law of the Father.

The Propaganda
of History

Black Reconstruction in America

This chapter must begin at the end. The conclusion of *Black Reconstruction in America* (1935) provides a key to understanding Du Bois's historical sensibility. The final chapter is entitled "The Propaganda of History." In one sense, it is merely a bibliographical essay on the historiography of the postbellum period. But, as the title indicates, Du Bois intends much more, for he calls into question the whole process of writing history. He claims that history as a profession has betrayed its ideal of a scientific discipline and instead become a tool of political and economic interests: "We shall never have a science of history until we have in our colleges men who regard the truth as more important than the defense of the white race, and who will not deliberately encourage students to gather thesis material in order to support a prejudice or buttress a lie."[1]

The role of the historian is carefully distinguished from other roles:

> In the first place, somebody in each era must make clear the facts with utter disregard to his own wish and desire and belief. What we have got to know, so far as possible, are the things that actually happened in the world. Then with that much clear and open to each reader, the philosopher and prophet has a chance to interpret these facts; but the historian has no right, posing as scientist, to conceal or distort facts; and until we distinguish between these two functions of the chronicler of human action, we are going to render it easy for a muddled world out of sheer ignorance to make the same mistake ten times over. (*Reconstruction*, 722)

Rhetorically at least, Du Bois has resolved the oppositions of earlier works—science and morality—by dividing them into distinct operations. Gathering information is separated from interpreting it. The matter is not so simple, though, since the gathering is not an end in itself but still the means to reform: "If we are going, in the future, not simply with regard to this one question, but with regard to all social problems, to be able to use human experience for the guidance of mankind, we have got clearly to distinguish between fact and desire" (722). In reality, three, not two, functions are under discussion: historian, prophet, and propagandist. The historian objectively examines the past, trying to clarify "what really happened." The prophet uses those facts to inspire changes in attitude and activity for the good of society. The propagandist distorts or suppresses facts to benefit some political, economic, or racial interest. In *Black Reconstruction in America*, Du Bois plays the first two roles in order to attack the third. By clarifying and interpreting, he calls into question American history as it has been usually, and wrongly, understood. But this effort at revision is itself necessarily a political act, since it challenges those who have had the power to control the present by narrating the past.

The full title of Du Bois's text, *Black Reconstruction in America: An Essay toward a History of the Part Which Black Folk Played in the Attempt to Reconstruct Democracy in America, 1860–1880,* suggests the multiplicity of aims he seeks to achieve. An essay toward a history suggests a return to the monographic tradition of *Suppression of the Slave-Trade*, in which a work was to be simply a part of the larger project of historiography to establish facts. The emphasis on the part played by blacks indicates an interpretation that blacks were not merely observers of American history but in some sense shapers of it. Finally, to label this story *black* Reconstruction and to assert that that rebuilding was of democracy makes the author a polemicist, since such phrasing implies that blacks are central to the development of democracy in America and that Reconstruction itself was not the corrupt "tragic era" white historians had named it but rather a progressive stage in the nation's history.

In the first aspect, identifying "what happened," Du Bois undertakes to document events through the use of archival materials, memoirs, and, with reservations, other histories of the period. He seeks to be scientific in the terms established by his German training. But the very definition of his subject involves a moral and political commitment. Howard Zinn has described this aspect of the historian's work: "How shall all this affect the actual work of the historian? For one thing, it calls for an emphasis on those historical facts which have hitherto been obscured, and whose recall would serve to enhance justice and brotherhood."[2] By undertaking a study of the role of blacks in this episode of American history, Du Bois is making assertions that were, at the time, radical: blacks had a history, they were active in that history, and their history is important. But beyond such assertions is the more significant generation of a narrative in which the race becomes a collective hero. Scientific truth leads here not only to moral and political truth but also to myth.

That Du Bois realizes the moral implications of what he is doing is made clear in his prefatory note:

> It would be only fair to the reader to say frankly in advance that the attitude of any person toward this story will be distinctly influenced by his theories of the Negro race. If he believes that the Negro in America and in general is an average and ordinary human being, who under given environment develops like other human beings, then he will read this story and judge it by the facts adduced. If, however, he regards the Negro as a distinctly inferior creation, who can never successfully take part in modern civilization and whose emancipation and enfranchisement were gestures against nature, then he will need something more than the sort of facts that I have set down. But this latter person, I am not trying to convince. I am simply pointing out these two points of view, so obvious to Americans, and then without further ado, I am assuming the truth of the first. In fine, I am going to tell this story as though Negroes were ordinary human beings, realizing that this attitude will from the first seriously curtail my audience. (*Reconstruction*, ix)

Du Bois cannot begin with a defense of the significance of his subject. Instead he must take up a more basic question: whether blacks are part of human history at all. By answering in the affirmative, he sees himself defying the dominant society. The assumption of black humanity and the writing of its history are radical political and social gestures, regardless of one's method or ideology. No matter how "objective" his presentation, Du Bois of necessity operates in a morally and politically charged context. In setting up his axioms, Du Bois defines the terms of evaluation of his work. If it is not well received, as he anticipates, the fault will lie with his racist critics and not with his method. His is the true science because it grounds itself in logic, fact, and environment, not in irrational prejudice. Only critics with the same sensibility as his can properly judge what he says. Moreover, he defines his own role self-sacrificially: he chooses the truth over professional success. He deliberately restricts his audience by refusing to accommodate prejudice. Thus, he becomes heroic like the race whose heroic tale he narrates.

The methodology adopted in this study is, appropriately, the historical materialism of Marx. Such a "scientific" system reinforces Du Bois's interest in economics and provides him with a vocabulary for discussing self-interest that minimizes the overtly moralistic tone of his earlier work. The language can be found in the table of contents: "The General Strike," "The Black Proletariat in South Carolina," "The Duel for Labor Control on Border and Frontier."

But the analysis involves more than renaming events. Du Bois examines the period from 1850 to 1880 in terms of economic interest and class struggle. He makes a primary division between capitalists and laborers and then explores the conflicts between and within these classes. He was criticized at the time and later for a faulty application of Marxist methods, especially in his treatment of racial conflict.[3] It is more useful to see Du Bois modifying the system to fit the situation and his own ideological and narrative purposes. He uses the method of historical materialism without accepting its description of reality. He adapts a European model to the circumstances of the postbellum, racially divided American South. The book is ultimately non-Marxian, but for more subtle reasons than critics have allowed. Du Bois cannot finally accept the deterministic and materialistic underpinnings of standard Marxism, because these violate the voluntarist, idealist, and moralistic foundations of his own perception of reality. To the extent that Marxism offers a coherent, rational theory of history, it is useful to Du Bois; but when the theory threatens to undermine human responsibility and potential, it becomes inappropriate.

Mid-nineteenth-century Americans are divided in the text into six categories, much like character types: abolitionist-democrats, Northern capitalists, Northern laborers, Southern planters, black laborers, and poor whites. Each group represents both a political and economic interest, though economics tend to be more important. The most political group, as indicated by the name, is the abolitionist-democrats: "This movement was not primarily a labor movement or a matter of profit and wage. It simply said that under any condition of life, the reduction of a human being to real estate was a crime against humanity of such enormity that its existence must be immediately ended" (*Reconstruction*, 20). The movement nonetheless had an economic base. "The abolition-democracy was the liberal movement among both laborers and small capitalists, who united in the American Assumption, but saw the danger of slavery to both capital and labor" (184).[4] What the reformers were after, in effect, was the nationalizing of free enterprise based on small business and free labor. The right of all persons to sell their labor or the products of that labor for what they could get was the basic economic premise.

The combined beliefs in moral and economic freedom made abolition-democracy a powerful force. The idea that moral strength increases in alliance with self-interest continues here as in Du Bois's earlier works. This power is manifest in the two men he selects to symbolize the movement, Charles Sumner and Thaddeus Stevens: "Charles Sumner was at the time fifty-five years of age, handsome, but heavy of carriage, a scholar and gentleman, no leader of men but a leader of thought, and one of the finest examples of New England culture and American courage. His speech laid down a Magna Charta of democracy in America" (193). The description, while defining one kind of hero for this epic, also fits the author of the passage. Du Bois assigns himself, implicitly or explicitly, the same qualities in various places in his writings; as is so frequently the case, the protagonist here follows the model of the storyteller. Here is the idealist, who refuses compromise on black rights but tends to ignore economic considerations. This limitation must be compensated for:

> The second seer of democracy was Thaddeus Stevens. He was a man different entirely in method, education and thought from Charles Sumner. We know Stevens best when he was old and sick, and when with grim and awful courage he made the American Congress take the last step

which it has ever taken toward democracy. Yet in one respect Stevens in his thought was even more realistic than Charles Sumner, although Sumner later followed him; from the first, Stevens knew that beneath all theoretical freedom and political right must lie the economic foundation. (197)

Stevens is a realist inspired by a moral vision; this is the Du Bois who adds Marxist analysis to the struggle for a new moral order. Historically, the idealist and the realist make Reconstruction a reality, just as their narrator seeks economic and racial justice in the Great Depression. The difference is that the earlier men, in order to enact their vision, necessarily engage in compromises fatal to their creation. Thus, their part of the tale plays out a classical tragedy.

The sources of their failure are their own economic roots. Abolition-democracy was a petty-bourgeois movement and, as such, at cross-currents with Northern labor:

> Here, then were two labor movements; the movement to give the black worker a minimum legal status which would enable him to sell his own labor, and another movement which proposed to increase the wage and better the condition of the working class in America, now largely composed of foreign immigrants, and dispute with the new American capitalism the basis upon which the new wealth was to be divided. Broad philanthropy and a wide knowledge of the elements of human progress would have led these two movements to unite and in their union to become irresistible. It was difficult, almost impossible, for this to be clear to the white labor leaders of the thirties. They had their particularistic grievances and one of these was the competition of free Negro labor. Beyond this they could easily vision a new and tremendous competition of black workers after all the slaves became free. What they did not see nor understand was that this competition was present and would continue and would be emphasized if the Negro continued as a slave worker. On the other hand, the Abolitionists did not realize the plight of the white laborer, especially the semi-skilled and unskilled worker. (20–21)

Northern workers suffer from economic myopia; they recognize only their immediate and not their long-term self-interest. Rather than seeing a unitary labor problem, they allow themselves to be manipulated into a division of labor and racial interests. Blacks, not capitalists, become the source of their problems and the targets of their hostilities. They perceive the Civil War as a contest between capitalist systems, with their interests represented by neither side. Possible sympathy for the North based on the potential threat of the expansion of slavery into free-labor territory is neutralized by the prospect of millions of freed blacks taking away "white" jobs. Anti-black riots during and after the war in major Northern cities were one result of this economic fear. The abolitionist-democrats, who held to the same gospel of free labor but whose interests tended to favor capital, failed to grasp the depth of fear and to accommodate their rhetoric and principles to the laborers' situation. This failure on both sides to seize the moment on the highest moral ground produces, as is so often the case in Du Bois's narratives, violence and ultimate defeat.

What abolitionism did accommodate itself to was Northern capitalism, and this adaption was the source of its greatest success and its inevitable failure. In developing this relationship Du Bois reverts to the moral absolutism of *The Suppression of the Slave-Trade*, although his ideological position is overtly very different. The earlier book castigated the constitutional slave-trade compromise as a surrender to Southern immorality. In *Black Reconstruction*, political necessity is recognized by the author, but his moralistic impulse remains strong. The abolitionist-democrats turn to capitalists because they could make no other agreement:

> When now they were offered alliance with Northern industry, temporary military control, instead of civil government, and then immediate citizenship and the right to vote for Negroes, instead of a period of guardianship, they accepted because they could not refuse; because they knew that this was their only chance and that nothing else would be offered. Their theory of democracy led them to risk all, even in the absence of that economic and educational minimum which they knew was next to indispensible. (186)

The bargain was made with the devil:

> The new industry had a vision not of work but of wealth; not of planned accomplishment, but of power. It became the most conscienceless, unmoral system of industry which the world has experienced. It went with ruthless indifference towards waste, death, ugliness and disaster, and yet reared the most stupendous machine for the efficient organization of work which the world has ever seen. (182)

Here is the moral base of Du Bois's economic analysis; he cannot escape the equation of self-interest, an economic concept, with selfishness, a moral concept. Given this equation, he has to insist that industrialists act willfully and not within the framework of natural or economic law. His effort to apply "scientific" Marxist analysis is complicated by this impulse, since he seems to give morality a place in the base rather than the superstructure. What should be read here is Du Bois's commitment to his own moral vision, which adapts methods to his purposes rather than follows a fixed system of interpretation.

That moral character is not merely an abstraction becomes clear when Du Bois sets up the conflict between Northern and Southern capitalists:

> The Southern planter in the fifties was in a key position to attempt to break and arrest the growth of this domination of all industry by trade and manufacture. But he was too lazy and self-indulgent to do this and he would not apply his intelligence to the problem. His capitalistic rivals of the North were hard-working, simple-living zealots devoting their whole energy to building up an industrial system. They quickly monopolized transport and mines and factories and they were more than willing to include the big plantations. But the planter wanted results without effort. He wanted large income without corresponding investment and he insisted furiously upon a system of production which excluded intelligent labor, machinery, and modern methods. He toyed with the idea of local manufactures and ships and railroads. But this entailed too much work and sacrifice. (37)

Du Bois is not satisfied with demonstrating divergent tendencies in economic development, though this is his overt purpose. Such tendencies must be grounded in different moral characters. The planter does not merely fail to make capital investments; he willfully chooses not to engage his economic intelligence. Operative here seems to be the same moral geography that informed *The Suppression of the Slave-Trade*: the farther south one goes, the lazier and more morally indifferent one becomes. A similar character typology shapes some of his fiction; *The Quest of the Silver Fleece* portrays its Northern and Southern whites in virtually identical terms. Du Bois plays off the cavalier and Yankee stereotypes here. The Yankee may be shrewd and money-oriented, but he has some sense of limits and moral propriety. The cavalier tends to excess both in morality and economics, as the passage cited above indicates.

The typology also facilitates a moral continuum that transcends economics. Every group in the narrative—abolitionist-democrats, Northern labor, Northern capital, Southern planters, poor whites, black laborers—acts according to its self-interest. But that term has moral connotations and, without modification, would imply the moral equality of the groups. Since he cannot accept such a formulation, Du Bois must designate group qualities in order to make distinctions. Such qualities include courage, hard work, incorruptibility, belief in education, belief in democracy, and belief in brotherhood. Judging by these standards allows the creation of a hierarchy, with blacks at the top and white Southerners at the bottom. Such a pattern clearly serves to validate its creator's moral and ideological vision rather than define historical reality in any "objective" sense.

When this moral system is used in conjunction with the principle of self-interest, important results are produced. Black self-interest works to the good of all because it embodies high moral values. At the other extreme, the self-interest of the planters is self-destructive, because it blinds them to the complex workings of the moral, economic, and political order. Somewhere in the middle, the Northern capitalist is economically successful because of his diligence but eventually doomed because of his antidemocratic and exploitative practices.

The necessity of this hierarchy becomes apparent when Du Bois begins, after a long prelude, his discussion of Reconstruction proper. The issues, activities, and dramatis personae are complex, but his categories provide clarification as well as a basis for judgment. The operation of this method can be best seen through examination of an individual chapter. "Transubstantiation of a Poor White" has Andrew Johnson as its title character, but it includes in its analysis all the groups in the typology. It opens, not with a portrait of Johnson, but with a summary of the economic basis of the war:

> If Northern industry before the war had secured a monopoly of the raw material raised in the South for its new manufactures; and if Northern and Western labor could have maintained their wage scale against slave competition, the North would not have touched the slave system. But this the South had frustrated. It had threatened labor with nationwide slave competition and had sent its cotton abroad to buy cheap manufactures, and had resisted the protective tariff demanded by the North. (237)

The interactions are complicated, but at the level of economic analysis, the causes of the war are readily apparent. Conflicting economic interests cannot be resolved peaceably. Civil war comes because slavery as an economic system threatened industrial development and therefore had to be eliminated.

But this interpretation does not satisfy Du Bois because it takes virtually no account of blacks:

> The results of the war left four million human beings just as valuable for the production of cotton and sugar as they had been before the war—but during the war, as laborers and soldiers, these Negroes had made it possible for the North to win, and without their actual and possible aid, the South would never have surrendered; and not least, these four million free men formed in the end the only possible moral justification for an otherwise sordid and selfish orgy of murder, arson and theft. (238)

Blacks not only are crucial for Northern victory; they give it meaning. The economic conflict of the page before has become a "sordid and selfish orgy." The pursuit of self-interest has at most a negative meaning; only when it is put in the service of some ideal, such as freedom, can it have positive value. Blacks provide the means for this transvaluation.

Du Bois in effect tries to have it both ways. While Northern capital fights the war primarily for "trade and wealth" (238), using "freedom" only as a rallying cry and eventually betraying blacks, those same blacks nonetheless shape the true meaning of the war and Reconstruction.

A similar tension evidences itself in the portrayal of Andrew Johnson. He is depicted as the ultimate poor white, an actualization of the "white trash" stereotype. He suffers the Southern tendency to excess without redeeming social graces. Du Bois discusses his excessive drinking, his demogogic oratorical style, his lack of political subtlety, and his intense prejudices. These prejudices include a love-hate relationship with the planting class and a refusal to recognize black humanity. The costs of these biases were high: "It was the drear destiny of the Poor White South that, deserting its economic class and itself, it became the instrument by which democracy in the nation was done to death, race provincialism deified, and the world delivered to plutocracy. The man who led the way with unconscious paradox and contradiction was Andrew Johnson" (241).

This tragedy occurred partially because of Johnson's intense ambivalence toward the Southern aristocracy. To explain this attitude, Du Bois finds economics inadequate; psychological analysis is also required:

The very inferiority complex which made him hate the white planter concealed a secret admiration for his arrogance and address. . . . In fact, personally, Johnson liked the slave-holders. He admired their manners; he enjoyed their carriage and clothes. They were quite naturally his ideal of what a gentleman should be. He could not help being tremendously flattered when they noticed him and actually sued for his favor. As compared with Northerners, he found them free, natural and expansive, rather than cold, formal and hypocritical. (254–56)

Johnson holds to a Southern version of the American assumption: even the least of poor whites can aspire to the position of Southern planter.

The roles of ideology and psychology are crucial for Du Bois's interpretation. By such means, he continues his quest for the rational explanation for greed and prejudice that perpetually eludes him. The discourse of psychology offers him a way to read the subjective aspects of Johnson's thought and action, thus bringing them within the discursive universe of reason. If successful, according to his interpretive scheme, they can then be subjected to the problem-solving techniques of modern science. He can thus create the possibility of an intelligent resolution of heretofore insoluble difficulties.

Johnson's attitude affected the political alignments of the time. During his administration, the abolitionist-democrats were joined by Northern industrialists in opposing the presidential reconstruction plan. This alliance was based on a mutual fear of a politically revived South that would oppose the legislation necessary to build a national industrial and commercial economy. Industrialists feared the effects on their profits, while abolitionists feared the reenslavement of blacks. On the other side were the planters who wanted to regain their property and labor source, and poor whites, such as Johnson, who saw an opportunity to gain influence by siding with the planters.

But racial prejudice reshaped even these areas of economic and political interests. Northern capitalists wanted a docile labor force and were not concerned with political rights. When a compromise became possible in 1876 that permitted both industrialization and white supremacy, Northern support for blacks evaporated. As for the South, even self-interest could not overcome racism:

Of course, the Southerners believed such persons [capable blacks] to be exceptional, but all that was asked of them at this time was to recognize the possibility of exceptions. To such a reasonable offer the nation could and would have responded. It could have paid for the Negro's land and education. It could have contributed to relief and restoration of the South. Instead of that came a determination to reestablish slavery, murder, arson, and flogging; a dogmatic opposition to Negro education and decent legal status; determination to have political power based on voteless Negroes, and no vote to any Negro under any circumstances. This showed the utter absence of common sense in the leadership of the South. (275)

History here is judged by a standard of reason joined to morality and justice. The South's behavior is willfully irrational; it substitutes dogmatism for "common sense." It works against its own long-term interest by surrendering to racism.

This is the position adopted by Johnson. Regardless of his populist ideals, he was limited by racial bigotry. "Andrew Johnson could not include Negroes in any conceivable democracy. He tried to, but as a poor white, steeped in the limitations, prejudices, and ambitions of his social class, he could not; and this is the key to his career" (242). This class ideology, which in fact works to the detriment of poor whites, is one that Du Bois consistently finds in white laboring classes and one that necessarily modifies his Marxist perspective.

But lack of class consciousness does not make one less culpable individually, especially for failures due to racism. Northern white laborers are held responsible for riots and Southern workers are accountable for lynchings, even though both groups are encouraged by local capitalists for economic reasons. In just this manner, Johnson cannot avoid the judgment of history, despite his commitment to the American Assumption:

> The Transubstantiation of Andrew Johnson was complete. He had begun as the champion of the poor laborer, demanding that the land monopoly of the Southern oligarchy be broken up, so as to give access to the soil, South and West, to the free laborer. He had demanded the punishment of those Southerners who by slavery and war had made such an economic program impossible. Suddenly thrust into the Presidency, he had retreated from this attitude. He had not only given up extravagent ideas of punishment, but he had dropped his demand for dividing up plantations when he realized that Negroes would largely be beneficiaries. Because he could not conceive of Negroes as men, he refused to advocate universal democracy, of which, in

his young manhood, he had been the fiercest advocate, and made strong alliance with those who would restore slavery under another name. (322)

Johnson's tragic flaw is racism; he knew what was right and had the opportunity to enact it, but bigotry prevented that. The explanation and the meaning of this parable of the nation's history is clear:

> This change did not come by deliberate thought or conscious desire to hurt—it was rather the tragedy of American prejudice made flesh; so that the man born to narrow circumstances, a rebel against economic privilege, died with the conventional ambition of a poor white to be the associate and benefactor of monopolists, planters and slave drivers. In some respects, Andrew Johnson is the most pitiful figure of American history. A man who, despite great power and great ideas, became a puppet, played upon by mighty fingers and selfish, subtle minds; groping, self-made, unlettered and alone; drunk, not so much with liquor, as with the heady wine of sudden and accidental success. (322)

Johnson is the victim of two illusions, the American dream and white supremacy. He is, as is repeatedly the case in Du Bois's work, a kind of prodigal son who loses his great opportunity by following false fathers. Whatever success he attains is deceptive, and consistently in Du Bois's histories, life stories, and fiction, such men are shown to be empty and often pathetic.

The nobler way is the path of the group largely missing from the discussion so far: blacks. As the book title indicates, this is their story. But their role can only be understood in the context of the other groups involved, for the claim Du Bois makes is a complex one: blacks were largely responsible for the achievements of Reconstruction, but not so important as to be held responsible for the scandals that accompanied those achievements. Furthermore, black self-interest is not really self-interest at all; rather it is the general good. Blacks are the exceptions to the rules of economics and thus worthy, in Du Bois's view, of idealization. What he does in effect is offer here the alternative to the nation's flawed choices that was not present in *The Suppression of the Slave-Trade*; the tale now has a hero to accompany its villains and tragic figures.

The need for the paradoxical claims about blacks is dictated by the Bourbon historiography mentioned at the beginning of this chapter. The double charge was made that blacks were incompetent and corrupt. To counteract this indictment, Du Bois adduces hundreds of pages documenting the efficient and beneficent design of Reconstruction legislation and the effectiveness and integrity of black political figures:

> Consequently, with Northern white leadership, the Negro voters quite confounded the planter plan; they proved apt pupils in politics. They developed their own leadership. They gained clearer and clearer conceptions of how their political power could be used for their own good. They were unselfish, too, in wishing to include in their own good the white worker and even the ex-master. Of course, all that was done in Constitution-making and legislation at this time was not entirely the work of black men, and in the same way all that was done in maladministration and corruption was not entirely the fault of the black man. But if the black man is to be blamed for the ills of Reconstruction, he must also be credited for its good, and that good is indubitable. In less than ten years, the basic structure of capitalism in the South was changed by his vote. A new modern state was erected in the place of agrarian slavery. And its foundations were so sound and its general plan so good that despite bitter effort, the South had to accept universal suffrage in theory at least, and had to accept the public school system. It had to broaden social control by adding to the landholder the industrial capitalist. . . . The Negro buttressed Southern civilization in precisely the places it was weakest, against popular ignorance, oligarchy in government, and land monopoly. (621)

Blacks come close to canonization. If "transubstantiation" was an ironic term for Andrew Johnson, its use here would be straightforward. Despite their experience of slavery for generations, blacks have few faults, many virtues, and they consistently return good for evil. Conscious of the conventional wisdom about Reconstruction, Du Bois must make large claims for the race in order to gain any respect for it. In a sense, he destroys one myth by creating another. But he is careful to ground his myth in historical reality. Black labor, while it gained a certain degree of power, still thought in the old Southern economic terms: "But Southern [black] labor was still thinking in terms of land and crops and the old forms of wealth, and was but dimly conscious of the new industry and the new wealth" (587). But changes were coming: "Economic revolution did not come immediately. Negro labor was ignorant, docile and conservative. But it was beginning to learn; it was beginning to assert itself. It was beginning to have radical thoughts as to the distribution of land and wealth" (590). Unlike white Southerners, blacks were capable of learning, of gaining a sense of the long-term interests that were involved; this is further evidence of their virtue.

At one level, the great promise and equally great threat of black Reconstruction was to be found in these beginnings. "It was not, then, that the post-bellum South could not produce wealth with free labor; it was the far more fundamental question as to whom this wealth was to belong to and for whose interests laborers were to work" (591). The question was an economic one; either former landholders would somehow regain their property and thereby their wealth and power or else an economic democracy would be created.

The latter was a contradiction of the American assumption, since it would redistribute land and wealth by political policy rather than free enterprise and therefore would be problematic for most of the key groups in the society. It also contradicted the other key assumption, white supremacy, since it implied the equality of all laboring people.

Inevitably, then, black Reconstruction was doomed, though by violence rather than inherent weakness: "It is argued that Negro suffrage was bad because it failed, and at the same time that its failure was a proof of its badness. Negro suffrage failed because it was overthrown by brute force. Even if it had been the best government on earth, force, exercised by a majority of richer, more intelligent and more experienced men, could have overthrown it" (631). *Black Reconstruction*, then, is the story of white, not black, failure. Violence is the logical end of the irrationality by which the white South chose to operate. Whites failed to grasp the opportunity to realize American ideals and settled instead for unreason:

> If that part of the white South which had a vision of democracy and was willing to grant equality to Negroes of equal standing had been sustained long enough by a standing federal police, democracy could have been established in the South. But brute force was allowed to use its unchecked power in the actions of the whites to destroy the possibility of democracy in the South, and thereby make the transition from democracy to plutocracy all the easier and more inevitable. (632)

The relationship between race and class remains complex. Racism, though it can be used by economic interests, also generates its own system of rules and even creates modes of economic exploitation. The North, for example, accepts the Southern ideology for reasons that are not economic; like the South, it fears that political power will lead to miscegenation and social equality. In response to these fears, it creates its own rationalizations:

> Under such circumstances, it was easier to believe the accusations of the South and to listen to the proof which biology and social science hastened to adduce of the inferiority of the Negro. The North seized upon the new Darwinism, the "survival of the Fittest," to prove that what they had attempted in the South was an impossibility; and they did this in the face of the facts which were before them, the examples of Negro efficiency, of Negro brains, of phenomenal possibilities of advancement. (631)

Du Bois refuses to reduce racism to a function of economics. While it can be manipulated for economic reasons, it clearly involves more than this. Furthermore, by not reducing it to economics, he can make moral arguments against it that are not necessarily linked to self-interest. On its own terms, racism leads to the perversion of truth and science. The willful distortion of understanding is not only dishonest but also powerfully destructive:

> And so the South rode the wind into the whirlwind and accomplished what it sought. Did it pay? Did it settle either the Negro's problem or any problem of wealth, labor, or human uplift? On the contrary, it made the government of the South a system of secret manipulations with lying and cheating. It made its religion fundamental hypocrisy. And the South knows today that the essential Negro problem is just as it was—how far it dare let the Negro be a modern man. (632–33)

As always in Du Bois's narratives, evil must be paid for through self-destruction. The long view of history is one of an almost Old Testament moral order. If the right does not clearly prevail, at least the wrong does not always prosper.

Aligned with this perspective is the other reason for distinguishing race and economics: the black ideal. If blacks are "merely" another class of self-interested human beings, then they exist in no special relationship to truth and their oppression has no necessary meaning. Du Bois's moral vision cannot permit such a conclusion. The history of blacks not only has a meaning for him; that meaning is also his key to

American history itself. Blackness is his ordering principle; it provides the ethical ground for judgments about character, politics, economics, and finally the national identity.

Blackness is the measure of courage. The race is a "black Prometheus," who, "bound to the Rock of Ages by hate and humiliation, has his vitals eaten out as they grow, yet lives and fights" (670). A standard is created by which to judge all men:

> And yet, despite this, and despite the long step backward toward slavery that black folk have been pushed, they have made withal a brave and fine fight; a fight against ridicule and monstrous caricature, against every refinement of cruelty and gross insult, against starvation, disease and murder in every form. It has left in their soul its scars, its deep scars; but when all is said, through it all has gone a thread of brave and splendid friendship from those few and rare men and women of white skin, North and South, who have dared to know and help and love black folk. (708)

The idealism inherent in the analysis is made evident here. The meaning of what blacks did during Reconstruction is not limited to history; it transcends "mere" existence and enters the realm of essence. Success or failure in history is less important than the moral values that were enacted in that particular period, for that enactment "proves" that Du Bois's value system has validity. Furthermore, the rewards for such goodness are not necessarily tangible; they are, rather, "treasures laid up in heaven," to use the biblical language implicit in Du Bois's statements. Moreover, whites who associate themselves with blacks attain a kind of sainthood by that association.

In addition, blackness is the measure of political and economic democracy. Reconstruction offered the nation the opportunity to transcend its emerging plutocracy and, led by blacks, to create a new order. Instead, oppression became entrenched and global:

> One can only say to all this that whatever the South gained through its victory in the revolution of 1876 has been paid for at a price which literally staggers humanity. Imperialism, the exploitation of colored labor throughout the world, thrives upon the approval of the United States, and the United States gives that approval because of the South. World war waits on and supports imperial aggression and international jealousy. This was too great a price to pay for anything which the South gained. (706)

Two key Du Bois motifs are played here. One is the often apocalyptic effects of immorality, especially racism and self-interest; the end of irrationality is violence and death. The destruction of black rights produces world war. The second theme is moral economics. More fully developed in *John Brown* (discussed here in chapter 8), the argument is that the cost of oppression is always greater than the price of liberty. Through such a concept, Du Bois can effectively join the polarities of his discourse in interpreting history.

Finally, blackness is the measure of the nation itself:

> The attempt to make black men American citizens was in a certain sense a
> failure, but a splendid failure. It did not fail where it was expected to fail.
> It was Athanasius contra mundum, with back to the wall, outnumbered ten
> to one, with all the wealth and all the opportunity, and all the world against
> him. And only in his hands and heart the consciousness of a great and just
> cause; fighting the battle of all the oppressed and despised humanity of
> every race and color, against the massed hirelings of Religion, Science,
> Education, Law, and brute force. (708)

Beginning in history, Du Bois again ends in myth. Marxian analysis is not sufficient, because Du Bois's vision involves a morality that is more basic than science and therefore must take into account self-sacrifice as well as self-interest, the future as well as the past. Blackness, as reality and ideal, is the criterion of truth. But the very emphasis on sacrifice and morality reflects the narrator's commitment to the Law of the Father. Just as Athanasius did, blacks take on the minions of the dominant order—Religion, Science, Education, Law, and force—not because they represent an order to be destroyed, but rather because they have become perversions of that order. The capitalized terms all are emblems of the trinity of beauty, truth, and goodness that Du Bois always argues for. They have been turned to functions of greed and racial hatred rather than their original noble purpose. Du Bois's narrative is designed in part to deconstruct the discourse of domination and create one of reason, morality, and democracy, which he sees as the authentic and original discourse.

Such a perspective makes clear the necessity of the chapter on historiography. History is his chosen means of revealing truth. Furthermore, he believes that creating the future is only possible by understanding the past. Therefore, historical reconstruction as a scholarly pursuit is both political and prophetic. Those who write history in a sense create reality, because their judgments and interpretations form the story of where the world has been, where it can go, and who has won life's key battles. Historians, in Du Bois's view, are the true legislators of the world.

He explicitly contends that historiography itself has been used to promote self-interest and racism:

> If history is going to be scientific, if the record of human action is going to be set down with that accuracy and faithfulness of detail which will allow its use as a measuring rod and guidepost for the future of nations, there must be set some standards of ethics in research and interpretation. If, on the other hand, we are going to use history for our pleasure and amusement, for inflating our national ego, and giving us a false but pleasurable sense of accomplishment, then we must give up the idea of history either as a science or as an art using the results of science, and admit frankly that we are using a version of historic fact to influence and educate the new generation along the way we wish. (714)

To the bibliographical essay he appends a bibliography that is a parody of conventional apparatus. The categories include "Standard—Anti-Negro (These authors believe the Negro to be sub-human and congenitally unfitted for citizenship and the suffrage)" (731) and "Propaganda (These authors select and use facts and opinions in order to prove that the South was right in Reconstruction, the North vengeful or deceived, and the Negro stupid)" (732). In this manner, Du Bois emphasizes his view that the writing of history has become a self-serving ideological gesture. But in the process, he raises questions about his own commitment to history as science. As we will see again in his definition of literature, he appears to become himself a propagandist for a particular view in his effort to subvert the propaganda of others.

History for him becomes a tool for political change rather than a science or an art, to use his own terms. He contends, obviously, that his interpretation comes closer to truth, but the moral imperative that drives his narrative in fact problematizes the whole project of historiography. It also reveals his own self-interest in his telling. In fighting historiographical distortion, he aligns himself with his subject. He argues for truth, not interests. As a historian, he faces the oligarchy that controls the historical discourse of the nation, just as his black reconstructionists faced powerful economic and political forces. Like them, he is Athanasius *contra mundum* and Prometheus bringing light and fire in defiance of the gods. He enters history by writing history; he becomes truth by speaking truth. He becomes part of the myth he has created.

4

· · · · · · · · · ·

Inscribing the Race

· · · · · · · · ·

The Historical Drama of Africa and the Diaspora

· · · · · · · · ·

Crucial to an understanding of the discourse Du Bois sought to create is the meaning for him of the term *race*, both as an abstraction and as an aspect of history. Here, as elsewhere, a dialectical process is at work: he seeks to overthrow the discursive control of the dominant culture but must use its assumptions to do so. Thus, both in shaping a definition of "race" that will subvert racism and in generating a narrative of black racial history, he feels compelled to operate from within a Eurocentric ideological framework.

For Du Bois, race as a concept was always problematic, as it seems to have been in the late nineteenth and early twentieth centuries for many writers and scholars. Within that discursive universe, the nature of race was widely discussed in scientific, social, political, linguistic, and literary circles, but virtually no one within the debates contended that it was anything other than a fundamental human reality. Race can be defined as fundamental, inheritable differences between large groups of people. These are at minimum physical differences such as skin color, hair texture, and bone structure, but historically they have been held to include linguistic, intellectual, moral, cultural, and, especially important for Du Bois, spiritual differences. My argument is that Du Bois had to operate within the available discourse and in fact needed race to accomplish his ideological purposes.[1]

The debate over race around the turn of the century was multifaceted, involving as it did questions of both the nature and meaning of human differences. Issues included the origins of races, the evolutionary and biological meaning of race, and the roles of language and culture as either determinants or consequences of race. The field of physical anthropology developed specifically to quantify difference through craniometry, hair analysis, and examination of brain weight and condition.[2] At the same time, differences were assigned hierarchical status. Both social and progressive Darwinists believed that history demonstrated the superiority of white civilization over all others; they disagreed over what responsibilities that civilization had to its "inferiors."[3] In contrast, those George Fredrickson has labeled "romantic racialists" believed that the very qualities used to designate blacks as inferior—simplicity, closeness to nature, submissiveness, loyalty—instead made them morally superior to a greedy, violent, arrogant white society.[4] Related to this view was that of Johann Gottfried von Herder, an eighteenth-century German philosopher who argued that the crucial differences among groups were spiritual rather than physical. Each race had its own spiritual essence, which was its contribution to civilization. Herder also complicated the notion of race by identifying it with national groups rather than physical ones.[5]

What this brief and superficial survey should make clear is the complexity of racial discourse at the time Du Bois was writing "The Conservation of Races" (1897) and *The Souls of Black Folk* (1903). At that historical moment, the issue was not the reality of race, but the particular racialist position to be taken. What can be seen in Du Bois's writings is a kind of deconstruction and reinscription of "race" as a signifier. It is important to keep in mind that "Conservation of Races" was presented to the American Negro Academy and that fully a third of the essay lays out what Du Bois saw as the goals and principles of the organization. His comments on race should be read as the philosophical ground for his definition of the Academy. They have, in other words, a specific institutional and ideological purpose.

The ground they establish is a shifting one. Du Bois considers several of the approaches described above and notes the problems with them. Nonetheless, he asserts, "The final word of science, so far, is that we have at least two, perhaps three, great families of human beings" ("Conservation," 816). A page later, the number changes: "We find upon the world's stage today eight distinctly differentiated races, in the sense in which History tells us the word must be used. They are, the Slavs of Eastern Europe, the Teutons of middle Europe, the English of Great Britain and America, the Romance nations of Southern and Western Europe, the Negroes of Africa and America, the Semitic people of Western Asia and Northern Africa, the Hindoos of Central Asia and the Mongolians of Eastern Asia" (817–18). But even this list is not exhaustive since there are "minor race groups," including American Indians, Eskimos, and Polynesians. Such a list is curious since it suggests ties based variously on geography, language origins, religion, and prehistoric migration patterns, as well as conventional hereditary concepts. It also has a Eurocentric bias, since half the groups fit into the "white" category of the original divisions.

The apparent confusion of number and kind is only reinforced by Du Bois's explicit definition of the key term: "What, then, is a race? It is a vast family of human beings, generally of common blood and language, always of common history, traditions and impulses, who are both voluntarily and involuntarily striving together for the accomplishment of certain more or less vividly conceived ideals" (817). The striking aspect of this statement is the extent to which it subverts itself. Even before considering its application to the groups identified, its syntax renders it virtually meaningless. "Generally" makes "blood and language" expendable; "impulses" makes the already imprecise history and traditions very vague; "voluntarily" and "involuntarily" muddy "striving together"; and "more or less" undermines "vividly." Within the groups specified, it is difficult to see how the Romance nations share "common blood," Africans and Afro-Americans common language, Asians a common history, "Semitic people" (taken as those of Jewish and Arab descent) common traditions, and any of the groups common "impulses." If one considers the three large groups mentioned earlier—Caucasian, Negro, Mongolian—the problems are even greater.

Such apparent rhetorical imprecision enables Du Bois to give an aura of scientific authority to his definition without trapping himself within a specific theory. To this he adds, through reference to "ideals of life," an echo of Herder, whose theory is most amenable to Du Bois's project. To assert simultaneously an ideal and its obscurity allows Du Bois both to claim for blacks standing in civilization and to claim for himself the power to specify that standing. That specification is the program he outlines for the American Negro Academy, consisting of elite leadership, higher education, moral probity, and scientific study of race problems. Thus, his theorizing about race is not primarily an engagement in the ongoing discourse, but a breaking down of that discourse so as to inscribe a set of values and principles that would enhance the struggle against racism and, in that process, enhance his position as a leader of the race. He needs the existence of race to have someone to lead, and, moreover, the dominant society could not accept erasure of the term. Because of the latter reality, he needs to manipulate the concept so as to make difference an opportunity rather than a threat. His attempt to do this in "The Conservation of Races" comes through liberating the signifier "race" from its presumed signified.

Several survey works that Du Bois produced during his life demonstrate the need for a flexible and ideologically useful definition of *race*. Each requires the term to justify its historical narrative but also manipulates it to undermine racist perspectives. Thus, *The Gift of Black Folk* (1924), which focuses on black contributions to American history, *The Negro* (1915), *Black Folk: Then and Now* (1939), and *The World and Africa* (1946), all of which treat Africa and the African diaspora, are works that are simultaneously history and propaganda. They seek to establish the facts of black participation in history and to critique European and white American cultural, political, and economic hegemony. This dual purpose means that, on the one hand, *race* must be a substantive term in order to give black Americans and Africans a positive identity to which achievements can be attributed. On the other hand, that difference that is "race" must not be so essential as to call into question the thesis of a common humanity that Du Bois is so desirous of proving.

The Gift of Black Folk was part of a Knights of Columbus series intended, in the words of Edward F. McSweeney, general editor, "as a much needed and important contribution to national solidarity." [6] The series was devoted to recording the contributions of a variety of ethnic groups to the making of the nation, in the context, as McSweeney suggests, of developing immigration restriction legislation (*Gift*, 27–28). More generally, its purpose was to counteract the post–World War I intolerance of difference that encouraged such laws.

Du Bois's work clearly fits into this pattern. He traces not only the practical contributions of blacks in America, but also, as in other works, the less definable "spiritual" gifts. His view, in fact, is that America could not be without blacks:

> This essay is an attempt to set forth more clearly than has hitherto been done the effect which the Negro has had upon American life. Its thesis is that despite slavery, war and caste, and despite our present Negro problem, the American Negro is and has been a distinct asset to this country and has brought a contribution without which America could not have been; and that perhaps the essence of our so-called Negro problem is the failure to recognize this fact and to continue to act as though the Negro was what we once imagined and wanted to imagine him—a representative of a subhuman species fitted only for subordination. (ii–iii)

The "we" of the last sentence suggests Du Bois's rhetorical (and polemical) strategy: he narrates as one within the hegemonic order, one who envisions blacks as other and thus inferior. From this position, he seeks to move a like-thinking audience to a more empathetic view. But to do so, he must operate within a frame of reference comprehensible to that audience.

The first three chapters are devoted to concrete contributions in exploration, labor, and military service. Here names, economic statistics, and historical events serve as the more or less objective evidence supporting his position. Even slavery is represented primarily as an economic structure in which black labor provided the basis for industrial development. Even more accommodating to the audience within this section of the book is the racialist characterization of blacks. Two brief passages on black labor make the point: "As a tropical product with a sensuous receptivity to the beauty of the world he was not as easily reduced to be the mechanical draft-horse which the northern European laborer became" (53–54); "The black laborer brought [from the tropics] the idea of toil as a necessary evil ministering to the pleasures of life. While the gift of the white laborer made America rich, it will take the psychology of the black man to make it happy" (79). Such statements fit nicely into the emerging discourses of the Harlem Renaissance and the Jazz Age, in which the virtue of blacks is their resistance to industrial civilization, but they can also be read as simply positive twists on the racist stereotypes of blacks as lazy and childlike. Whites, in this view, are the real workers, whose toil, drudgery though it may be, has created modern society.

Such verbal compromise seems part of a negotiation going on within the text in which Du Bois offers such possible concessions in order to gain a more crucial point. The central chapters, on slavery and Reconstruction, make the key argument that blacks have defined democracy for America and have thereby shaped the meaning of the nation:

> Dramatically the Negro is the central thread of American history. The whole story turns on him whether we think of the dark and flying slave ship in the sixteenth century, the expanding plantations of the seventeenth, the swelling commerce of the eighteenth, or the fight for freedom in the nineteenth. It was the black man that raised a vision of democracy in America such as neither Americans nor Europeans conceived in the eighteenth century and such as they have not even accepted in the twentieth century; and yet a conception which every clear sighted man knows is true and inevitable. (135–36)

Far more than one contributor among many to the story of America, blacks in fact *are* the narrative. With their exclusion, democracy could be defined in terms of economic status or physical power. Their insistence on freedom required not merely an expansion of the idea but a "reconstruction" of it to its fullest meaning. By claiming that even the most scorned and abused of people had rights, they changed the terms of American political discourse.

For Du Bois, this discursive shift is vital, for it permits a positive reading of American history that the actual events do not strongly support. Much like his spirituality argument, this one allows him optimism in the face of the injustice, inhumanity, and failure of democracy that constitute historical reality and that he helped to expose. Even Reconstruction, the period to which he devoted much of his research efforts and on which much of his argument must stand, must be read ambiguously. He shows here, as elsewhere, that the black contribution was primarily moral. Blacks are shown to promote education and the franchise and general social welfare, but not to have decisive political power. In an environment in which Reconstruction was generally considered the American Dark Ages—Claude Bowers's *The Tragic Era* was published five years later—it was essential to Du Bois's purpose to keep blacks as untainted as possible.

The strategy is twofold. The first part is to acknowledge the corruption of the period, but to minimize the black role in it as well as to place the real responsibility elsewhere. Du Bois goes to great lengths to show the extent of corruption before the war and to show its national pervasiveness after, thus establishing that corruption was neither racial nor ideological. Furthermore, blacks were not in positions to reap significant wealth. But, more important, black corruption is itself attributable to the far vaster white evil: "We may not forget that among slaves stealing is not the crime that it becomes in free industry. The slave is victim of a theft so hateful that nothing he can steal can ever match it. The freedmen of 1868 still shared the slave psychology" (227–28). As is generally the case in Du Bois, the sins of the white fathers are the sources of black problems.

The second part of the strategy is to demonstrate that the moral, social, and political achievements of Reconstruction were such that the reactionary governments that overthrew it kept the program largely intact for several years. The irony of history is that whites were the main beneficiaries of the black commitment to democracy and education. He notes that the state constitutions were only replaced years later, that the schools that were set up became the first true public systems in the South, largely benefiting the children of working-class and poor whites, that the social welfare facilities provided care for the first time to the mentally ill and the physically handicapped, and that, most fundamentally, meaningful democracy existed for the first time in the South.

The argument then shifts to more abstract issues by way of consideration of black womanhood, folk song, and literature. These brief chapters are clearly intended to show black cultural efforts, but it is apparent that Du Bois does not believe he has a strong case here. For example, he interprets the labor of black women as placing them in the vanguard of the quest for women's economic independence, and he details the efforts of Harriet Tubman and Mammy Pleasants for black freedom. At the same time, he spends several pages on the black woman as "concubine," to a large extent responsible for the mixing of the races in America. He describes this not as an act of violence, but simply as historical reality. Similarly, he discusses all writing by blacks as "literature," with a disclaimer about the lack of opportunity to do something finer: "The time has not yet come for the great development of American Negro literature. The economic stress is too great and the racial persecution too bitter to allow the leisure and the poise for which literature calls" (305).

The real contribution, the "spiritual gift" of blacks, is of course the most important, given the qualifications made about other efforts, because it can least effectively be challenged with historical evidence. But even here the definition of the dominant culture must be acknowledged:

> Above and beyond all that we have mentioned, perhaps least tangible but just as true, is the peculiar spiritual quality which the Negro has injected into American life and civilization. It is hard to define or characterize it— a certain spiritual joyousness; a sensuous, tropical love of life, in vivid contrast to the cool and cautious New England reason; a slow and dreamful conception of the universe, a drawling and slurring of speech, an intense sensitiveness to spiritual values—all those things and others like to them, tell of the imprint of Africa on Europe in America. (320)

All the qualities listed here align with the dominant culture's construction of blacks as a racial image. They do not take into account individual or regional differences; they cannot, for example, accommodate the highly rational New Englander who wrote the words. Rather than repudiate the perspective of his largely white audience, Du Bois chooses to adopt a racialist position that permits him to implicitly critique the "American civilization" blacks have contributed to. By affirming the terms of racial difference, he can free blacks from complicity in the materialist, philistine, aggressive culture that America has become. By assigning certain qualities to blacks, he is by implication associating their opposites with whites. Thus, the dominant society becomes hard, impatient, money-oriented, profane, and death-loving. He makes the point most clearly in a statement on blacks and American religion: "It [the black race] has kept before America's truer souls the spirit of meekness and self abasement, it has compelled American religion again and again to search its heart and cry 'I have sinned;' and until the day comes when color caste falls before reason and economic opportunity the black American will stand as the last and terrible test of the ethics of Jesus Christ" (338–39).

From being one race among others in American society, blacks have become the surrogate for Christ on earth. They are not contributors but the measure of America, the means by which it is to be judged. And even though the tone of this text is moderate and rational, the final sentence above suggests an apocalyptic subtext. The means of avoiding judgment are clear: reason, economic opportunity, and the end of color caste. Acceptance means the creation of true democracy, the infusion of idealism and spirituality into the culture, and the generation of a rational and moral economic order. Rejection means death for the nation:

> Listen to the Winds, O God the Reader, that wail across the whip-cords stretched taut on broken human hearts; listen to the Bones, the bare bleached bones of slaves, that line the lanes of Seven Seas and beat eternal tom-toms in the forests of the laboring deep; listen to the Blood, the cold thick blood that spills its filth across the fields and flowers of the Free; listen to the Souls that wing and thrill and weep and scream and sob and sing above it all. What shall these things mean, O God the Reader? You know. You know. (Postscript)

The divine reader, having been given the narrative of the past and its interpretation by the prophet-historian, is given the responsibility of creating the future.

The Negro (1915), *Black Folk: Then and Now* (1939), and *The World and Africa* (1946) do on the global level what *The Gift of Black Folk* attempted for the nation. Essentially variations of the same text, they survey the history of Africa and the African diaspora, emphasizing the variety and achievement of the black past. The discourse on Africa at the time was largely dominated by colonialist perspectives, especially those of the British and French. Whether these views were primarily imperialist or liberal, they assumed the backwardness of African cultures and the need for "civilizing" influences. Sir Harry Johnston, a leading authority during the "high" colonial period (1885–1914), said of Africans: "The Negroes of Tropical Africa specialized in their isolation and stagnated in utter savagery. They may even have been drifting away from the human standard back towards the brute when migratory impulses drew the Caucasian, the world's redeemer, to enter Tropical Africa."[7] This passage comes in what Du Bois indicates in the "Suggested Reading" section of *The Negro* is among the best of the existing studies of Africa. As much recent analysis of colonial or "Africanist" discourse has demonstrated, Africa was a "blankness" to be filled according to the needs of the creator of the discourse rather than a place and culture comparable to Europe. One aspect of the present argument is that Du Bois seeks to displace that discourse in part by generating his own Africa.[8]

At the same time, Du Bois was actively involved in the Pan-African movement. That movement had a variety of aspects, from the emigrationist efforts of Edward Blyden and Henry Turner to Marcus Garvey's "Back to Africa" schemes and the reformist and often elitist Pan-African congresses originated around the turn of the century and carried by Du Bois and others up to the post–World War II liberation period. Even Booker T. Washington got into the act on occasion.[9] The thrust of these endeavors was the improvement of conditions in Africa in the context of colonialism. One assumption that frequently shaped the discussion was that Africans were incapable of achieving the standards of modern civilization on their own. What was needed, depending on who was making the argument, was a reform of colonial practices, immigration to the continent by black Americans who had the skills essential to economic and social progress, or a recognition of the racial and spiritual connections of all people of African descent. Du Bois, over his sixty years of involvement in Pan-African activities, asserted all of these, singly or in combination. If Skinner is correct in concluding in his analysis of U.S. policy toward Africa that the Pan-African movement was primarily engaged in symbolic gestures, since European powers had little interest in the programs proposed, then Du Bois's actions are part of an essentially dramatic discourse on Africa contained in *The Negro, Black Folk: Then and Now*, and *The World and Africa*.

Two possible sources for *The Negro*, or at least two pieces that offer interpretive clues to Du Bois's thinking, were written by Franz Boas and Josiah Royce, both of whom Du Bois knew for many years. Boas presented an address at the 1906 Atlanta University commencement entitled "The Negro Past." In it he argues that knowledge of their African heritage would give young Afro-Americans a sense of pride in their race that would counteract the racists' claims of black inferiority. Recognizing the glories of that past would give them confidence in their possibilities for the future. This confidence is necessary because another lesson of history is that prejudice is eliminated very slowly and only as a result of long and difficult effort. Awareness of the past then will provide assurance for the future and determination in the present.[10]

Josiah Royce's emphasis, in an essay entitled "Race Questions and Prejudices," is psychological rather than historical. Examining and dismissing all of the historical and pseudoscientific arguments for race prejudice, he makes the point that such bias is a state of mind reinforced by certain emotions. He indicates that human beings regard those different from themselves as "portentous" others. This reaction is necessary if one is to be prepared to deal with those others. The degree of difference makes this sensitivity more intense and more easily convertible to antipathy. The more unlike oneself the other is, the more likely he or she will be a threat. When this instinct is given a name, it begins to take on an aura of social acceptability. An initial fear of difference that has no other justification eventuates in an institutionalized hostility. Naming defines the fear but brings about no knowledge of the original other. Thus, for example, white Southerners have created a system of racial discrimination and violence based not as they claim on an intimate knowledge of blacks, but rather on fear of African-American difference. The solution as Royce sees it is to recognize the fear for what it is and to overcome it through authentic knowledge.[11]

It may be said, then, that Du Bois has a twofold purpose in these books, influenced by the ideas of his friends: he wants to provide blacks with a past that is as distinguished as that of any other group, and he wants to demonstrate to whites that blacks are not such an unknown quantity, that in fact they are not significantly different from themselves. He asserts that the real source of black inferiority, in the sense of a failure to meet the highest standards of modern civilization, is the barbarous treatment accorded Africans by "civilized" whites. The central act of violation was the slave trade. The story of Africa, like that of all Du Bois's historical works, is a vast drama. In this case, the people of a whole continent are brought down by the nefarious actions of others. Africans and their descendants, history shows, have been just as capable of civilized achievement as anyone; their failings are historical, not genetic. This "true" story exposes white claims of superiority as the bravado of the fearful. Acknowledgment of the "error" of racism can help actualize the repeatedly asserted black ideal of brotherhood.

But accomplishment of the other purpose, black pride, requires the suggestion that blacks are not merely as good as, but often superior to whites. One racist contention has always been that any African or Afro-American achievement was prima facie evidence of white ancestry. Du Bois contends that, on the contrary, "black blood" is most responsible and, furthermore, that white ancestry has resulted in the most barbarous African groups. In speaking of West Africans, he confronts directly the "Aryan" theory:

> Effort has naturally been made to ascribe this civilization to white people. First it was ascribed to Portuguese influence, but much of it was evidently older than the Portuguese discovery. Egypt and India have been evoked and Greece and Carthage. But all these explanations are far-fetched. If ever a people exhibited unanswerable evidence of indigenous civilization, it is the west-coast Africans. Undoubtedly they adapted much that came to them, utilized new ideas, and grew from contact. But their art and culture is Negro through and through. (*The Negro*, 38)

He extends the argument by hypothesizing that European civilization may well be African in origin:

> This "Aryan" theory has been practically abandoned in the light of recent research and it seems probable now that from the primitive Negroid stock evolved in Asia the Semites either by local variation or intermingling with other stocks; later there developed the Mediterranean race, with Negroid characteristics, and the modern Negroes. The blue-eyed, light-haired Germanic people may have arisen as a modern variation of the mixed peoples produced by the mingling of Asiatic and African elements. (12)

Thus, if anything, it is whites who are the mulatto declension from racial purity. While Du Bois concedes that there is sketchy evidence to support his thesis, the point clearly is made that racial theorizing opens a multitude of possibilities. Such multiplicity of interpretations in fact undermines the whole process and exposes its ideological foundations.

He does not really want to engage in reverse-racist polemics, since such a position would undercut his ultimate objective of brotherhood. In fact, he wants to argue that race is not a viable concept in the ways it is usually presented. He repeats in *The Negro* the argument of "The Conservation of Races": "it is generally recognized to-day that no scientific definition of race is possible" (7). The quantifiable physical elements usually associated with race—skin color, facial and cephalic features, hair texture—are so variable as to be meaningless. The only useful distinctions, as before, are historical and "spiritual":

> Race is a dynamic and not a static conception, and the typical races are continually changing and developing, amalgamating and differentiating. In this little book, then, we are studying the history of the darker part of the human family, which is separated from the rest of mankind by no absolute physical line, but which nevertheless forms, as a mass, a social group distinct in history, appearance, and to some extent in spiritual gift. (9)

While *Black Folk: Then and Now* and *The World and Africa* emphasize cultural rather than spiritual differences, the fundamental definition remains the same. Environment and history have generated the distinctions labeled "race." From this perspective, conventional attempts to attribute superiority or inferiority to a whole group of people are meaningless except as an ideological function. The only legitimate question is the success of a group in adapting to the necessities of history and geography.

This adaptability is the foundation for Du Bois's large claims for African achievement. "The inhabitants of this land have had a sheer fight for physical survival comparable with that in no other great continent, and this must not be forgotten when we consider their history" (10). Under these circumstances, any cultural accomplishments take on a heroic quality. Much of *The Negro* and the later works is devoted to depicting such cultural heroism. In every age and in every corner of the continent, Du Bois points to indigenous elements of high civilization despite the lack of geographic barriers to invasion. By every measure of culture—agriculture, industry, language, art, and social and political organization—Africa meets high standards. He provides a catalogue of heroic African figures to supply individuality to the general picture.

In the areas of agriculture, industry, and commerce, Du Bois goes to some trouble to demonstrate both the antiquity and the superiority of

African skills. He quotes other authorities at length as to the vitality, organization, and success of these endeavors. The "dark" continent is reported to be the original site for the domestication of farm animals, for the smelting of iron, and for much of the ancient world's trading activity. All of this occurred, it is repeatedly said, while Europe was still overrun with barbarians.

On family and social relations, Du Bois depends entirely on secondary sources and is quick to counterbalance any appearance of unfavorable traits: "While women are sold into marriage throughout Africa, nevertheless their status is far removed from slavery. In the first place the tracing of relationships through the female line, which is all but universal in Africa, gives the mother great influence. Parental affection is very strong, and throughout Negro Africa the mother is the most influential councilor, even in cases of tyrants like Chaka or Mutesa" (74). What is crucial to Du Bois's narrative strategy here is the dissociation from slavery, since Africa's decline will later be attributed to the European slave trade.

Religion is more problematic for a Eurocentric audience, but even here a solution is found. "Fetishism" is admitted to be the chief religious practice of the continent, but it is not "savage" if one examines it closely: "It is not mere senseless degradation. It is a philosophy of life. Among primitive Negroes there can be, as Miss Kingsley reminds us, no such divorce of religion from practical life as is common in civilized lands. Religion is life, and fetish an expression of the practical recognition of dominant forces in which the Negro lives" (74). A superficial sign of African barbarism becomes an indicator of virtue. Africans prove in fact to be more spiritual than Europeans because they incorporate belief into their everyday lives, something that Du Bois throughout his writings suggests that whites fail to do. In addition, Africans show signs of developing a monotheistic religion, and some even have a concept of "dying divinity." In effect, these people have an instinct for Christianity even without being exposed to it.

Similarly, the discussion of African aesthetics links the two traditions. European craftsmanship serves as the frame of reference. Given the emphasis in "The Conservation of Races" and *The Souls of Black Folk* on the artistic sensibility of blacks, its significance in *The Negro* is understandable. Africans did not merely smelt iron; they fashioned it into useful yet imaginative items. Work in pottery "would be fertile in suggestion to every art craftsman in Europe" (81). They were equally creative in brass, bronze, and gold: "All the work of Benin in bronze and brass was executed by casting, and by methods so complicated that it would be no easy task for a modern European craftsman to imitate them" (80). The conclusion then is not surprising: "Perhaps no race has shown in its earlier development a more magnificent art impulse than the Negro" (80). Africa is clearly seen as having the possibility of equaling or surpassing Europe culturally. Here as elsewhere, blacks are seen as approaching the level of European civilization even with their different history.

But it is precisely on this point that Du Bois's narrative becomes problematic. Europe is in fact the norm for defining civilization. The discussion of African culture does not accept it on its own terms but seeks to demonstrate how "European" it is. A progressive theory of culture is assumed: "We must now gather these threads together and ask what manner of men these were and how far and in what way they progressed on the road of human culture" (62). The terminology used to describe conflict and interaction throughout African history— "hordes," "heathen," "primitive," "uncivilized"—is part of the discourse of European historiography and implies a universalist conception of civilization. Moreover, in describing architecture in ancient Zymbabwe, Du Bois uses the language of European art history. In the very effort to define the significant achievement of Africa, to measure its true place in history, he must suppress any assertion of its difference. Authentic otherness in effect cannot be accommodated within the purposes of the text. To prove the familiarity that will invalidate racism requires positive identity in which difference is only a local variation.

Such an approach is also essential for the larger narrative design. Africa must be shown to be developing along recognizable cultural lines so that its decline can be fully explained and appreciated. The key question for Du Bois is why, given the levels of greatness actually achieved and even higher ones that could have been expected, Africa is now so little regarded and her people seen as less than human. The answer is the slave trade. It cut off the natural civilizing process in the service of "Christian" greed. Slavery was not unknown in pretrade Africa; in fact, the practice was universal. But it was neither harsh nor degrading:

> Slavery as it exists universally among primitive people is a system whereby captives in war are put to tasks about the homes and in the fields, thus releasing the warriors for systematic fighting and the women for leisure. Such slavery has been common among all peoples and was widespread in Africa. The relative number of African slaves under these conditions was small and the labor was not hard; they were members of the family and might and did often rise to high position in the tribe. (86)

Even with the systematic slavery introduced by Islam, the possibility of progress remained: "In fiction and in truth the black slave had a chance. Once converted to Islam, he became a brother to the best, and the brotherhood of the faith was not the sort of idle lie that Christian slave masters made it" (87).

The claims made here are oversimplifications; introducing a slave into the family or into the dominant religion did not change the fact of slavery. But such historical reality would complicate the mytho-poeic purposes of the book. *The Negro* attempts to prove the equality of blacks by showing their achievements and by placing the blame for their limitations elsewhere. To make blacks morally complex figures would obscure this essentially melodramatic endeavor.

White Christian civilization becomes the villain of this human drama. Du Bois can find no grounds to excuse Europe and America:

> These were not days of decadence, but a period that gave the world Shake-speare, Martin Luther, and Raphael, Haroun-al-Raschid, and Abraham Lincoln. It was the day of the greatest expansion of two of the world's most pretentious religions and of the beginnings of the modern organization of industry. In the midst of this advance and uplift this slave trade and slavery spread more human misery, inculcated more disrespect for and neglect of humanity, a greater callousness to suffering, and more petty, cruel, human hatred than can well be calculated. We may excuse and palliate it, and write history so as to let men forget it; it remains the most inexcusable and despicable blot on modern human history. (90)

Du Bois points out the economic explanations for the trade, but his attacks on self-interest in earlier works make it clear that economics is not an adequate justification for the treatment Africa received. The effects were devastating: the population was decimated, native industry was disrupted, war became a constant state of affairs, artistic skills were lost, and political and social institutions were destroyed. It was nothing less than the violation of a continent:

> Such is the story of the Rape of Ethiopia—a sordid, pitiful, cruel tale. Raphael painted, Luther preached, Corneille wrote, and Milton sung; and through it all, for four hundred years, the dark captives wound to the sea amid the bleaching bones of the dead; for four hundred years the sharks followed the scurrying ships; for four hundred years America was strewn with the living and dying millions of a transplanted race; for four hundred years Ethiopia stretched forth her hands unto God. (95)

The objective of such language is not to offer facts or even to interpret the facts that are available; it is rather to persuade through the discourse of melodrama. The simple statements of European cultural achievement, juxtaposed to the vivid litany of African suffering and the violation of the feminine continent, rebukes the indifference of those great white European fathers to ongoing inhumanity. Du Bois represents history as a straightforward conflict of good and evil, assuming an audience not concerned with historiographical controversies but with clear-cut moral choices. *The Negro* in this sense is a work of popular literature which combines certain informative passages with simplified historical drama. The goal of such writing is political persuasion and not historical accuracy.

The political stance being defended, here and in *Black Folk* and *The World and Africa*, is anti-imperialism. Both the commentary on Africa and, in later chapters, on the black American experience (which follows the same pattern of white evil and black accomplishment) are designed to deny the racist claims of twentieth-century European colonizers. In a sense, all three books point toward the anti-imperialist arguments of their last chapters. The cruelties of slave trading and slavery itself are implicitly attacks on the exploitation of labor, in whatever guise. The cataloguing of black achievement is a refutation of the racist ideology used to justify imperialism. The history of black insurrection suggests a potential threat to continued white domination.

In essence, Du Bois returns in this series of texts to his assertion of a morality of economics. International exploitation has no other justi-fication than greed: "On the other hand, back of practically all these experiments stands the economic motive—the determination to use the organization, the land, and the people, not for their own benefit, but for the benefit of white Europe" (*The Negro*, 143). Claims of racial superiority, Christian mission, and civilizing motives are all ex post facto rationalizations for one of the basest of human instincts.

The battle against evil, specifically the self-interest and racism of the dominant culture, now takes in the entire world. Not just America but all of Western civilization has to be told the truth it prefers to ignore. And not just black Americans but all nonwhite people must be made proud of their histories and confident of their futures. "There is slowly arising not only a curiously strong brotherhood of Negro blood throughout the world, but the common cause of the darker races against the intolerable assumptions and insults of Europeans has already found expression" (146).

That this is an ongoing battle is evidenced by Du Bois's decision to publish essentially the same book in two revised, rewritten, and retitled versions years later. *Black Folk: Then and Now* (1939) and *The World and Africa* (1946) primarily update the narrative rather than reconceive it, despite the fact that his political views by the late thirties and forties had become more radical. In 1939, he can base his emergent position on the same moral principles as he did not only in *The Negro*, but also *The Suppression of the Slave-Trade* from 1896:

> Poverty is unnecessary and the clear result of greed and muddle. It spawns physical weakness, ignorance, and dishonesty. There was a time when poverty was due mainly to scarcity, but today it is due to monopoly founded on our industrial organization. This strangle hold must be broken. It can be broken not so much by violence and revolution, which is only the outward distortion of an inner fact, but by the ancient cardinal virtues: individual prudence, courage, temperance, and justice, and the more modern faith, hope and love. (*Black Folk*, 383)

The irony, of course, is that this is the same moral order upon which classical capitalism and Western civilization based the claim to national and global superiority and exploitation. Moreover, the terms Du Bois uses to articulate his call for action belong to the Judeo-Christian discursive tradition alien to those non-Western cultures he seeks to liberate. The use of such language generates a fundamental ideological tension at the very moment Du Bois seeks to be most transparent in his message. A work devoted to the repudiation of Western individualism and "Christian" exploitation and the advocacy of pluralism and native socialism and artistry must speak its urgency and high seriousness in the universalist words of the white fathers, thereby validating the very order it rejects.

Du Bois goes so far in *The World and Africa* to define the issue in Puritan terms: "This is the modern paradox of Sin before which the Puritan stands open-mouthed and mute. A group, a nation, or a race commits murder and rape, steals and destroys, yet no individual is guilty, no one is to blame, no one can be punished!" (42) The labeling of the slave trade as "sin" and of the observer as a Puritan implies the real nature of Du Bois's project. He is not writing, as he suggests, "a history of the world from the African point of view" but rather the story of the fathers' sins from the perspective of the son. His purpose is the purification of Western civilization through its own "ancient cardinal virtues" rather than a displacement or dismemberment of it. He seeks not separation but cultural reformation. The history of Africa and the slave trade are the evidence of a sinful nature that has been denied. Du Bois is the prophet who will not remain mute, who must expose the reality. But the means of doing so—historiography and moral assertion—are those defined by the culture he attacks. His Africa and his African Americans are, in these narratives, the foils in the melodrama of the white fathers. They are the vehicles by which Western culture is tested and found wanting. They lack true otherness; they are incorporated within Du Bois's version of the master narrative. That narrative is the ancient one of sin and salvation, with the Law of the Father as the measure of good and truth. Even the act of inscribing the race that the dominant order has erased from history necessarily becomes implicated in the dominant discourse.

5

· · · · · · · · ·

The Propaganda of Art

· · · · · · · · ·

Ideology and Literary Practice

· · · · · · · · ·

Du Bois tended to see himself as a man of letters, one who demonstrated significant literary skills regardless of the subject matter. He also was specifically a writer of literature, with a number of published poems, stories, parables, reviews, and novels, as well as many more writings that were never published. He sponsored the work of others in a variety of ways—publication in *The Crisis*, creation of literary prizes, recommendations to foundations—and corresponded extensively with both established and unknown authors. He was, quite self-consciously, one of the father figures of the Harlem Renaissance, offering to several of the writers support, publicity, and often criticism, both public and private. He was also a theorist and historian of black writing. It is this role of definer of Afro-American literature that is the focus of this chapter.

Du Bois's definition of black writing, based on key essays, reviews, correspondence, and literary practice, is a complex one. On the one hand, he was very traditional and even genteel. He wrote to would-be contributors to *The Crisis* about the flaws in their metric patterns or their plot structures. In a confidential letter to the Guggenheim Foundation, he advised against a grant to his friend Georgia Douglas on the basis, not of her artistic abilities, but of certain weaknesses in her character.[1] His reviews of some of the work of Langston Hughes, Claude McKay, and Jean Toomer criticized them for the lack of moral seriousness in their writing.[2]

On the other hand, he spoke for the freedom of the artist. In this, he could be as straightforward as Hughes in "The Negro Artist and the Racial Mountain." [3] As we will see in the discussion of "The Criteria of Negro Art" (1926), he asserted that one of black writing's key problems was the repression of authentic black voices. He questioned the status of the existing literary canon and at the same time posited both ideological and economic reasons for the relative lack of black literary achievement. He also broke with conservative tradition by praising Toomer, for example, for the sexual honesty of his writing. Finally, some of his own work was seen as breaking out of literary conventions. He was invited in 1930 to contribute to an anthology of pre-1912 experimental poetry; in agreeing, he commented to editor John McDermott, "My poetry has simply been a part of my urge to express myself, and has been written quite unconscious of any accepted form." [4] Moreover, his blending of narrative modes renders his long fiction problematic, as later chapters will show.

But it is his articulation of the racial nature of black literature and the responsibility of the black artist in "The Criteria of Negro Art" that is his best-known and most controversial statement. His claim seems quite dogmatic: "I do not care a damn for any art that is not propaganda." [5] In the context of its paragraph, in which he asserts that "all Art is propaganda" and that he has always used his own literary skills for propagandistic purposes, the statement appears to take an unequivocal ideological position. On its own, it is consistent with emerging Marxist aesthetics and anticipates the black arts movement of the 1960s in its recognition of the ideological nature of art.

It is important, however, to put this paragraph in the framework of the whole essay and to test the theory against Du Bois's actual literary practice. Doing so reveals a complex aesthetic position. Initially in the essay, he ties the issue of art to politics, specifically black rights. But he does so not to reveal art's political character but to suggest its role in expressing human ideals. Art helps to name the ideal ends for which the political struggle is carried on. Rights are the means, not the ends. Without the values articulated through art, black equality would be essentially meaningless:

> If you tonight suddenly should become full-fledged Americans; if your
> color faded, or the color line here in Chicago was miraculously forgotten;

suppose, too, you became at the same time rich and powerful;—what is it that you would want? What would you immediately seek? Would you buy the most powerful of motor cars and outrace Cook County? Would you buy the most elaborate estate on the North Shore? Would you be a Rotarian or a Lion or a What-not of the very last degree? Would you wear the most striking clothes, give the richest dinners and buy the longest press notices? ("Criteria," 994)

Clearly such results are not desirable to the speaker. He believes that blacks have a special understanding of the underlying philistinism of American society, precisely because they have been excluded from the material rewards of that society. The political, economic, and social conditions that make the rights struggle necessary have also generated a moral-aesthetic view that is superior to that of whites. The key issue of the essay is the hyphenation of the previous sentence. What does beauty have to do with black (or any other) morality and truth? In itself, beauty is apparent in various forms:

> I remember tonight four beautiful things: The Cathedral at Cologne, a forest in stone, set in light and changing shadow, echoing with sunlight and solemn song; a village of the Veys in West Africa, a little thing of mauve and purple, quiet, lying content and shining in the sun; a black and velvet room where on a throne rests, in old and yellowing marble, the broken curves of the Venus of Milo; a single phrase of music in the Southern South—utter melody, haunting and appealing, suddenly arising out of night and eternity, beneath the moon. (995)

What is noteworthy about this list is that while all the images are within human culture and are synaesthetic in character, human beings are absent from all of them. They are at the same time historical and dehistoricized. They also cross cultural and racial boundaries; African and African-American artistry is given equal standing with great works of Western civilization. The absence of human beings aids in such an equation because it enables the reader to focus on the product rather than the producer. Beauty thus abstracted from the particulars of human history can be universal.

The problem with beauty is that such an abstraction is artificial:

> What has the Beauty to do with the world? What has Beauty to do with Truth and Goodness—with the facts of the world and the right actions of

men? "Nothing," the artists rush to answer. They may be right. I am but an humble disciple of art and cannot presume to say. I am one who tells the truth and exposes evil and seeks with Beauty and for Beauty to set the world right. That somehow, somewhere eternal and perfect Beauty sits above Truth and Right I can conceive, but here and now and in the world in which I work they are for me unseparated and inseparable. (995)

The concession of some transcendent realm of disembodied, ahistorical beauty is clearly a rhetorical device. The position of the pure aestheticists is irrelevant, since it has nothing to do with present reality. Du Bois takes a pragmatic position here, though not a materialist one. He believes in beauty and sees it as the end to be pursued, but that work must be done within human reality. Once aesthetic considerations are brought within history, then they condition and are conditioned by other essential factors—race, economics, and ideology among them. When such contextualization takes place, then black experiences take on the character of classic literature. The tragedy of miscegenation, the irony and pathos of black success arousing white hostility, and the epic heroism of black soldiers fighting for causes defined by the dominant society are cited as great black narratives waiting to be shaped into black literature. Racial history thus becomes not an aesthetic limitation but a wellspring of beauty.

The problem then is not in the material, but in the politics of telling. Even when black artists can overcome the presumption of their inferiority (by both blacks and whites), Du Bois argues, there is an encouragement to moral and political quiescence. The very transcendence and universality claimed for art becomes a mechanism for the suppression of black artistic honesty. The claim is made by critics that racial distinctions are not made in art; work that reaches a certain standard will be recognized and appreciated regardless of the race of the artist. Du Bois points out two problems with this view. First, even if it were true, blacks who seek to become artists are discriminated against by the institutions that provide professional training. Second, black experience is not considered aesthetically appropriate material. Du Bois cites the example of a writer whose black story is rejected by a magazine; he then changes the color of the characters and the story is both published and praised. Du Bois's essential position, then, is that art in America is a product of American history and defined by the dominant culture. Since that culture is white and Eurocentric, it will consistently denigrate work that is not like itself.

The difficulty for Du Bois is to find a ground on which to argue for the value of black expression. He does this by returning to the "universals" he has just problematized:

> And what have been the tools of the artist in times gone by? First of all, he has used the Truth—not for the sake of truth, not as a scientist seeking truth, but as one upon whom Truth eternally thrusts itself as the highest handmaid of imagination, as the one great vehicle of universal under-standing. Again artists have used Goodness—goodness in all its aspects of justice, honor and right—not for sake of an ethical sanction but as the one true method of gaining sympathy and human interest. The apostle of Beauty thus becomes the Apostle of Truth and Right not by choice but by inner and outer compulsion. Free he is but his freedom is ever bounded by Truth and Justice; and slavery only dogs him when he is denied the right to tell the Truth or recognize an ideal of Justice. (1000)

This restructuring of the philosophical trinity effectively serves Du Bois's rhetorical purposes. The artist needs truth and goodness in order to achieve beauty. The proper use of them as tools does not reduce art to exposition or moral assertion; rather, it is only through them that the highest art can be achieved. Without them, artists are not free to express their visions. Thus, it must be logically argued, the black art-ist must present the truth of black experience and the need for black freedom in order to be true to his or her own voice. With different conditions, the same would be said of any other group of artists.

But curiously, this logical sequence is not the next step in Du Bois's argument. Though presented as part of it, the next point seems a hyper-bolic non sequitur: "Thus all Art is propaganda and ever must be, despite the wailing of the purists. I stand in utter shamelessness and say that whatever art I have for writing has been used always for pro-paganda for gaining the right of black folk to love and enjoy. I do not care a damn for any art that is not used for propaganda. But I do care when propaganda is confined to one side while the other is stripped and silent" (1000).

Only if we equate "truth" and "goodness" with "propaganda" does the claim follow from the previous statement. "Propaganda" would be understood by Du Bois's audience as implying a distortion of truth rather than an expression of it. His examples of current popular drama and fiction only reinforce the confusion; in each work cited, white superiority and black degradation are emphasized. "In such cases, it is not the positive propaganda of people who believe white blood divine, infallible and holy to which I object. It is the denial of a similar right of propaganda to those who believe black blood human, lovable and inspired with new ideals for the world" (1000–1001). The comparison here is false. Clearly Du Bois believes that claims of the divinity of white blood are untrue and objectionable; much of his career is devoted to deconstructing such an image. It fits his definition of propaganda. But the second statement has for him momentous truth value. It is the denial of black humanity, not its affirmation, that is propaganda.

Du Bois engages in such rhetorical exaggeration precisely because black art, if it tells the truth and raises ethical questions based on that truth, will consistently be seen by readers from the dominant culture as propaganda, since it will be a repudiation of the racial ideology of that culture. Cultural hegemony requires that black reality be interpreted to meet the culture's needs and not those of some abstraction called truth. Distortion becomes the truth, and any other version is labeled propaganda.

Du Bois points out that white artists are restricted to certain images when they treat racial subjects: "The white public today demands from its artists, literary and pictorial, racial prejudgment which deliberately distorts Truth and Justice, as far as colored races are concerned, and it will pay for no other" (1001). Similarly, the black audience limits the options of black artists because of its conservative views of sexuality and religion. In addition, the negative images portrayed in white work have made blacks afraid to accept anything less than completely positive views of themselves. Thus, any artist dealing with racial subject matter, regardless of attitude or approach, is necessarily engaged in a political gesture, "propaganda."

The moral necessity, then, is the promotion of aesthetic freedom. Only by encouraging black artists to speak what they know can the richness of black humanity be made known to the world. "I do not doubt that the ultimate art coming from black folk is going to be just as beautiful, and beautiful in the same ways, as the art that comes from white folk, or yellow, or red; but the point is that until the art of black folk compells [sic] recognition they will not be rated as human" (1002). Black art is not a special case, in any aesthetic, moral, or ontological sense; it only seems so because racial ideology demands that it be so. Du Bois adopts here an essentially conservative aesthetic position for radical purposes. Art is universal and eternal; for those very reasons, black achievement in art is proof of black humanity and equality.

The problem for Du Bois when it comes to concrete literary practice is that his genteel aesthetic runs counter to the modernist tendencies of much twentieth-century black writing.[6] Neither in his evaluations of others nor in his own literary efforts could he quite make the connection between the two. The almost postmodern insights of "The Criteria of Negro Art," with its assumption of an ideological component to art, cannot be effectively translated into a critical stance that accommodates the significance of Jean Toomer, Langston Hughes, or Richard Wright nor into an artistic practice that could transcend the romance-mimesis traditions.

His standards of evaluation are largely based on content; form is often problematic for him. Thus, in "The Younger Literary Movement," he can praise Toomer's sexual frankness and certain poetic phrases used to define character, but his criticisms of Cane—its objectivity, stylization, and difficulty—are precisely the points that mark the work as something truly new in black literature. Du Bois uses a moralistic discourse, one very similar to the one he employs in his historical works, in questioning Toomer's artistry. Like white Southern gentlemen, Cane is "splendid" but "careless." Like the black bourgeoisie, Toomer "offends often by his apparently undue striving for effect" ("Younger," 1209). The difficulty becomes obscurantism: "I cannot, for the life of me, for instance see why Toomer could not have made the tragedy of Carma something that I could understand instead of vaguely guess at; 'Box Seat' muddles me to the last degree and I am not sure that I know what 'Kabnis' is about" (1210). The underlying desire here seems to be for a transparency of language that is consistent with the transparent nature of truth and morality. The beauty of words is a virtue as long as it enhances rather than problematizes its subject. "Effects" or opacities are corrupt because they obscure the truth.

In his review of The New Negro, he provides historical context for the publication and then restates the position of "The Criteria of Negro Art." He recounts past experience with the racial ideology of *The Survey*, the magazine that originally published a special number on the emerging Harlem Renaissance. Most of the review in fact is devoted to this background, which serves to suggest the progress blacks have made in becoming a recognized part of American culture. Alain Locke is credited with a skillful job of editing the material, but none of the work contained in the collection is discussed either individually or collectively. Instead, Du Bois uses the "literary" (as opposed to historical) part of the review to question Locke's aesthetic philosophy:

> With one point alone do I differ with the Editor. Mr. Locke has been newly seized with the idea that Beauty rather than Propaganda should be the object of Negro literature and art. His book proves the falseness of this thesis. This is a book filled and bursting with propaganda but it is propaganda for the most part beautifully and painstakingly done; and it is a grave question if ever in this world in any renaissance there can be a search for disembodied beauty which is not really a passionate effort to do something tangible, accompanied and illumined and made holy by the vision of eternal beauty.[7]

Since Du Bois does not cite any instances of such propaganda, it is difficult to determine what he means by the term. Certainly, it is not likely to include the contributions of Rudolph Fisher, Eric Walrond, Arna Bontemps, Claude McKay, or Toomer, all of whom he criticized at one time or another for incomplete, negative, or decadent portrayals of black life.

But again it is the moral and political issues that are crucial:

> Of course this involves a controversy as old as the world and much too transcendental for practical purposes, and yet, if Mr. Locke's thesis is insisted on too much it is going to turn the Negro renaissance into decadence. It is the fight for Life and Liberty that is giving birth to Negro literature and art today and when, turning from this fight or ignoring it, the young Negro tries to do pretty things or things that catch the passing fancy of the really unimportant critics and publishers about him, he will find that he has killed the soul of Beauty in his Art. (*New Negro*, 141)

The same standards that were used to evaluate the Founding Fathers in *Suppression of the Slave-Trade* are used in the assessment of Locke.

To ignore issues of justice and goodness is to fall into decadence; to compromise with those indifferent to such issues is destructive of the very ends one is trying to achieve. Beauty becomes in essence a facilitator of truth and goodness; it "makes holy" those pursuits. But the pursuit of beauty in and for itself is insufficient when there is "practical" work to do. While Du Bois indicates that this question is open, he clearly has closed it for the present historical moment of black art. It is now "too transcendental" and will result only in "pretty things." These assertions carry an inherent contradiction in defining for beauty both a sanctifying role and a trivializing one. The position is more clearly ideological than the one taken in "Criteria," and that may have to do with Du Bois's perception that in fact *The New Negro* signals a renaissance. If in fact a major stage of black creativity is developing, it becomes vital to control the ways new talent is going to be used. The language of deprecation ("decadence," "too transcendental," "pretty things," "unimportant critics and publishers") suggest an effort to wrest the definition of black literature from Locke, who serves as the father figure of the collection. The "falseness" of the editor's position, while it may appear attractive, will only "kill" the art. Only by submitting to Du Bois's position can black artists achieve true significance.

Du Bois's literary practice in poetry and short fiction reinforces the view that the truth content of literature has priority over formal aesthetic considerations. His statement from the letter to John McDermott about his lack of concern for form suggests his disdain for either aestheticism or modernism. Thus, "propaganda," in the sense of a primary interest in communicating his moral and social message, dominates his work. Of the twenty-five previously published poems collected in *Creative Writings*,[8] sixteen are either explicit statements or obvious allegories of Du Bois's political positions. Of the rest, one is an assertion of black pride ("Song of the Smoke") and one a paean to Africa, both with clearly ideological implications. Of the seven remaining works, six significantly concern suffering or death. The pattern of the short prose pieces is even stronger. Of the thirty-three pieces that can be labeled narrative fiction, only two are not "propagandistic."

Given this emphasis, it is not surprising that the aesthetic element in these works is primarily ornamental rather than formal. Alliteration, almost to the point of parody, is one of the most common devices. A quatrain from "In God's Gardens" illustrates the point:

Lo! sense its sleep-sown subtle breath,
Where wheel in passioned whirl above
All lingering, luring love of love—
All perfume born of dole and death.
(*Creative Writings*, 27)

Such patterning of sound calls attention to itself as poetic discourse in an exaggerated fashion. Similarly, the multiplication of rhymes often seems more a marker of versification than a formal necessity:

I am the Smoke King
I am black!
I am swinging in the sky,
I am wringing worlds awry;
I am the thought of the throbbing hills,
I am the soul of the soil-toil kills,
Wraith of the ripple of trading rills;
Up I'm curling from the sod,
I am whirling home to God;
I am the Smoke King
I am black. (10–11)

A characteristic of the language is its archaic quality. The poetry is filled with "thees," "O's," "farewells," sentence inversions, invocations to spirits, and the sentimental phrasings of the genteel tradition. The imagery is consistently abstract, even when the reference is to a particular person or place. Thus, the memorial to Paul Laurence Dunbar could refer to any artist, and "A Day in Africa," except for the presence of a lion, could refer to any landscape of the imagination:

The sun grew sad. I watched
The mystic moon-dance of the elves
Amid the mirth-mad laughter of the stars;
Till far away some voice did wind
The velvet trumpet of the night—
And then in glooming caves
I laid me with the lion,
And I slept. (17)

It would seem, contrary to the contentions of "The Criteria of Negro Art," that beauty is in fact a means to truth and not the reverse. A "poetic" language can make a polemical point striking in ways that an argumentative discourse cannot. Certain aesthetic and religious expressive forms allow for the articulation of emotion and moral indignation in ways that are controlled yet not repressed; such expression can be found in the parodic version of "My Country 'Tis of Thee" and in the ritual form of "A Litany for Atlanta."

In the short fictions, the emphasis on message is even stronger. Allegory is the dominant mode, with several versions of the story of Christ revoicing it as a statement on racism. Either the Christ child is black, or Christ, in modern times, appears to preach a gospel of tolerance and equality. Nearly half the narratives are such Christian allegories. Others are less narratives than brief, ironic anecdotes focusing on particular issues of race or greed, such as white liberal hypocrisy, black education, or economic exploitation. In virtually none of the narratives is there any significant effort at characterization, plot development, or other facets of fiction making. The pieces exist to make a moral or political point. They are, in Bakhtinian terms, monologic rather than dialogic.[9]

The question again, as in the poetry, is why a literary form is needed at all if the message is the same as that of the expository and polemical writings. The answer seems to lie in part in the audience for these works. All except one were published in either *Horizon* or *The Crisis*. They thus were part of the campaign for black rights. They allowed Du Bois to set up dialogues with racists of various kinds in which he could control the outcome of the exchange. They allowed him to give his views the highest moral sanction by having Christ voice them. He could generate hypothetical situations to validate the arguments made elsewhere. In these ways, literature could be made to serve the principles of reason and morality while offering readers the variety of poetic or fictive discourses.

But there is a deeper issue involved: a fundamental distrust of aesthetics. Poetry for Du Bois means putting words together in certain conventional sound and image combinations, and fiction seems to mean either allegory, as in the short pieces, or, as the first two novels demonstrate, romance. His literary assumptions leave no room for the complexity and ambiguity that is usually associated with great art. His reviews suggest that it is precisely these qualities that are most troubling in the work of others. He could excoriate Claude McKay for his negative images of blacks or praise Jessie Fauset for her morally serious ones, but Jean Toomer frustrated him. *Cane* was clearly artistically important, but it could not be reduced to a paraphrasable message.

Two of Du Bois's own narratives help to illustrate his perspective. One, "Spanish Fandango," juxtaposes artistry with racial reality. The narrator, after a day of morally serious activity, gathers with two friends "in an upper room at midnight." The friends are both artists, an author and an actor. The setting suggests the liminal character of the experience. It is specifically identified as a sacred space outside the normal day's reality. The activities are pleasant and gentlemanly: eating, a little drinking, entertaining stories, and reminiscences. Then one of the men takes down a guitar and plays a fandango:

Have you ever heard Dabney play the Spanish Fandango? Dear God! There will be threads of smoke, and sprawling, indistinct men; a tiny tuning as of drops of musical rain and then a swell of silvery sound softening to a wail. The swish and swirl of dark and lacy skirts and flicker of slim young limbs, all crimson beauty. There are skies and trickling waters, lifting and falling to music—whispering and crying; soft, so soft, that at last they drift away to utter music almost soundless, pulsing in ecstasy, with now and anon the rough whir and roll of the recovering bass, out of which the silvery music emerges—re-born, alive, wailing, dancing and dying—. (*Creative Writings*, 120)

Just as the setting removes the episode from mundane reality, so the description of the music uses a language outside the essentially mimetic prose of most of the story. The scene and language contrast sharply with the return to the world the next morning. Here the narrator experiences racial discrimination and conflict. His manhood in this reality is not a given but something to be contended for in a confrontation with whites. The relatively simple act of riding on a train requires what the narrator calls "war." This profane space has its own rituals, but they are ones of negation and degradation imposed by the dominant society. The description of them suggests that they, unlike the night in the upper room, are part of the usual experience of the participants. What is noteworthy in this narrative is the irrelevance of the sacred to the profane. Nothing in that night can be used for the conflict of the day. It gives no strength or strategy or consolation. The beautiful gains its value precisely by remaining separate from harsh reality. One implication of this point is that art that does engage the world is a pale reflection of ideal beauty and therefore subject to different standards of evaluation. The ideal has nothing to do with history or ideology, but everything in the daylight world is necessarily contaminated by them. For Du Bois, there must be a space that is pure because reality is too corrupt to be tolerated otherwise. In order to live in a condition of racism, hypocrisy, and greed, he must posit a transcendent realm. Thus, in aesthetic terms, he reasserts the binary oppositions that shape his other work.

"The Case" reveals the problematic nature of ambiguous art for him. The story is one of the few that do not offer a clear moral message. It takes the form of a mystery, with a frame narrator, who listens to a train porter tell of the death of a beautiful young woman. The narrative structure is a variation of one used by Du Bois's local-color contemporaries, both black and white, in which a white gentleman repeats a tale told to him by a black menial. Du Bois changes the pattern somewhat by making the black speaker literate and articulate; the narrator even comments that the black man speaks "excellent English." The porter's story, then, is not quaint, and he does not lend himself to condescension by either the narrator or the reader.

This racial point is made subtly and is not a focus of the story; in fact, the story has little to do with race. The narrator, seeking entertainment on a boring journey, asks the porter to tell him a story of life on the train. The porter points out significantly that "we get stories now and then but only parts of them, just glimpses you know" (64). He then tells of an attractive young woman he encounters at a station who at a later stop gets on his train. He seats her next to the only other passenger in the car, a young clergyman. The two of them have a very pleasant conversation until, a few hours later, the train stops and word comes that police officers are searching for someone. The woman quietly asks the porter to conceal a case she has with her, and then, when questioned by the police, pretends to be the clergyman's wife, a ruse he goes along with. After the officers leave, she asks the porter to send a cryptic telegram. As they enter the Charlotte station, the woman gets her case back from the porter, and at that moment the train crashes, killing her. A stranger, whom the porter recognizes from the original point of departure, takes the case and slips away. The porter explains to the narrator that he never learned who the woman was or what was in the case. The story ends with this failed closure.

The story is unique in Du Bois's literary canon, both published and unpublished, in its deliberate open-endedness, a quality it stresses at both the beginning and the end with the porter's comments about "pieces of stories." It would seem to repudiate aesthetic "propaganda" in favor of artistic freedom. There is no clear paraphrasable moral or any discernable allegorical code to be deciphered. But in the very process of generating such art, Du Bois, through the patterning of the tale, seems to problematize it. The young woman is a beautiful text that everyone seeks to read. The porter interprets her as one who "wasn't exactly a lady" (64), a reading that, coming from a black man about a white woman, initially angers the narrator, who shortly thereafter concedes the point. The porter also attempts to construct a narrative of her eventual arrival on his train. The clergyman interprets her as a potential wife, a reading that, after the encounter with the police, she repudiates when she rejects his rather melodramatic proposal. Finally, of course, the narrator, as surrogate for the reader, seeks the completion of her tale, the clue that will make her meaning clear.

The story is made problematic because Du Bois associates the ambiguities and the woman with corruption. Her moral and social standing are questioned from the beginning; she seeks to conceal both material goods and her identity and purpose; she engages the innocent in her deception; she fears contact with the law; and, in true melodramatic fashion, dies at the moment of the apparent success of her conspiracy. Her deceit symbolically flouts the order of patriarchal society—class, religion, marriage, and law. In the process, she makes others complicitous in her putative criminality. The porter and the clergyman aid her deception; the police are taken in by it; even the narrator initially wants to defend her honor as a white woman. In this reading, beauty that cannot be subsumed by clearly definable truth is necessarily corrupt and corrupting. The object of desire for all the male characters, in the sense that they seek to possess her through their constructions of her, is the source of untruth and immorality. Her failure to submit to their word leads to her death. The story thus becomes a cautionary tale about beauty and art. The artist must be free to create beauty, to follow the logic of "The Criteria of Negro Art," but that freedom is dialectically tied to the responsibility to depict the good and the true. Artistic freedom must never become poetic license.

Du Bois's aesthetic, then, is one in which beauty is essentially feminine in the sense that his views of it follow the patriarchal categories of woman as virgin, wife, and whore. Art is something too pure for this harsh male world, something transcendent that is to be admired but not touched, making it largely irrelevant. Or it is "propaganda," something impure but very real and useful in the world of men; in this role, it can aid in the struggle for morality, although it can also serve immorality. Art in this sense is passive, like a "good" wife, in that everything depends on the possessor and not the possession. The third possibility is that it can be deceitful and decadent, existing for itself and not as ideal or tool. Beauty in this basically modernist sense is corrupt and corrupting; it turns men from the serious business of creating a new social and moral order to pointless self-indulgence and dishonesty. As consideration of his novels reveals, Du Bois repeatedly seeks ways to bring beauty in the form of literature under the control of truth and goodness, but, as we will also see, beauty is not to be so readily contained.

Race and Romance

The Quest of the Silver Fleece
and Dark Princess

The Quest of the Silver Fleece (1911) and *Dark Princess* (1928) are romances in several senses of the term. Their central plots involve virtuous men and women who achieve fulfillment in each other only after a series of trials and separations. Each work offers unusual settings and circumstances and often melodramatic plot elements. Finally, each uses its love story as an allegory to express certain values of the author. All of this is done in a literary discourse of high seriousness. Du Bois clearly manipulates this popular form to articulate his political ideas.

At the same time, he interweaves materials that give the works a realistic aspect. In the early novel, these materials are primarily economic, while in the later one they are mainly political. These place the novels in the context of the muckraking writing of the time, with the focus on the corrupting and destructive effects of corporate capitalism and machine politics. These materials seem to pull in opposite directions from the romantic elements, a tension consistent with the moral-ideological and positivist-rationalist dialectic of much of his writing. We will see, however, that the realism itself takes on allegorical qualities as Du Bois situates his "factual" material, some based on his own sociological research, in the context of the larger moral drama.

The Quest of the Silver Fleece presents itself in the tradition of the sentimental romance. Its hero is pure, strong, and incorruptible; its heroine is beautiful and mysterious; they are united only after having their virtue tested by antagonistic forces. More specifically, Du Bois writes his own version of the Southern romantic novel so popular in the late nineteenth and early twentieth centuries. This form required a representation of the South as a once-idyllic land in which white domination produced harmony; harmony is restored in the postbellum period by the symbolic reconciliation of North and South through the marriage of the central characters.[1] Du Bois's work is a deconstruction of this master narrative and simultaneously a reinvention of it from a black and socialist perspective. The North-South alignment is shown to be self-destructive, while harmony is achieved through the uniting of the black elite and the masses in a cooperative utopia. At the same time, Du Bois presents a family romance in which the patriarchal white society, which has raped and exploited the feminized black masses, is overcome by the black son, a coup aided by the black woman and finally acknowledged by the white father. Thus, the harmony created represents a new order of reason and justice.

In a prefatory note to *The Quest of the Silver Fleece*, Du Bois says:

> He who would tell a tale must look toward three ideals: to tell it well, to tell it beautifully, and to tell the truth. The first is the Gift of God, the second is the Vision of Genius, but the third is the Reward of Honesty.
>
> In *The Quest of the Silver Fleece* there is little, I ween, divine or in-genious; but, at least, I have been honest. In no fact or picture have I con-sciously set down aught the counterpart of which I have not seen or known; and whatever the finished picture may lack of completeness, this lack is due now to the story-teller, now to the artist, but never to the herald of the Truth.[2]

On one level this statement is the novelist's traditional disclaimer: he realizes his limitations as an artist, but at least he is sincere and forth-right in the pursuit of truth. He has also made the conventional dis-tinction between form and content, thereby giving himself claims to writing a novel worth reading, even if it is not well structured.

But in the context of his other works, his note announces the desire to have the work read simultaneously as romance and realism. By sepa-rating narrative ("to tell it well") and language ("to tell it beautifully") from content ("to tell the truth"), he is able to make his fiction do two things at once. He can describe explicitly and in realistic detail certain activities and institutions such as political machinations and the cotton industry. On the other hand, he can pay homage to the genteel traditions of fiction by telling a love story, which also serves, allegorically, to reveal moral truth.

Within the overall polarity of realism and romance, a further division occurs between black and white. We have critical portraits of urban black political figures and harsh, "realistic" descriptions of the activities of white businessmen and politicians. In terms of romance, Du Bois tells of a failed love affair between two white characters and a successful one between two blacks.

The "realistic" sections of the novel deal principally with politics and cotton. The political elements concern black office-seekers, though these characters are associated closely with their white counterparts. The middle third of the novel places the hero, Blessed Alwyn, in Washington, D.C. Here he first discovers the necessity of racial politics in gaining even a civil service job. A young black woman is willing to exchange vital political information for Bles's appointment. In return, he becomes her companion, and she begins to manage his career. Through everything, he remains astonishingly naive, unable to grasp the principles of self-interest or political manipulation. He relies wholly on his moral instincts and necessarily fails in Washington.

But this very naïveté provides the narrator with a sounding board for political criticism. Caroline Wynn, the woman in this subplot, is one of those talented, educated blacks whom Du Bois has described in earlier works. She broods over the injustice of racism:

> A bitterness dawned in her eyes. The whole street was a living insult to her. Here she was, an American girl by birth and breeding, a daughter of citizens who had fought and bled and worked for a dozen generations on this soil; yet if she stepped into this hotel to rest, even with full purse, she would be politely refused accommodations. Should she attempt to go into this picture show she would be denied entrance. She was thirsty with the walk but at yonder fountain the clerk would roughly refuse to serve her. It was lunch time; there was no place within a mile where she was allowed to eat. The revolt deepened within her. (*Quest*, 314–15)

But this frustration does not lead to a reformist ideology:

This was the thing poor blind Bles was trying to attack by "appeals" for "justice." Nonsense! Does one "appeal" to the red-eyed beast that throttles him? No. He composes himself, looks death in the eye, and speaks softly, on the chance. (315)

Her response is to pursue self-interest with an attendant degree of self-hatred. As long as Bles's career is on the rise, she supports him, even to the extent of becoming engaged to him. But when his moral principles require that he attack the political bosses, she abandons him and attaches herself to the black politician most adept at manipulating the situation. She is fully aware of her actions; she admits her selfishness and mourns her loss, saying, " 'Bles Alwyn, the Fool—and the Man. But by the grace of the Negro Problem, I cannot afford to marry a man' " (324–25).

The characterizations of her new fiancé and his fellow conspirator demonstrate the narrator's progressivist distaste for conventional politicians. Sam Stillings is a former house servant who serves no interest except his own: "Stillings was a type. Up from servility and menial service he was struggling to climb to money and power. He was shrewd, willing to stoop to anything in order to win. The very slights and humiliations of prejudice he turned to his advantage" (241).[3] His associate is from a similar mold. "Mr. Teerswell was handsome and indolent, with indecision in his face and a cynical voice" (243). These two stage-manage Bles's political downfall, working closely with white Southerners and Northern conservatives. Their rewards for this feat were high (for blacks) political appointments and, for Stillings, betrothal to Caroline Wynn.

This subplot reveals a set of attitudes necessary for its political realism. It assumes that all those engaged in politics are interested in nothing other than money and power. Every figure involved in such activity in the novel is corrupt and self-serving. Those few who are idealistic about government are shown to be impotent in the face of the onslaughts of the powerful. The absoluteness of characterization and moral values indicate that political "realism" here is in fact another allegory of good and evil. Its claims to mimesis are based more on its depiction of corruption than on correspondence to political practice. Bles is an innocent moving through the "swamp" (to use the dominant trope of the book) of self-interested, exploitative behavior and managing to retain his virtue.

Similarly, economics, represented by the cotton industry, is allegory in the guise of mimesis, even though this part of the novel was what Du Bois knew best from his scholarly research.[4] Cotton is, in a sense, the thread that holds the work together. Every character, in one way or another, is in quest of this silver fleece. Southern landowners build their wealth and power on profits made from it. Black laborers work virtually as slaves in growing it. Poor whites see it as the source of their poverty. Northern industrialists envision it as one more raw material to be exploited for their profit. It is the economic basis of Southern racism and Northern tolerance of that racism and alternating black resistance and submission to the oppressive Southern system.

Northern capitalism symbolizes in the book the highest form of self-interest, since it requires a high level of sophistication and involves so many lives. The manipulations of Stillings and Teerswell pale beside the operations of John Taylor's cotton combine. Taylor, by the end of the novel, is able to control the product from the fields to the completion of the manufacturing process. In doing so, he controls the fate of labor, both black and white, and of landowners. The narrator carefully depicts Taylor as a sober-minded, hard-working man who nonetheless is willing either to corrupt or to destroy others for his own financial benefit. He is also willing to tolerate the Southern system of racial oppression as long as it reinforces his own control. But he has a set of rules under which he consistently operates, as do all the characters. As an example, when Zora, the black heroine, takes the white landowner Cresswell to court to force him to honor a contract, Taylor's testimony supports her. His business principles permit manipulation and exploitation, but fundamental to them is the sacredness of the contract. He will not violate this rule, even though his refusal undermines the system of racism he otherwise accepts.

Such narrative sensitivity to the culture of economics also informs the characterization of the landowner, Colonel Cresswell. He is old enough to have held slaves in the antebellum South, and he is portrayed as never having quite accepted the outcome of the Civil War. He still treats the blacks working his land as though they were slaves and Northerners as though they were the enemy. He only submits to partnership with John Taylor because his son Harry convinces him that it is the only way to survive under the new economic order. He is not corrupt so much as morally tired. He tries to maintain an old system of values in a new age, and his actions are consistent with those values. Blacks are not to him real human beings; therefore exploiting and deceiving them are not violations of his integrity. But he is also paternalistic toward them, making certain that they do not starve or suffer much pain. He has qualms about the rise of poor whites, not only because they threaten his political and economic power, but also because they have the potential to do violence to "his" blacks; this qualm is realized in the most explicit scene of the book, the lynching of two black men: "A hundred or more shots rang out; then slowly and silently, the mass of women and men were sucked into the streets of the town, leaving but black eddies on the corners to throw backward glances toward the bare, towering pine where swung two red and awful things. The pale boy-face of one, with soft brown eyes glared up sightless to the sun; the dead, leathered bronze of the other was carved in piteous terror" (425). This scene is the logical end of the colonel's system of values, though that very system makes him resistant to such implications. The narrator brings together in this and other characterizations the intricate pattern of social, political, economic, and racial realities that constituted the white side of the cotton story.

Despite these complexities, the economic realism depends on character types and on fully articulated, conspiratorial motives for their behavior. John Taylor, as the Northern industrialist, is predictably cold, calculating but unsubtle, and personally moralistic, while the Cresswells are aristocratic, passionate, exploitative, and paternalistic. The merging of the two, in finance and marriage, is clearly an emblem of the development of the new South. Du Bois has his characters describe explicitly the mechanisms by which they take control of the wealth of post-Reconstruction society. This conspiratorial element, in which motive, strategy, and behavior are fully articulated by the principal actors, is a pattern of all of Du Bois's long fiction. He sacrifices nuance and psychological complexity in order to lay bare the self-interested essence of the evil in his texts.

Significantly, the major black characters are the least realistic in the novel. They provide the main love story, but even more Bles and

Zora serve allegorical functions in Du Bois's vision of the black past and future. As a romantic set, they contrast with the white pair composed of Mary Taylor and Harry Cresswell. In fact, the comparisons are even more complex, since Bles, the moralistic Southern black man, is comparable to Mary, the moralistic Northerner; while Zora, the poor, ignorant, illegitimate, but passionate swamp girl, is set against Harry, the wealthy, well-born, well-educated, but passionate son of the manor. The two love stories also play off a set of sentimental conventions: the fallen woman and the reformed rake. These polarities—wealth-poverty, black-white, male-female, experience-innocence, morality-immorality, North-South—function as demonstrations of the moralism that shapes the text. Moral truth is operative in the political and economic exposés, but to make it overt would call into question their mimetic appearance; such is not the case with the romances.

This difference is possible because the sentimental tradition lends itself to moral assertion.[5] On the level of the love stories themselves, the narrator employs idealizations of character. Mary Taylor is a well-educated, naive New England woman who comes to the South to teach in a school for black children. She is the White Virgin: "She was a pretty young woman of twenty-three, fair and rather daintily moulded. In favorable surroundings, she would have been an aristocrat and an epicure" (*Quest*, 27). But she is not in such an environment; she is in rural Alabama, though not for neo-Abolitionist purposes:

> But from the offer that came to teach Negroes—country Negroes, and little ones at that—she shrank, and indeed, probably would have refused it out of hand had it not been for her queer brother, John. John Taylor, who had supported her through college, was interested in cotton. Having certain schemes in mind, he had been struck by the fact that the Smith School was in the midst of the Alabama cottonbelt. . . . And so, howsoever reluctantly, she had gone. (26–27)

Mary is portrayed throughout as innocent but officious. She is the primary target of satire, which suggests Du Bois's underlying moral design. In fact, all of the white characters, with the exception of Sarah Smith, the matron of the school, are seen unsympathetically; they are either ridiculous, as Mary is in the South, or pernicious, as the Cresswells are. The chapter on the meeting of Mary and Harry reveals the pattern. He goes to the school to warn Miss Smith about taking too many of his black child laborers into her school. Instead of the older woman, he meets Mary. "Miss Taylor noticed his riding breeches and leggings, his white linen and white, clean-cut, high-bred face. Such apparitions were few about the country lands. She felt inclined to flutter, but gripped herself" (83). The scene quickly becomes a parody of a meeting of lovers. His lies appear to be chivalrous gestures:

"He mentioned your being here and I thought I'd drop over and welcome you to the South."

"Thank you," returned Miss Taylor, reddening with pleasure despite herself. There was a real sincerity in the tone. (84)

His paternalistic attitudes toward blacks immediately become her own: "Mary Taylor suddenly felt herself a judge of character" (86).

A darker view of Cresswell emerges as he leaves the school. He rides past Bles, who refuses to offer obeisance to this paragon of Southern manhood: "How dares the black puppy to ignore a Cresswell on the highway? If this went on, the day would surely come when Negroes felt no respect or fear whatever for whites. And then—my God! Mr. Cresswell struck his mare a vicious blow and dashed toward town" (89). His character is later made even more explicit:

The unregulated fire of energy and delicacy of nervous poise within him continually hounded him to the verge of excess and sometimes beyond. Cool, quiet, and gentlemanly as he was by rule of his clan, the ice was thin and underneath raged unappeased fires. He craved the madness of alcohol in his veins till his delicate hands trembled of mornings. The women whom he bent above in languid, veiled-eyed homage, feared lest they love him, and what work was to others gambling was to him. (196)

He is the classical rake, Southern-style, which he finally admits to Mary. But this confession does not offend her; quite the contrary, it makes him even more desirable:

"I have not been a good man—Mary; but I love you, and you can make me good."

Perhaps no other appeal would have stirred Mary Taylor. She was in many respects an inexperienced girl. But she thought she knew the world; she knew that Harry Cresswell was not all he should be, and she knew too that many other men were not. Moreover, she argued he had not had a fair chance. All the school-ma'am in her leaped to his teaching. What he needed was a superior person like herself. (207)

In a true sentimental novel, her vision would be realized, after much tribulation. To some extent her wishes do come true: the cotton combine makes them wealthy, and Harry is elected to Congress. But his character is not changed, and, moreover, his past sins must be paid for. He is syphilitic, and their only child is a stillborn monster. Mary follows her husband one night and confronts him in a gilded brothel. In the end, she returns to the South alone, her beauty gone and her marriage shattered.

In an inversion of the ideology of conventional Southern romances, this plot line suggests the destructiveness of Northern acceptance of the white South's self-image. Mary has a romantic conception of the South, one reinforced by self-interest. She accepts Harry's view of Southern conditions and of blacks and chooses to ignore the harsh realities. This moral obtuseness constitutes as sure a sin as Harry's flagrant immorality. She would correct his surface symptoms without getting at the root cause of the disease: a Southern system of exploitation and prejudice. Harry's syphilis, immorality, and indifference to Mary's suffering, as well as her lost beauty and the stillborn child, reveal the deconstructive nature of Du Bois's use of his fictive model.

The love of Bles and Zora functions very differently, both in plot structure and allegorical significance. Bles's naïveté has already been discussed. In many ways, it is like that of Mary Taylor. He lacks any firm sense of the nature of evil, believing that education and hard work necessarily lead to individual and social progress. Caroline Wynn says of him that "Miss Smith has gone and grafted a New England conscience on a tropical heart" (265), but in fact the only thing Southern about him is his birthplace. The New England conscience is clear from the opening pages of the book, where he fails to understand Zora's singing or her talk of dreams and white demons. He also has a preconceived set of moral principles, which he applies regardless of their effects on other people.

Zora, in the initial pages of the novel, appears as a precursor of the mysterious, primitive women of some Harlem Renaissance literature.[6]

Like Harry Cresswell, she lives a life of instinct rather than conscience; she has no qualms about lying or stealing. Her first entrance into the story emphasizes her sensuality:

> Amid this mighty halo, as on clouds of flame, a girl was dancing. She was black, and lithe, and tall, and willowy. Her garments twined and flew about the delicate moulding of her dark, young, half-naked limbs. A heavy mass of hair clung motionless to her wide forehead. Her arms twirled and flickered, and body and soul seemed quivering and whirring in the poetry of her motion.
>
> As she danced she sang. He heard her voice as before, fluttering like a bird's in the full sweetness of her utter music. It was no tune or melody, it was just formless, boundless music. . . . The crimson light fell full upon the warm and velvet bronze of her face—her midnight eyes were aglow, her full purple lips apart, her half hid bosom panting. (*Quest*, 14–15)

Like Mary, Bles wants to tame his wild companion. But he at least has the sense to begin the domestication before marriage. He virtually forces Zora to begin learning how to read and then, after a time, to attend Miss Smith's school. The central plot of the story, in fact, is the education of Zora; the process is begun by Bles, carried on by Miss Smith, and brought to completion by Mrs. Vanderpool, a Northern woman of the world. Only when all the stages are finished is she permitted to marry Bles.

The device of the fallen woman is used to facilitate this long procedure. Mary's officiousness and Bles's moral absolutism combine first to reveal that Zora had once been sexually violated by white men and then to encourage the young man to abandon his love:

> "I asked you what it meant to be pure, Bles, and—and you told—and I told you the truth."
>
> "What it meant!—what it meant!" he repeated in the low, tense anguish.
>
> "But—but, Bles—" She faltered; there came an awful pleading in her eyes; her hand groped toward him; but he stepped slowly back—"But, Bles—you said—willingly—you said—if—if—if she knew—"
>
> He thundered back in livid anger: "Knew! All women know! You should have *died!*" (169–70)

The dialogue could be taken from almost any sentimental novel, and in most the fallen woman would in fact die. But Du Bois has other purposes in mind. The scene frees both characters to go out into the larger world to gain a much more profound knowledge. Just before this revelation, they had been raising a cotton crop in the midst of the swamp to make money and pay for Zora's schooling. Such activity in the book's moral universe has undertones of selfishness. When Bles leaves, none of it matters any longer, and Zora silently submits to the Cresswells' expropriation of the cotton.

She also moves in with Miss Smith, and it is in this relationship that in fact "a New England conscience is grafted onto a tropical heart." Zora loses most of the qualities of her former life in the swamp. The New England spinster with a stern moral code and a sense of personal sacrifice becomes the model of womanhood. When the young woman has adequately learned this new pattern, she becomes a personal maid for Mrs. Vanderpool, who takes her to Washington and New York. Here she is provided with an opportunity to overcome her parochialism, which she does by extensive reading and careful attention to political and social events.

In Washington, she also has a religious experience, but of a very special kind. She listens to a black minister of the social gospel:

"Behold the Lamb of God that taketh away sin. Behold the Supreme Sacrifice that makes us clean. Give up your pleasures; give up your wants; give up all to the weak and wretched of our people. Go down to Pharaoh and smite him in God's name. Go down to the South where we writhe. Strive— work—build—hew—lead—inspire! God calls. Will you hear? Come to Jesus. The harvest is waiting. Who will cry: 'Here Am I, send me!' "

Zora rose and walked up the aisle; she knelt before the altar and answered the call: "Here am I—send me." (295)

Three elements of this message are significant for Zora. The call for hard work and sacrifice is an opportunity to put into practice the essentially patriarchal middle-class values she has acquired through her extended period of education. The smiting of Pharaoh is sublimated revenge for the exploitation she has personally suffered. And, finally, her gesture of sacrifice is an act of purification. Metaphorically at least she can return to that state of chastity that Bles so strongly believes in.

These three elements are the themes of the last third of the novel.

She returns to the South and becomes, if possible, an even sterner spinster than Miss Smith. She conceives the idea of remaking the swamp into a black socialist community. She works constantly and urges and demands that others do the same. She sacrifices all personal ambition and desire to the cause of the community. She even resists the advances of the returned Bles.

Furthermore, she engages in financial dealings with Colonel Cresswell, and when he proves as devious toward blacks as ever, she takes her business elsewhere. She even defeats him in the court case mentioned above. Having studied both business and law, she is able to appeal to the rules of economic conduct in order to win the support of John Taylor. Her actions, because they are in defense of the community, receive the approbation of a narrator who generally views economic activity as inherently immoral.

Finally, the hard work and sacrifice have the desired romantic effect. She wins the heart of Bles, who says in the concluding scene, "She is more than pure" (433). The fallen woman has regained her virtue through hard work, personal sacrifice, and financial acumen. She is to marry and live happily ever after in her middle-class, socialist home.

But this romantic ending is premised on certain compromises of the realistic parts of the novel. For example, the very consistency with which John Taylor applies the rule of contract in defense of Zora casts doubt on his economic intelligence. He is elsewhere presented as carefully manipulating the Southern racial situation to his economic advantage. Yet here he undermines with a word that system that is so profitable to him.

In a more important instance, Colonel Cresswell undergoes a change that makes possible the continuation of the school that he has sought to destroy for years, as well as Zora's economic experiment, which he knows is destroying white supremacy. In an inadequately explained gesture, he leaves both his plantation and a large sum of money to the school and cancels all debts owed him. Moreover, in his final breath he acknowledges his paternity of some of the blacks on the plantation. This deathbed conversion is nowhere prepared for in the narrative.

What it does do, however, is provide a key to another level of meaning in the novel. The romance of Bles and Zora is in fact an allegory of the black experience and a vision of the black future. Angus Fletcher has said of allegory:

Considered also as a nonmetaphysical semantic device, whether leading to apocalypse or not, allegory likewise appears to express conflict between rival authorities, as in times of political oppression we may get "Aesop-language" to avoid censorship of dissident thought. At the heart of any allegory will be found this conflict of authorities. . . . Allegories are far less often the dull systems they are reputed to be than they are symbolic power struggles.[7]

What is encoded in the romance of Bles and Zora is a radical political vision. Zora speaks of white power early in the novel: "They don't really rule; they just thinks they rule. They just got things,—heavy, dead things. We black folks is got the *spirit*. We'se lighter and cunninger; we fly right through them; we go and come again just as we wants to. Black folks is wonderful." (*Quest*, 46) This statement is in fact the thesis of the novel. Mary's stillborn child is literally a "heavy, dead thing" that symbolizes the sterility and death of white power based on greed and exploitation. Repeatedly the book emphasizes the ephemeral nature of white authority. The old aristocracy is being supplanted by white laborers, who in turn fail to destroy the new black community that is emerging and that tends to absorb willing whites.

The "realistic" elements suggest that greed is the true source of white power and that it is destined to fail. Likewise, the black politicians are viewed negatively because they are pursuing what amounts to a shadow of a shadow. A consistent pattern in Du Bois's writing is that self-interest is entropic, and that pattern holds here. John Taylor then is conceding the new order of things when he supports Zora, and the colonel's deathbed gesture is simply the acceptance of justice as the one great historical reality. It carries the message that the meek have in fact inherited the earth.

The story of Zora and Bles is the story of the black masses and the talented tenth. Zora begins in the dark swamp of superstition, ignorance, illegitimacy, immorality, and lassitude and through careful guidance and desire makes the swamp and herself into centers of wisdom, education, community, moral probity, and hard work. Meanwhile, Bles gains knowledge of his own strength through overcoming the temptations of money and power; he learns the importance of the group ideal and returns to combine this sensibility with Zora's new-found self-respect and politico-economic strength. Their projected marriage is the confirmation of this racial unity. Together they literally rule the earth. The old system of exploitation, greed, and corruption has been supplanted by a moral utopia.

But this meaning is rendered problematic in the very process of its creation. The swamp, which is Zora's origin, is both the site of corruption and wildness that must be changed to make life there productive and the source of creativity and magic that give its inhabitants vitality. In the former case, it is identified with Elspeth, Zora's grandmother and the generator, along with white men, of moral chaos. The daughter's own status as fallen woman comes from this maternal space. Thus, the logic of the allegory is that the black masses are feminized and always already corrupted. In the latter case, the magic cotton seeds, Zora's beauty and song, and the awareness of ephemeral white power also are derived from the swamp. In order for the new order to be accomplished, the swamp must be drained and destroyed, Elspeth must die, and Zora must give up sensuality and song. In effect, all aspects of desire, both positive and negative, must be annihilated in order to create a rational society. Du Bois is necessarily caught in a web of figuration in which his rather straightforward allegory becomes a prison house of language. The son, with his New England conscience, succeeds in supplanting the order of the father by unsexing the mother-daughter, and then, in the name of morality, remaking her into an image of himself.

At the same time, this utopia comes into being only by means of that patriarchal order it has replaced. Miss Smith, the New England spinster responsible for the grafting of conscience onto heart, implants an ideology of self-sacrifice and Eurocentric culture. More directly, the worldly Mrs. Vanderpool provides the money for buying land, the capitalist Taylor gives the purchase legal standing, and the Southern aristocrat Colonel Cresswell leaves money and land to secure the future of the community. Thus, its origins are as much in the fathers as in the sons and daughters. The rewards of evil are as much responsible as those of good. Such gestures, in their narrative surprise, suggest a desire to move outside of the very political economy the text presents as fundamental to society. Self-interest "magically" becomes self-sacrifice. Moreover, self-sacrifice is penance by both the fathers and the children who have overthrown them. The justification for the new order is that its rules of purity and sacrifice efface the desire responsible for the sins of the patriarchs. But such values appear to preclude symbolically a future. Not only the syphilitic Harry and the morally obtuse Mary, but also the chaste and virtuous Miss Smith and Bles and Zora remain childless at the conclusion. The victory of the virginal sons and daughters over the wanton fathers appears Pyrrhic. Having lost their lightness and cunning to moral seriousness, they may have made themselves "heavy, dead things."

The Dark Princess is in many ways a rewriting of The Quest of the Silver Fleece. Its hero must prove himself before being rewarded with the beautiful, exotic heroine. Like Bles, Matthew Towns faces the temptation of political power but ultimately rejects it for a higher ideal. The temptation is again in the form of a woman aligned with a political operative, and it is rejected for the dream of a new world, also symbolized by a woman. The crucial difference lies in the nature of this new world. In *Quest*, it was a Southern utopia, for which Zora, the emblem of the black masses, must be united with Bles, sign of the talented tenth. In *Dark Princess*, Towns is joined to the princess, ruler of Bwodpur and symbol of the international nonwhite world. Thus, this romance allegorizes the emergence of what now would be called a Third World sensibility. Those who must be overcome are not Southern racists and Northern industrialists, but the global system of imperialism and economic exploitation run by white Americans and Europeans. Curiously, Du Bois does not offer any character equivalents of Colonel Cresswell and John Taylor. Thus, the dominant order against which the protagonists struggle remains abstract and vague. Ironically, this allows Du Bois to be more specific than before about the effects of domination and the details of an alternative order.

Dark Princess is simultaneously more fantastic and more realistic than its predecessor. Du Bois's own summary of the work reveals its contradictory thrusts:

"Dark Princess" is a story of the great movement of the darker races for self-expression and self-determination. It stretches from Banares to Chicago and from Berlin to Atlanta, but centers in two persons, a Princess of India seeking light and freedom for her people and an American Negro seeking first to escape his problem and then to understand it. The main movement of the story takes place in America where the hero is first a medical student and then a Pullman Porter. Through entanglement in radical propaganda he is sent to jail but pardoned by the efforts of a leading Negro politician of Chicago. He becomes a ward politician in that city, then a member of the legislature and finally, through the manipulation of a shrewd woman whom he has married, has the nomination to Congress in his grasp. But his political success has meant his moral degradation, and when the Indian Princess with her great dream of world unity for the darker races dramatically reappears in his life, he surrenders all to become a common laborer. Groping thus in the depth for light and understanding, these two fighters for the common good are finally called to the supreme sacrifice of parting but in the end are brought back together in the person of a child who is crowned in Virginia, "Messenger and Messiah of all the Darker Worlds!"[8]

Realism is apparent in the depiction of Chicago politics. The author is not content to develop one minor incident but rather tries to suggest how the whole system of black politicking and patronage operates. Matthew Towns is shown as a ward politician who acquires and maintains control over his section by finding jobs and doing other favors for the people in the neighborhood. He also protects certain kinds of criminal activity and pays off policemen. In return, he gets not only votes but also occasional gifts. Du Bois even implies that this system functions better than any that reformers would introduce.

Towns advances in this world on the basis of his success, becoming the protégé of Sammy Scott, the black politician who controls most of the black vote in Chicago. With the assistance (and often guidance) of Sara Andrews, Scott manipulates and is manipulated by the white power structure of the city. This complex relationship involves a very careful use of the color line in which blacks are shown to be necessary to white power but not threatening to it. Sammy tends to be satisfied with petty corruption and the accumulation of wealth, but Sara sees great possibilities in the emerging economic "super-power."

Sara is an important development of the Caroline Wynn figure in *The Quest of the Silver Fleece*. Unlike her predecessor, Sara is not content merely to marry a politician; she actively engages in the games of power in the city. She is the one who points out to Sammy that he "will never learn that big business pays better than crime" (*Princess*, 141). She studies economic issues and learns how to gain advantage from them. She also creates Matthew's political career, purely for reasons of power, since she is depicted as devoid of emotion:

Sara Andrews was thin, small, well tailored. Only at second glance would you notice that she was "colored." She was not beautiful, but she gave an impression of cleanliness, order, cold, clean hardness, and unusual efficiency. She wore a black crepe dress, with crisp white organdie collar and cuffs, chiffon hose, and short-trimmed hair. Altogether she was pleasing but a trifle disconcerting to look at. Men always turned to gaze at her, but they did not attempt to flirt—at least not more than once. (109)

But Du Bois is ambiguous in his characterization of Sara, as to a lesser extent he was with Caroline Wynn. On the one hand, she represents that part of the black bourgeoisie that is alienated from the race and concerned only with personal wealth and power. On the other, she is the strongest character in the book, stronger even than the princess. She has suffered discrimination, she is educated, she is self-made. She relies on little more than inner drive and native intelligence to succeed in a world dominated by men, especially white men.

What this complex depiction suggests is Du Bois's own ambivalence about the black middle class. To some extent it had succeeded in rising out of the mass and had achieved a degree of culture. But it had failed to realize the ideal of the selfless and self-sacrificing talented tenth. It was Du Bois's own class, and he was disappointed that it had become so thoroughly inculturated into American materialism. Only by robbing its representative in the novel of human warmth can he sustain his criticism of it. Sara must be denied emotion if the good and evil of the romance are not to become completely confused.

The realism of the political world and the tight structure of the book are necessary to the credibility of the love story, for that story is filled with grand passions, impossible coincidences, and an improbable conclusion. The brief outline Du Bois offers in the preface does not do justice to his narrative. After being told that he cannot complete medical school because he would have to do clinical work in obstetrics with white women, Towns angrily leaves the country and seeks solace in Europe. In Berlin, he saves the East Indian princess from the insulting behavior of a white American, and she then introduces him to a conference of Asian and Arab dignitaries who want to overthrow white imperialism.

At their request, he returns to America to determine if blacks are prepared to participate in such a world revolution. He contacts a West

Indian named Perigua, who plans to blow up a train carrying members of the Ku Klux Klan. Towns, enraged at the Klan's lynching of a friend, aids in the plot, but, just as the train nears the spot of the explosion, he learns that the princess is aboard. He stops the train and goes to jail for his part in the conspiracy, even though there is little evidence against him.

Enter Sara Andrews, who sees political possibilities in Towns's pardon. He becomes a politician and rises quickly, sacrificing more and more of his integrity as he advances. Finally, he is on the verge of being nominated for Congress, but this step will require that he surrender entirely to powerful interests. At this critical moment the princess again appears, now in the guise of a union organizer. She saves him from corruption, and they go off together to a love nest.

She leaves after a short time to prepare for a return to India, but he remains and becomes a ditch digger in Chicago. They write long letters about the evils of imperialism and the rise of true democracy. A new conference is called at his mother's Virginia home. When he arrives, he finds that she has borne his child, the new maharajah. They marry, she dons the crown jewels she has been secretly carrying around, and they presumably live happily ever after.

Just as the romance of *The Quest of the Silver Fleece* could be seen as an allegory of the union of the masses and the talented tenth, so *Dark Princess* can be seen as the joining of black America with the rest of the nonwhite world. The local socialism of the earlier work becomes here global industrial democracy. The princess's life as a union official and Matthew Towns's roles as porter, small-time politician, and menial laborer indicate a belief in a proletarian consciousness. Matthew tells the Berlin conference that they must believe in the masses, since they are the source of any natural aristocracy. Acceptance of his view comes when they meet at the home of his illiterate mother and sanction his marriage to the princess. The birth of the child is a literal sign of the fertility of a union of the masses and the elite.

The novel then can be read as a vision of incipient socialist democracy. Herbert Aptheker, in the introduction to the 1974 reprint, says that the reader should note "in particular, his [Du Bois's] defense of democracy and his impassioned rejection of elitism in all forms, leading him in this book to express his belief in both the possibility of and need for socialism" (17). But this reading ignores the elitist and patriarchal subtext of the novel. First, none of the characters of major importance is proletarian, as Zora conceivably was at the beginning of *The Quest of the Silver Fleece*. Matthew, supposedly from a Virginia farm, has been educated at Hampton Institute and in the schools and colleges of New York City. When the story opens, he has nearly completed his medical school training. Sara, light enough to pass as white, is a self-made member of the black bourgeoisie and, like Sammy Scott, a powerful political figure. The princess is the ruler of a small but wealthy kingdom in India.

Beyond their middle-class or aristocratic situations, none of these characters achieves or reflects a proletarian sensibility. Matthew goes to Europe when he is forced to leave school, and there he becomes interested in art. At the Berlin conference of Third World dignitaries, the dinner discussions focus on German music and the latest developments in European art. Evident in the arguments on imperialism is a belief, not in the masses, but in the superiority of the elites of the nations represented. Even Matthew's disagreement, which is viewed as rampant democracy, is based only on a Jeffersonian defense of the right of natural aristocracies to develop.

Furthermore, Matthew and the princess only play at being members of the working class. He takes the porter's job largely to do research for the conference, and he constantly carries with him an envelope he knows contains a large amount of money given him by the princess. When he later becomes a ditch digger, he alternates in his letters to her between lyrical praise of touching the earth and despair over the drudgery of it all. To counteract one of his depressions, he takes a week off to visit museums of the city. When he returns to work, he is amazed to find that he has been fired. The princess becomes, not merely a worker, but a union leader, a post she resigns immediately after she takes Matthew away from Sara and when she decides to devote her full time to lovemaking. In addition, she carries with her a bag containing a million dollars' worth of jewels.

Despite their pretensions, labor is not a serious matter for these characters. They idealize it, and when it becomes too real or inconvenient, they dismiss it. Their real attitude is expressed in a letter Matthew writes. In the midst of a dissertation on "We Common People," he says, "Whether we will or not, some must rule and do for the people what they are too weak or silly to do for themselves" (283–84).

The novel is, in fact, a bourgeois fantasy, complete with sexual fulfillment. Matthew experiences three moments of frustration, each associated somehow with the princess. First, he is kept from intimate physical contact with white women by being prevented from taking the obstetrics clinic. This episode conjures up all the miscegenational obsessions of white America. The episode only makes sense in the context of white fantasies of black potency and rape. This racial obsession denies Matthew the potency of his vocational dream. At this point, having left the United States, he sees the princess being accosted by a white man and is literally able to strike back at a representative of his oppression. He is rewarded by being brought into the conference of Third World nations.

In the next major episode, the hero again enters the fantasy of someone else, this time that of Perigua, the revolutionary. The plot to blow up the KKK train contains obvious Freudian elements. The train is to enter the Cumberland Gap and, at the end of the gap, to go through a tunnel. As it emerges from the tunnel, a bomb is to explode, blowing up the tunnel and the train. Unfortunately for Perigua, the bomb goes off too soon, and, furthermore, Matthew stops the train before it reaches the explosion point—a striking case of both premature ejaculation and coitus interruptus. Again, the princess offers Matthew a chance to prove his manhood. He not only stops the train (because she is on board) but also refuses to implicate others because of her. This time she directly recognizes his masculinity: "They looked at each other. He let his eyes feast on her for the last time—that never, never again should they forget her grace and beauty and even the gray line of suffering that leapt from nose to chin; suddenly she sank to her knees and kissed both his hands, and was gone" (105).

Finally, Matthew leaves prison, only to enter the political fantasy of Sara Andrews. Sara, as already suggested, has sublimated all her sexual energy into the quest for political power. Even when she weds the hero, no evidence is offered that the marriage is ever consummated. Sara's moment of fulfillment is to come when Matthew is nominated for Congress; but again the princess intervenes. Although he has been tempted by Sara's dream, he realizes his own inadequacy and humiliation: "Then slowly shame overwhelmed him. He was paying a price for power and money. A great, terrible price. He was lying, cheating, stealing. He was fooling these poor, driven slaves of industry. . . . He had meant now to meet the delegation brusquely and tell them railingly that they were idiots, that he could do little" (297). The princess enters and his manhood is revived; the castrating effects of Sara are ended: "There was a silence of a thousand years, a silence while he again found her lips and kept them, and his arms crept along the frail, long length of her body, and he cried as he whispered in her ears" (209). At this point they are interrupted, but instead of hiding, they walk straight through the crowd and into the night. They go to Matthew's private apartment, where they spend days in sexual and spiritual communion.

Matthew is driven, not by the dream of democratic socialism, but by physical desire for the princess. His success in each episode is his demonstration of the stereotypically masculine virtues of physical force, silence, and sexual potency. And these are rewarded in material ways: he marries a princess, fathers a king, and leads a global political movement. Beginning in impotence, he ends in wealth, power, and status of the highest order. Like a good capitalist, he has delayed gratification so as to invest in a highly profitable future. He has struggled on alone, with the help of a good woman (who is, stereotypically, both mother and mistress), and his persistence and individualism have paid off handsomely. The marriage, a social convention, is the joining, not of the black masses with the Third World masses, but of the black bourgeoisie with Asian aristocracy, an association with little meaning for either socialism or democracy.

At the same time, Du Bois has been able to play out fantasies of violence and revenge against the dominant order. The white man in Berlin, the KKK, and the political machine are all patriarchal emblems that he assaults on the way to engendering a new patriarchal order. In support of this latter point, Towns and the princess see a Japanese dignitary who has tried to keep them focused on the goal of social change as the model of future leadership:

"I did not tell you, but yesterday my great and good friend, the Japanese baron whom you have met and dislike because you do not know him, came to see me. He knows always where I am and what I do, for it is written that

I must tell him. You do not realize him yet, Matthew. He is civilization—he is the high goal toward which the world blindly gropes; high in birth and perfect in courtesy, filled with wide, deep, and intimate knowledge of the world's past—the world, white, black, brown, and yellow; knowing by personal contact and acquaintanceship the present from kings to coolies. He is a man of lofty ideal without the superstition of religion, a man of decision and action. He is our leader, Matthew, the guide and counselor, the great Prime Minister of the Darker World." (261–62)

He is the idealized patriarch, stripped of greed and power-hunger and concerned only with the betterment of humanity. His membership in the "darker world" is insignificant; all the qualities used to describe him—aristocracy, gentlemanliness, knowledge, and reason—are those commonly associated with Eurocentric culture. The terms are virtually identical with those used elsewhere to describe the virtues of certain radicals, Southern gentility (when not defiled by slavery and racism), Europeans who have not surrendered to colonialism, and the talented tenth, including of course Du Bois himself. What we are offered, in other words, is the universalizing of certain aspects of patriarchal order. This, linked with fulfilled desire for the feminine other, engenders narratives that are fantasies of an overthrown father and a new fatherhood in the guise of brotherhood.

The masculine phrasing here is deliberate. While in both of these novels women characters are the mechanism for the final success of the hero, they function primarily as helpers in the redefinition of the patriarchal order. Moreover, both Zora and the princess are always already corrupted, Zora through promiscuity and the princess by an earlier arranged marriage. Only through the purification of hard work, selflessness, and nurture of the son can they be made acceptable. They must become maternal in order to serve as proper partners for him. As political symbols, such characterizations suggest that the racial other remains irrational and defiled. The difference for Du Bois is that it can be brought to its fulfillment through the guidance of men such as himself.

Such an interpretation is obviously at odds with Du Bois's arguments for his political values, and his sincerity is certainly not in question. His art as propaganda clearly spells out, especially in dialogue, the terms of a new socialist democratic society. But the very casting of it as allegory opens up ambiguities that it should preclude. The necessities of narrative compel strategies of deferral, conflict, and figuration that subvert the ideological design. Straightforward, reasoned visions of the future, when informed by allegory, become sexualized, violent fantasies of power that reveal despair, narcissism, desire, and anger at the very heart of rational optimism.

7

· · · · · · · · ·

Revisions and Visions

· · · · · · · · ·

The Trilogy as History

· · · · · · · · ·

The Black Flame (1957–61), Du Bois's trilogy about post-Reconstruction America, is perhaps the most complicated, if not sophisticated, of his writings. Cast in the form of novels, the books are a blending of history, fiction, social commentary, political criticism, and autobiography. The plot, in one sense, is merely a thread on which are hung his assorted observations about American life. To some extent, Du Bois concedes this point in a postscript to the first volume:

> The basis of this book is documented and verifiable fact, but the book is not history. On the contrary, I have used fiction to interpret those historical facts which otherwise would not be clear. Beyond this I have in some cases resorted to pure imagination in order to make unknown and unknowable history relate an ordered tale to the reader. In a few cases I have made slight and unimportant changes in the exact sequence of historical events and in names and places. In no case have these changes altered, to my mind, the main historical background.[1]

Art here has been brought into the service of social science. If Du Bois's description of his design is accurate, then he has moved beyond the genteel notions of literature that created the tensions of his earlier novels. He no longer feels required to attach his realistic observations to a love story. He will speak the truth straightforwardly and not make concessions to those interested only in a pleasant tale.

In his roles as historian and sociologist, Du Bois has presented himself as a scientist, though, as we have seen, his work is seldom positivistic. He prefers to gather facts, determine relationships, and then offer a theory. But such a method is not available to the author of *The Black Flame*. First, he is very old: eighty-nine at the time of publication of the first volume. Second, he lacks the research money and facilities: "If I had had time and money, I would have continued this pure historical research. But this opportunity is running out" (*Ordeal*, 316). Most important, he has some doubts about the possibilities for complete knowledge. He himself knows a great deal and knows how to find out much more. "But even with all this, much, indeed most, is missing: just what men thought, the actual words they used, the feelings and motives which impelled them—these I do not know and most of them will never know. These facts are gone forever" (316).

He asserts an ideal notion of historiography, knowing all the while that the things he sees as unavailable have virtually always been unavailable to historians. Nonetheless, he goes beyond even the standard he set in *Black Reconstruction*. The historian should concern himself with gathering facts; any intrusion of his subjectivity is unacceptable. The degree of objectivity demanded here is more extreme than any ever practiced or even proposed in his writings; it is a return to the ideal of "cold-blooded science" of his student days.

Given the impossibility of meeting this standard and the other limitations on his research, he proposes calling his work "fiction" rather than "history." But the distinctions he makes between these terms are very similar to the ones between interpretive and documentary history, which, in the light of work by Hayden White, are themselves false.[2] The historian presents and interprets information and "relates an ordered tale," much as Du Bois himself did in *John Brown* and *The Negro*. The storyteller, as indicated in *The Quest of the Silver Fleece* and *Dark Princess*, does not render a pure creation of his fancy; quite the contrary, he stays as close to the facts as possible. The novelist, in other words, is a historian who feels the necessity to speak even if he cannot prove everything he says.

But the postscript also suggests other strategies at work. Its disclaimer, like that of *The Quest of the Silver Fleece*, argues that the writer is not telling a tale at all but recounting real events. The novel form, in other words, is a measure of the historian's humility and deserves attention for its truth content, if not its art. But there is also a conflict-ing, if not contradictory, reason for the choice of genre. He recognizes the necessity of storytelling, with its referential character, but also of the "pure imagination." By making this gesture, he justifies otherwise inexplicable sections of the trilogy. The books are filled with conspiracy scenes and mystic visions and moral judgments. These are generally not justified by either plot or historical "fact." But for Du Bois they are the keys to the meaning of the novels. By allowing for the imagination, he can express his moral indignation and his version of the apocalypse without being accused of emotional excess or subjectivity. He puts the words in the mouths of madmen and conspirators, so that he can say what he feels must be said but what would be scandalous and perhaps even irresponsible to say in his own voice. To the roles of historian and novelist he adds that of prophet.

The three volumes under consideration—*The Ordeal of Mansart* (1957), *Mansart Builds a School* (1959), and *Worlds of Color* (1961)—cover the historical period 1876 to 1954. As works of history, Du Bois sees them completing a much larger trilogy:

> In the great tragedy of Negro slavery in the United States and its aftermath, much of documented history is lacking because of the deep feeling involved and the fierce desire of men to defend their fathers and themselves. This I have sought to correct in my study of the slave trade and of Reconstruc-tion. . . . I would rescue from my long experience something of what I have learned and conjectured and thus I am trying by the method of historical fiction to complete the cycle of history which has for a half century engaged my thought, research and action. (*Ordeal*, 316)

Du Bois manages to have it both ways. The current work is placed in the company of *The Suppression of the Slave-Trade* and *Black Recon-struction*, but it is not to be measured by the standards of those earlier studies. Its justification lies in the experience, insight, and integrity of its author and not in the conventions of genre. For the purposes of analysis, however, it is useful to make the divisions Du Bois implicitly refuses: history, fiction, prophecy.

As historical documents, the novels range widely in the period they cover. They mention or analyze American politics, economic systems, black religion, art and literature, education, obscure black figures, the NAACP and its internal politics, the two world wars, racism, vacationing in Paris, British aristocracy, Franklin Roosevelt, Booker T. Washington, Marcus Garvey, Harry Hopkins, Southern political figures, and Madame C. J. Walker of hair-straightener fame. In some cases subjects are raised and disposed of within a short paragraph. At times, the only apparent order is chronology, but even this is sometimes violated when events in one volume continue later in the narrative. The overall order, however, is that *The Ordeal of Mansart* covers 1876 to 1912, while *Mansart Builds a School* covers World War I and the pre-Roosevelt years, and *Worlds of Color* spans the years 1935 to 1954. Another order is apparent in the gradual expansion from a regional setting in the first book to a national one in the second and a global one in the third. Neither the time nor space structure is rigid, and the works are constantly threatened with disintegration into a compendium of obscure facts.

Despite this cataloguing tendency, Du Bois does concern himself with certain basic issues: capitalism, international socialism, the black elite, and the conflict of race and class. As always, he sees economics as a basic question, though now with a more strictly Marxist emphasis; and again, as always, he is concerned with how economics influences and is influenced by race. The history Du Bois writes here is, in other words, very much like the history he has been writing from the beginning.

A brief comparison of *The Quest of the Silver Fleece* and *The Ordeal of Mansart* can suggest the extent to which the trilogy is a work of history rather than fiction. The two works cover approximately the same time period and have as one theme the economic conditions of the post-Reconstruction South. The earlier work treats the theme strictly within the confines of created characters and plot. The white planting class, for example, is revealed to readers through the lives and actions of the Cresswells. In contrast, the Breckinridges of *Ordeal* think and converse in terms of documentable history. Much is told; very little is dramatized. As an illustration, when Colonel John Breckinridge, the landowner, sees black Tom Mansart approaching his home, he lapses into a thought process covering three pages in which the history of South Carolina Reconstruction is recounted, the economic motives of various groups are explored, and Wade Hampton is characterized (14–16). The colonel is nothing more than a cipher used by Du Bois to signify a certain white attitude and to justify the presentation of historical information. Whereas *Silver Fleece* builds upon the reader's knowledge, *Ordeal* and the rest of the trilogy assume very little awareness on the part of the reader. Everything must be stated and explained, even if such exposition has no relationship to the plot.

The intrusion of Wade Hampton in the passage referred to raises the issue of the role of actual historical persons in Du Bois's fiction. The placing of real people in fictional situations is a convention of the historical novel. It lends the fiction an aura of authenticity and human interest often associated with biography. But Du Bois is doing something different with the figures in his trilogy. They usually have little to do with the plot and frequently are brought in for their own sakes. The story of Madame C. J. Walker, for example, has no other function than to show how a black woman succeeded against the odds and achieved wealth and fame. In fact, as we shall see, such figures are often problematic for the meaning of the narrative.

Another reason for the appearance of "real" people is the author's desire to have the final word on certain subjects. His observations on Marcus Garvey and Booker T. Washington, two father figures whom Du Bois struggled against, reveal a mixture of historical and personal views. About the leader of the Universal Negro Improvement Association he observes, "Garvey was a demagogue with a core of sincerity, and deep color prejudice against whites and mulattoes; not so much unscrupulous as totally inexperienced."[3]

The anecdote about Washington comes close to gossip. It has nothing to do directly with the political differences between him and Du Bois; rather it clearly suggests that Washington was less than the virtuous character usually portrayed. Du Bois intimates that the Great Accommodationist had a strong predilection for white prostitutes. After giving a speech one night, Washington has a few drinks: "Suddenly he wanted the companionship of women. He wanted to sit beside somebody he did not fear, somebody who was not spying on him, who had no complaints. . . . The women were white so they could not tattle to Negroes—they could not take him to task for not helping all the black folk of the world."[4] Du Bois goes on to relate that the man becomes lost while seeking a certain brothel and eventually collapses of exhaustion. He notes that it is only with difficulty that the Tuskegee people explain away the incident. Such a story argues for the hypocrisy of Washington, but even more it appeals to miscegenational fantasies and thereby destroys Washington's character in the eyes of both blacks and whites. By telling this tale forty years after Washington's death, Du Bois gains the final, vindictive word on an ancient controversy.

Other figures fit more directly into the politico-economic theme of the trilogy. Tom Watson becomes the vehicle by which Du Bois examines the complex relationship of race, economics, and politics in the South. As a poor white, Watson was instinctively racist: "His inherited reaction was to despise if not hate Negroes" (*Ordeal*, 166). This inheritance did not, however, prevent him from facing what Du Bois sees as the more basic issue: "But knowing too well what poverty and ignorance had done to the white world, he had the courage to ask earnestly if the Negro was not only suffering from the same oppression, which re-inforced white degradation" (166).

Watson, with the assistance of Sebastian Doyle, a black minister, began to form a populist alliance that included farmers and laborers of both races. But such an alliance was doomed, Du Bois argues, because of the ability of capitalist front men like Ben Tillman to exploit the race issue:

Labor, North and South, was out of hand and even revolutionary. Its radicalism was at the point of ignoring and forgetting race hate, one of the strongest of human motives. Men talked in club and family circle; in Church and in the secret societies which in the South rose from solemn mummery to become fully calculated centers of white propaganda and action.

The South said: The trend to a Third Party must be stopped by splitting the labor movement. The obvious way to do this was by using the "natural and doubtless God-given difference of race" in the laboring class to keep them separated. Race difference must be emphasized and enforced by law. This, pleaded Science, was in the long run legitimate and would lead to the best human stock; this, argued Religion, is not hate and suppression but recognition of the "divine purpose" in history. (175–76)

Variations on this statement occur throughout the trilogy. Race is a consciously manipulated issue used to prevent laboring-class solidarity.

As long as the economic insecurities of white farmers and laborers can be translated into fears of black equality, then both groups will continue to be exploited. This argument is similar to the one put forth in *Black Reconstruction*. The dilemma of that earlier book, whether race or class is predominant, has apparently been decided. But we will see that the question is not so easily dismissed for Du Bois.

The question of who is running the "carefully calculated centers of white propaganda and action" is answered with a generalization: "Industry, organized and becoming monopolized, united in its efforts and descended on South and West. In the South it was opposed by the attempt to unite labor and small farmers. But labor was split by the Color Line and the small farmer was dominated by the big planter. There was no real union there. In the West united farmers beat the banks and railroads but the mining corporations tempted them with 'cheap money' " (178).

Wealth, as exercised by corporations, is the villain of the trilogy. Du Bois goes so far as to depict conspiratorial meetings among those who dominated the economic world. He never makes it clear whether he believes such cabals actually existed or whether he is using them metaphorically to indicate the manipulative capabilities of Big Money. In either case, capitalists and planters took advantage of the Southern situation. The impact was devastating: "Watson was beaten, Bryan was beaten, Socialism was buried, and triumphant organized private industry won the election and rushed into Colonial Imperialism through the Spanish-American War. So Revolution failed. So Tom Watson went mad" (179).

In the trilogy, Du Bois has a penchant for finding conspiracies and failed revolutions everywhere. Certainly the most spectacular of the latter was the New Deal. Franklin Roosevelt becomes a disciple of socialism, led by his sainted advisor, Harry Hopkins:

> As successor to Al Smith, Roosevelt inherited the philanthropic socialism of Florence Kelley and her Consumer's League, of Jane Addams and her leaders of Settlements among the poor, and of Frances Perkins and her factory laws. But Hopkins was closer to him and nearer to complete Socialism. Perhaps Roosevelt was drawn to him just because, in contrast to Roosevelt's own training, Hopkins was ill-bred, often ate with his knife and

swore. But he was a free inquiring soul, a Socialist who voted for Debs, and a free thinker, did not attend church and knew the mass of men because he was one of them. But he had added to what the class in which he was born knew. He studied poverty and disease face to face. He knew the Negro problem of the South by living with it. He was clear-headed and absolutely honest, and the only thing he placed above Truth was Loyalty—personal loyalty to friends. For this, he stopped at no sacrifice. (*School*, 336)

Du Bois's Hopkins could easily be a member of the talented tenth; he rose from the masses but devoted himself unselfishly to studying and rectifying the problems of the people. He was, in a sense, a white Du Bois. His socialism is not an abstract theory but the result of knowledge and experience. Like his portraitist, he has gone beyond genteel "liberal" socialism (significantly, represented here by women) to a more radical variety. On the basis of his integrity, intelligence, and ideology, he is the man to point the nation in the direction of revolution.

Such direction was both possible and necessary because of the character of Roosevelt:

Franklin Roosevelt was indeed two men in one. The sight of poverty in this rich land incensed him; he believed it entirely unnecessary and mainly the result of wrongdoing, conscious or unconscious. For remedy, he sympathized with the socialism of Harry Hopkins and of most of the greatest thinkers of his day. His thought was not socialism but it was socialistic. . . . The other Roosevelt was the English gentleman, with Dutch patroon reinforcement, who saw in the British empire the salvation of all that civilization meant to him, when the Prime Minister of Great Britain appealed to him for support in saving the British Empire from Hitler. (336)

Roosevelt is Tom Watson at a different level: "He could do right even if it clashed with inherited predilections" (335). Politicians of this sort can turn their good intentions to account only if they have proper guidance. In the trilogy, this guidance is toward socialism rather than, as in earlier works, toward racial pride or equality. To some extent, this shift is a logical continuation of what Du Bois had said before. As early as *The Quest of the Silver Fleece*, he envisioned a socialist future, although then it was in the context of local black achievement. *The Dark Princess* ended with the leaders of the nonwhite world united in favor of industrial democracy. What has occurred in *The Black Flame* is that the color line has been broken down, and socialism has become a global possibility.

But the form as well as the content of guidance to the future has changed. Ironically, given heroes like Hopkins, Du Bois has become more elitist than ever. Previously, his heroes, including himself, had undertaken to lead and educate the masses. Now, if the cases of Sebastian Doyle and Harry Hopkins are evidence, the heroes lead the politically powerful leaders who actually change history. The masses are the recipients of the actions of such men. The revolution will occur if and when the vanguard is effective.

That vanguard is opposed by an equally dedicated group of "reactionaries": "None can say how far Franklin Roosevelt would have gone in reorganizing the economy of the nation if the work of the first eight years of his reign had continued and expanded. We might now live in a different world. But war intervened and once again, as so often in the past, ruined the future of mankind."[5] The war is no accident. Earlier in the same chapter Du Bois describes a secret committee: "The members represented most of the chief international cartels which controlled the production and distribution of goods the world over" (*Worlds*, 168). This group concerned itself with the growing European conflict and the threat of socialism. The great hope was that Roosevelt would be defeated, since the New Deal was the great threat to capitalism in the West. Elections might end the "red" problem in the United States, but the Soviet Union was another matter. "By war alone can socialism finally be conquered" (170). Assuming, however, that Roosevelt was reelected and the Soviets did not capitulate quickly, then the conspirators had a plan:

1. To ask Japan to attack the U.S.A. without warning.

2. It was guaranteed that when Russia was conquered, Germany, Britain and France would protect Japan from injury and grant her necessary access to world trade.

3. When the U.S.A. declared war, British industry and finance, with the cooperation of American business interests, would see to it that the U.S.A. did not attack Germany or help Russia.

4. After the war, France and Italy as well as Germany were to be recognized as co-partners with Britain and the U.S.A. as leading directors of world trade, industry and finance. (171–72)

The first step in this program is deliberately designed to manipulate American racism: "On one matter alone today can American opinion be stampeded and that is race and color. . . . Still, an attack on white America by yellow Japan would unite the nation like a giant catalyst" (170–71). The same race hatred that defeated populism in the South is now being used on a global level to defeat socialism.

Du Bois's own obsessions are revealed in this historical interpretation. He constantly discusses, here and elsewhere, the conspiracy of capitalism, the hope for socialism, and the centrality of race. The conspiracy element functions metaphorically to show a central moral value. By creating secret committees and meetings in which the future is determined, he returns to the fundamental belief that self-interest is willful and not merely an amoral human drive. Humans have available to them various possibilities for action, and they consciously choose to exploit, manipulate, and deceive. In this sense, Du Bois's Marxism is tempered by his moralism. In the trilogy, it remains just as wrong to pursue one's own selfish ends as it was in *The Suppression of the Slave-Trade*, though sixty years of thought and experience separate these works. Furthermore, the correlation of economics and war remains a "fact" of the Du Boisian historical perspective. The conspiracies, then, are further demonstration that humans have choices to make in history and that those choices have a major impact on human existence.

But Du Bois also recognizes that nations as well as individuals play an important historical role. It is, in his view, the Soviet Union that foils the grand scheme of the international capitalists. Rather than fall meekly before the Germans, as had been expected, the Russians held Hitler's forces and even defeated them:

> It was a fearful victory. The Germans destroyed 72,000 towns and villages, leaving 25,000,000 people homeless. They demolished 32,000 industries; they tore up 40,000 miles of railroads with stations, telegraph and telephone offices; they destroyed 40,000 hospitals, 84,000 schools and 44,000 libraries; they ransacked 100,000 farms and drove off 70 million head of horses, cattle, sheep and goats. Their damage to state industrial enterprises has been estimated at $128 billion. Sixty-one of the greatest power stations were blown up. Coal mines and oil wells were destroyed. Public buildings, museums and churches were ruined. The Soviet Union lost seven million of its people in war, and perhaps as many more in civilian life. . . . The

war cost the Soviet Union $200,000,000,000. The U.S.A. gave her in net Lend-Lease about five percent of the sum. Never before in the history of man had a single nation sacrificed so much for the salvation of the world. (179–80)

The USSR has replaced blacks as a model of virtue and sacrifice. The Soviets preserve Western civilization in defiance of those who would destroy it for the sake of profit. Their action is comparable to that of the black reconstructionists who tried to build a democratic society in the postbellum South. And again, as in the case of those blacks, the Soviet Union is responsible for good and never for evil: "He learned how Russia was striving to achieve democracy. In this desperate, heart-breaking struggle with weak human nature, with crime and selfishness, the Soviet leaders could count on no aid or sympathy from the decency and religion of Europe or America" (20). Du Bois's position is premised on moral rather than economic or political values. The guardians of good struggle alone to reach certain ideals: altruism, self-sacrifice, brotherhood, truth. Capitalism is attacked less for its economic organization than for its endorsement of greed. Du Bois's radicalism, in other words, is founded on traditional, conservative moral grounds, on the Law of the Father.

Such a position does not, however, blind him to political nuances. His hero is specifically Stalinist Russia, and he attacks its ideological opponents:

> He began to realize that he has gotten it [information on the Soviet Union] largely from the American press and Leon Trotsky; that when Trotsky came to Mexico the American press was thrown open to him and American liberals swarmed about him. So that for years it was Trotsky who made up the minds of Americans on Russia. All this, of course, could not have been spontaneous. It must have been promoted and paid for. All American periodicals, all news services were open to Trotsky. The liberal movement became his agents. (201)

He goes on to argue that the press is controlled by big business, which profits from poisoning American minds about the great socialist experiment.

The emphasis on socialism as the new ideal is in one sense merely an expansion of the earlier black ideal. The trilogy is largely about black life in America, but, Du Bois contends, that life can achieve its fullest possibilities only through a global and socialist consciousness. Nonetheless, certain ambiguities are created when the author focuses on racial as opposed to economic matters. In several such cases, the portraits of strong black figures contradict the ideological stance. It is not surprising that Paul Robeson, an apologist for the Soviet Union, and A. Philip Randolph, the socialist union leader, emerge as historical heroes. What is more difficult to understand is the reason that Madame Walker, manufacturer of hair straighteners, and Heman Perry, founder of the Standard Life Insurance Company, are given the same high status. Black capitalists, it would seem, are not the same as white capitalists.

On the other hand, black capitalism itself is not to be admired: "Thus as political power faded there emerged a new escapism for educated and ambitious Negroes. In the South particularly, the better class not only turned from politics to business, but from industry to exploitation. A class structure began to appear among Negroes, differing from the past." (*Ordeal*, 282). Black business is ephemeral; those who engage in it delude themselves and the black masses if they believe that they can attain any real status in American society through moneymaking. Furthermore, such business will make its profits by exploiting other blacks, thereby perpetuating black oppression and suffering. In a representative passage, a black doctor is characterized:

> He became what was sometimes called a "commercial" physician. He had no deep human sensibilities or sympathies. He was strong, and callous. He calculated on making his profession "pay" in every way. He "strung along" those of his patients who could pay well for numerous visits over long periods of time. He was careful to select patients who could pay well, and to these he was always attentive. Poor patients he got rid of in various ways— by curing them quickly or by sending them to the city clinics; or sometimes by simply saying that he could do nothing for them. (*Worlds*, 217)

The black businessman has lost any sense he might have had of a black ideal. He has absorbed not only the dominant society's predilection for profit but also the selfishness and corruption that accompany capitalist enterprise.

Du Bois also suggests that a business orientation reflects a desire to escape one's racial identity. When Mansart's wife and others begin patronizing one of Madame Walker's shops, he accuses them of a lack of race pride and a desire to be white (*School*, 151). Furthermore, one of Mansart's sons sees wealth as a way of avoiding the implications of his color: "He didn't want to live in the South, he didn't want to teach school, and indeed, if the truth were known, he didn't want to be a Negro. The only way of escaping the penalties of being black was to make money, and he proposed to devote his life to that" (167).

The position taken here goes back as far as the essay "The Wings of Atalanta" that appeared in *The Souls of Black Folk*. There Du Bois argued that the city of Atlanta was paying too much attention to making money and too little to the virtues that made the South distinctive. His principal concern was for the black community, which he feared was willingly adopting the values of business-oriented whites. In the trilogy, blacks are again taking a lower road and denying themselves a greater destiny, which in this case means socialism. An ideal that transcends self-interest is still functioning, but Du Bois fears that that ideal is less and less effective.

A countercurrent runs through the novels, suggesting the author's divided loyalties between economics and race. The activities of Madame Walker, for example, are detailed from her early childhood to the establishment of her nationwide business. The history is recounted in an anecdotal manner that implies approval on the part of the narrator. Even though this is the business that encourages blacks to be "ashamed of their race," Madame Walker is portrayed as a heroine aiding her people: "Despite the opposition of churches, despite the fact that colored newspapers for a long time refused to carry her advertisements and that most colored people, while they resorted to her business shops, were ashamed to confess that they were having their hair straightened and arranged, there arose this new branch of work which gave Negroes an income and a chance for economic development" (116).

The same business that is exploitative serves the purposes of economic development. Arnold Rampersad has suggested that Du Bois displays a certain confusion with such dichotomous claims.[6] What is more likely is that not even a commitment to socialism keeps Du Bois from an appreciation of authentic black achievement. One point of the Walker story is that she rose from the masses. She became a member of the talented tenth who worked hard and who developed a legitimate service for blacks. Being rewarded for that service is just compensation for her efforts. The case here is similar to the "fair price" argument in the biography of John Brown. The issue is fairness and the meeting of community needs. It is when money rather than the community is the principal concern that in Du Bois's view business becomes immoral. Madame Walker's capitalism is justified because it encourages economic development and provides income within the black community; it is at once profitable and philanthropic. Such a sensibility is at the heart of the critique of capitalism in the trilogy. It also clearly problematizes the relationship of Du Bois the radical economic historian and Du Bois the moralist.

Very little has been said to this point about the trilogy as a work of fiction. The range and preponderance of historical data offered often leave the reader doubtful whether the narratives are fiction at all. The observations of the past several pages have been made with minimal reference to fictional characters or other narrative devices. This emphasis is justified in that Du Bois in the postscript clearly states his intentions: "Here lies, then, I hope, more history than fiction, more fact than assumption, much truth and no falsehood" (*Ordeal*, 316).

The question of narrative voice is at issue here, since that foregoing discussion consistently refers to Du Bois as the speaker in the text. The story is told by an omniscient narrator whose tone and ideology are those of Du Bois, as expressed in a wide range of nonfictive works, and who often borrows his own words from elsewhere. Frequently, it is difficult to distinguish this voice from those of certain characters, which suggests an author with little interest in character development. Characters are consistently identified by the ideologies they articulate or the allegorical roles they perform, all of which are colored by the biases of the narrator. Even "historical" figures are less persons than functions of a particular historical interpretation. Thus, the trilogy is clearly monologic in design and execution.

What this means for the trilogy is that even the purely fictional situations and characters are more concerned with history than literary structure. The dialogue of characters is more often intended to provide historical information than to reveal personality or develop plot. For example, a conversation about the outbreak of World War I quickly turns into a dissertation on black participation in America's wars. Similarly, Harry Hopkins has an evening's conversation with the fictional Revels Mansart in which the situation of blacks under the New Deal is discussed. Du Bois goes so far as to include an extended quotation from the *New Republic* (*School*, 345).

Characters in the trilogy largely lack what might be called a private consciousness. They concern themselves with the public events of the period in which they live. This lack of psychology exists despite the fact that it was the "inner life" that led Du Bois to fiction in the first place. After all, as the postscript states, it was "just what men thought, the actual words they used, the feelings and motives which impelled them" that could be expressed only through fiction. Such material is very limited in the fictional world of *The Black Flame*. The only necessary and sufficient motivations offered are greed, hatred, and idealism. Virtually every character, whether invented or historical, may be shown to react to one of these factors. This small range allows Du Bois to bring a kind of scientific logic to human subjectivity. He wants to offer a rational explanation for the irrationalities of human existence and action. In this sense, he has become a Marxist offering an economic reading of human psychology.

This helps to further explain the use of conspiracies. By setting up secret meetings, he can suggest the economic sources of capitalist behavior. Thus, the pre–World War II meeting described above analyzes the relationship between war and profits and demonstrates the economic fear of socialism that impelled such drastic action. In such scenes characters can be made to say forthrightly what they otherwise would never say or possibly even consciously think.

Of course, in such "scientific" fiction, characters have no unconscious. Either they themselves or someone else presents a rational explanation for what they do. Thus, we are again dealing with a largely allegorical world. Characters represent ideas or types and derive their meaning from their function in the grand scheme. For the vast historical canvas on which he works, Du Bois needs a complex scheme. He does not, for example, as in *The Quest of the Silver Fleece*, have only one Southern aristocratic family. He draws instead the Breckinridges, a conventional plantation group, and the Du Bignons, an old family of New Orleans. The Breckinridges resemble the Cresswells of the earlier work, demonstrating the same combination of arrogance, racism, and noblesse oblige in the post–Civil War world. The Du Bignons, on the other hand, represent the more complex attitudes of their French ancestors. They have a distaste for blacks but also have the sophistication and economic security to absorb a bit of the "tar brush," as the matriarch of the family phrases it.

We are also presented with the Scroggs family, several generations of poor whites; the Carmichaels, Northern black laborers; and the Mansarts, who represent various aspects of the black middle class. In each case the family name rather than individual traits designates the role to be played by the character. Any Scroggs, for example, will take a poor white perspective, regardless of situation.

The Mansarts represent the most complex idea, that of the black bourgeoisie. Each aspect of that socio-racial class is somehow articulated through family members. Further, in one way or another, we have met the Mansarts in Du Bois's earlier works. We have the successful but corrupt businessman in Douglass, the successful but corrupt politician in Revels, the embittered and doomed son in Bruce, the valiant warrior in Revels II, the straitlaced matron in Susan, the artist in Sojourner, the successful but corrupt minister in Roosevelt Wilson (Sojourner's husband), and the talented tenth in Manuel, the protagonist.

Each character exists principally as a focal point for the commentary of the author on a specific subject. The family as a whole and Manuel in particular serve to keep the trilogy from disintegrating into a string of unrelated observations. Nonetheless, the novels are less about the family than about representative events in the lives of individual members. The story of Douglass's escape to the North to go into business has virtually no relationship to the lives of others in the family. Although characters occasionally transcend a specific role, they do so only because they can be used for other purposes. For example, Revels is a successful politician. But before he functions as a focal point for Du Bois's critique of black politicians, he is used for a discussion of the difficulties of interracial marriage. After the problems of such a relationship are established, the wife conveniently disappears and Revels goes on to his political career and a different, intraracial marriage. When a new character is needed for a new purpose, the child of the first marriage miraculously appears. Later, Revels is also the vehicle through which Du Bois can have Harry Hopkins discuss socialism, blacks, and the New Deal. Each stage of the career of Judge Revels Mansart is isolated as much as possible from the others. Du Bois thus uses fictional characters in the same way he does historical ones: they help to explain his view of history.

These fictional characters are generally not masks for real people. They are composites of groups or individuals or sometimes simply types. Whenever he wants to talk about an actual person, Du Bois simply contrives a way to bring him or her into the story.

Such is not the case with himself. Even though he talks about the Booker T. Washington controversy, the Niagara movement, and the NAACP, and even though he quotes passages from his own articles and books, his own name never appears in the text. Often he refers to "a Negro editor" or "one Negro" or "a Negro author" when it is clear he means himself. But he cannot always be so circumspect, for it is clear to him that his actions and ideas frequently have a central place in the black experience. He therefore performs the interesting feat of giving to three different characters qualities of his own life.[7] The ostensible mask for himself is James Burghardt, a trained social scientist who teaches in the South, edits the *Atlanta Studies*, helps to found the Niagara movement, then moves on to the NAACP to become the editor of *The Crisis*. In Burghardt, Du Bois offers a character who is intelligent, analytical, and sensitive to the nuances of the race question. A clear notion of the significance of Burghardt is presented in an analysis of the NAACP:

> This new organization included the radical Burghardt as its only Negro official, who for that very reason wielded disproportionate influence. Without him no inter-racial effort could succeed. With him, his radical ideas must be pushed. This Burghardt from the first insisted on, when he proposed a monthly magazine to voice the program of the NAACP. The other officers hesitated. They not only feared the editor's ideas but they pointed out the cost. Burghardt assumed personal responsibility for this cost and in November, 1910, the *Crisis* appeared as a magazine of 18 pages. The maga-

zine spread like wildfire, not simply because it was readable but because it was timely for a people emotionally starved in a crisis of their development. (*School*, 67–68)

The facts of this passage are documentable history; it is an accurate recapitulation of the founding of the organization and its publication. But the interpretation offers us the classical Du Bois hero. Burghardt is morally courageous where others are hesitant. He is politically ahead of his time and willing to challenge conventional views. Moreover, his success demonstrates that he is spiritually aligned with blacks everywhere. The event is minor compared to the work of the black reconstructionists or the struggles of the Soviet Union, but the moral principles are the same.

A more subtle identification is made between Du Bois and Jean Du Bignon, the heroine of the trilogy to the extent that there is one. Rampersad has accurately noted that both Jean and Du Bois are devoted to sociology, each planning a revival of the *Atlanta Studies* in the 1940s.[8] Another connection that has not been observed is the legal action that is taken against each. In both cases, concern for and participation in the international peace movement leads to charges of being the agent of a foreign power; these patently false charges are easily disproved and the defendants are released.[9] But these historical identifications are minor compared to the spiritual associations. Jean is a Du Bignon, a member of that aristocratic New Orleans family mentioned earlier. As such, she is almost entirely white. The darkest relative in "recent" family history is a quadroon great-grandfather. Her own parents are at most octoroon. The emphasis on color and genealogy is important because Du Bois wants to minimize her inherited blackness. He thereby makes it possible for her to choose her racial identity, just as it was possible, according to *Dusk of Dawn*, for him to choose his.[10] For both of them, the element of choice introduces moral possibilities in what for others is simply genetic fate. By taking the more difficult path in insisting on her blackness, Jean becomes a saintly figure who willingly identifies with the suffering of others.

The sacrificial element in her character becomes apparent when she takes a position as secretary at Mansart's school. Even though she has a Ph.D. from the University of Chicago, she does not use either her whiteness or her education for personal gain. Like her creator, she sacrifices prestige and recognition for the betterment of her people:

> But the wide window looked on a beautiful stretch of yard, unkept but with natural glory of grass and vine and wild flower. Across it went an almost continuous stream of humanity; student, teacher and worker, and all colored. Jean sighed luxuriously; it was a relief to see color, unconfined, free, content. To glimpse seldom, if at all, the bloodless, straight features of that dominant world in which all her life she had been imprisoned, no longer set about her in unsmiling superiority. She felt at long last free in her own world. She sensed no incongruity in the fact that her face was white; she was only keenly aware that the people she wanted, to whom she felt nearest, were now about her and that for and with them hereafter she was to work. She was not unconscious of the fact that these people would not automatically or easily accept her, veiled as she was in a hated color of skin. Already the President's son had rejected her. But this she cast aside gaily. Acceptance would come. She would make it and it was the natural thing, for race was not color; it was inborn oneness of spirit and aim and wish; and this made this school her home; her very own. (*School*, 128)

It is not insignificant that here Du Bois reverses the image of the veil. Jean's problem is not being black; it is being white. Caught up in the darker world, she only fears that she will be taken for a member of the lighter one. This reversal carries over from earlier works in which the claim was sometimes made that being black was intrinsically better; it also is consistent with the negritude movement of African nationalists. White is the skin color to be despised. Jean's drop of black blood allows her to escape the "bloodless, straight features" of the world of the white fathers. This black world, if we follow the tropes of the passage, is natural, free, and sensuous; Jean seeks it as a release from the rigidity of white civilization. She can, of course, only do so by creating terms through which she can be part of it. Since nature and genetics have denied her, she redefines race as spirit, thus granting to herself that membership in the race that blacks would deny her. Thus, paradoxically, self-sacrifice becomes possible through self-assertion.

Du Bois has not given up his black ideal. The last statement in the quotation returns the reader to the articulations of that ideal in *The Souls of Black Folk* and *The Negro*. He attempts to bridge the gap between ideology and race by having Jean suffer for her radicalism as well as her racial choice. Socialism and blackness are equal to a third thing, brotherhood, and thereby equal to each other. This equation is imperfect, as Du Bois's own insights in the trilogy show, but it is one that he nonetheless insists upon.

The working out of this tension is most clear in the character of Manuel Mansart, the central character and the third one with similarities to his creator. The ideological transformations Mansart (Man's heart, Man's art) undergoes are roughly those of Du Bois. Beginning with a defense of Washington's accommodationism, he gradually moves through integrationism and ends his life as a Marxist. Like Du Bois, his international travel changed his perspective: "First of all, he himself began to have a conception of the world as one unified dwelling place. He was escaping from his racial provincialism. He began to think of himself as part of humanity and not simply as an American Negro over against a white world" (*Worlds*, 85). Arrival at this point, at which race is merely one fact among many, is achieved through a long, laborious process in which race plays a major role and, even after this point is reached, race is not so insignificant as it appears.

Manuel is born at the moment his father is lynched, and this fact is constantly brought back to him. He attempts to achieve in his life a balance between accommodation to the way the world is and faith in a different future:

So more or less unconsciously Manuel Mansart worked out a pragmatic solution of the race problem. He was going to avoid white folks when he could. When brought in contact with them he was going to be pleasant. He noted that a smile or cheerful greeting often changed the whole atmosphere. People, especially white people, liked his frank, black face and his ingenuous way. Part of his attitude was quite honest and natural, and part of it was more or less unconscious hypocrisy. He did not smile at white people because he liked them; in fact he usually smiled because he did not trust them, because he was watching to see what they were going to do, either to hurt him or in some way to stop his natural impulses. This did not always happen. Sometimes, in fact most of the time, he met very nice white people; they were kind to him; they gave him things and helped him. But he did not trust them too much. He knew that a time would come and often did, when they would be wretchedly unjust and he would have no method of defense. So he was careful of them; he cajoled them; he kept his temper; he kept out of their way. (*Ordeal*, 120)

This passage describes Manuel at twelve, but it clearly applies to his entire life. Such a portrait obviously is not that of the uncompromising hero that appears so often in Du Bois's work. But it is also not that of an "Uncle Tom," as Manuel is frequently labeled by other black characters. Rather, the characterization is related to that of Frederick Douglass and other Northern blacks in *John Brown*. These were the men who chose not to go to Harper's Ferry, not because they were fearful, but because they knew the price that blacks paid for rebellion. Their courage was displayed in other ways. The lynching of Manuel's father makes him similarly aware of the limits of black assertion.

Du Bois states the issue later in terms that show why Manuel cannot be the kind of hero found in other works:

Mansart now faced for the first time and inexorably the life problem with which he was destined to struggle three-score years and ten and yet never answer to his own satisfaction or that of anyone else: how shall Integrity face Oppression? What shall Honesty do in the face of Deception, Decency in the face of Insult, Self-Defense before Blows? How shall Desert and Accomplishment meet Despising, Detraction and Lies? What shall Virtue do to meet Brute Force? There are so many answers and so contradictory; and such differences for those on the one hand who meet questions similar to this once a year or once a decade, and those who face them hourly and daily. (275)

The passage suggests complex possibilities. What in fact happens in Mansart's case is that integrity, honesty, and decency are quietly rather than aggressively maintained. First, he must remain in the South despite the inducements of money and position. Unlike Jean, he cannot choose his race; but, like her, he can choose the road of sacrifice. In an interesting twist, Du Bois has him take Washington's advice to "put his buckets down" where he is. This choice is costly; he loses the respect of his children and must constantly face the racism of whites.

That racism includes a belief in black corruption. Mansart repeatedly must deal with the assumption that blacks, and especially influential ones, can be bought. White contractors and businessmen offer him kickbacks to arrange for them to profit from his school. The temptation is the self-interested hypocrisy that other members of the black bourgeoisie, including his own sons, submit to. But this character is above such inducements.

The point illustrates a major tension in the trilogy. The world is divided between the altruistic and the self-interested. Throughout the books, it is argued that economic self-interest is the basic motivation for characters. Even racism, Du Bois contends, has an economic source. And yet, the most positive characters—Roosevelt, Hopkins, Jean, Mansart—are motivated by moral idealism. Each of them is clearly shown to reject the appeal of self-interest and act instead out of moral necessity. Each chooses a noble course and remains true to it. At the heart of *The Black Flame*, then, is a tension between Du Bois's Marxism and his moralism, which itself is one ground for that patriarchal order the Marxism resists. The moral system refuses to be reduced to a superstructural element of an economic system. Mansart's adherence to this morality, despite his accommodationist attitude, is what separates him from others and gives him heroic status. He contradicts the premises of that "scientific" fiction Du Bois is writing and thereby enters the realm of the black ideal.

The envisioning of that ideal makes possible the most intriguing and difficult parts of the trilogy. Du Bois is not satisfied with either straightforward history or with the interpretive possibilities of fiction. Scattered throughout the novels are surreal and prophetic visions of the present and the future. These visions occur mainly to insane characters or to those who have temporarily suspended their rational faculties. Thus, Dr. Baldwin, an educator who has been put in an asylum, escapes and returns to the streets of Atlanta to prophesy:

"All this is written. It is an accumulation of hates and animosities; a clash of counter-striving covering centuries. Paradoxes have at last met. Europe, Asia, Africa and all the Americas have been preparing for this for centuries. It has announced itself in Trilogies: African slavery, Asiatic wealth and white Supremacy; Slums and Poverty, Ignorance and Crime, Disease and Death; Aristocracy and Power, Comfort and Luxury, Society and Gambling; Philosophy, Science and Technique. We have talked of Absolute, Final, Longest, Biggest, Highest. We have pretended to distinguish Truth,

Lies, Good, Evil. . . . The kingly crown was a wreath of colonies, studded with gold and diamonds and festering with tubercules, cancers and syphilis; packed with care and suspicion in ships and trains plastered with mud and oiled with human blood." (*School*, 28–30)

This same Dr. Baldwin is later said by the narrator to be responsible for the Atlanta fire, which destroys a square mile of the city.

Mansart himself has a dream with a built-in explanation of its allegory:

> Then, suddenly, with startling clearness, out there in the night he seemed to see a great green Spider nesting in Hell, weaving an impenetrable Web. It sat in a pool of blood, which had gushed down from China, flowed in from Spain and seeped through Mississippi. The Spider seemed to be spinning out thin tendrils of American gold, linking strand to strand. To the drying, stinking mess, the Spider added clods of British dirt and moistened all with the slime of France, until the spreading Web grew wide as the Earth and high as Heaven. It was too horrible. It seemed to divide the Darkness from the Light and the White World fought the Dark World and both faced Death. (*Worlds*, 163–64)

The economic grounds for both these visions is clear: they are attacks upon colonialism, imperialism, and racism. But the need for such passages in a work that insists upon its rational foundations is less clear. Rampersad persuasively argues that moral indignation informs the trilogy: "On behalf of what he considered to be the eternal verities, Du Bois had not faith but fanaticism. Like many others, he felt profoundly the wrongs inflicted by evil in the world. It is given to far fewer to simmer through life with hatred for those wrongs, but Du Bois was certainly one of these."[11]

Scientific explanations justify critiques of modern industrial society, but they do not get at the heart of the matter. The real question is finally a moral one: what happens to truth and goodness in a world built on greed? What happens is that things fall apart; there is no longer a center. Goodness and truth become functions rather than absolutes. In such a world neither the science nor the morality to which Du Bois devoted himself has any significant effect. The attraction of socialism is that it appears to transcend self-interest in a return to those "eternal verities." In the cases of Jean and Mansart, the link is made between socialism and the black ideal that served the same purpose in earlier works. The mad visions are expressions of anger that the old moral order has been destroyed by a dominant culture that is not salvageable. Du Bois directs his rage by voicing the apocalypse through insane or dreaming characters. The failure to control such expressions would itself be a surrender to the darkness; but the failure to articulate the rage would be a denial of moral responsibility. It is the role of the prophet to speak the truth, but that role is complicated by the belief in reason and facilitated by the devices of fiction.

An alternative to the chaos is offered. At the end of the second volume, Harry Hopkins has a vision, the only positive one in the trilogy. " 'Yes, I see the "City called Heaven." No poverty, homes for all, no fear of age, children in school, free music and theater, good food, and all men daring to say what they think' " (*School*, 365). This description comes close to the depictions of Du Bois's childhood in nineteenth-century Great Barrington, as the following discussions of the autobiographies will show. The order he is searching for existed once in that time and place. Good and evil were clearly distinguishable, and integrity and decency were never questioned.

The contemporary world lacks that coherence, and this fact engenders his hostility. The new world relies on selfishness, deceit, and hatred. The only hope lies with those who transcend such immorality. An elite that is not merely black but that has chosen to identify with the ideals of blackness, which are in fact the same moral principles as nineteenth-century patriarchal society, must be the guides to the future. The heroes of the trilogy—Roosevelt, Mansart, Jean, the Soviet Union—choose the higher pragmatism that will lead to a unification of the trinity of beauty, truth, and goodness. Chaos will be replaced by an ancient, ever-renewed order. The apocalyptic rage against the fathers is not because they are fathers, but rather because they have betrayed the basis of patriarchy. The sons must become the true fathers to re-establish the Law. The trilogy fuses history, fiction, and prophecy in a vision of this ideal. The nightmare of American life must be presented so as to justify a re-created American dream.

8

· · · · · · · · ·

History as Hagiography

· · · · · · · · ·

John Brown and the Black Self

· · · · · · · · ·

The story of Du Bois's biography of John
Brown begins in a conflict of authority and precedence. Du Bois was
asked by the publishing firm of George W. Jacobs to contribute a
volume to their National Biography series. After some negotiation, it
was agreed that he would write on Frederick Douglass. Shortly thereafter, the publisher, in a rather embarrassed tone, asked Du Bois to
change his topic, since Booker T. Washington, who had been contacted
first, had decided on Douglass. As the leading black figure of the time
(1908–9), Washington had to be given preference.[1] Du Bois then chose
to write about Brown. Thus, we have, in a series devoted to canoniz-
ing narratives of the fathers of the nation, a story of black hierarchy. It
should not be surprising, given what has been previously argued, that
the narrative that Du Bois generates both reclaims his position as the
voice of blackness and calls into question the social order that suppresses such voices. At the same time he defines a radical tradition of
speaking and acting that authorizes his stance.

The initial paradox of the book is that the life story of a white man
becomes the vehicle for the articulation of a black perspective. Du Bois
carries this out in two interrelated ways: by asserting a black point of
view and by identifying Brown with black experience. This is made
quite explicit: "The view-point adopted in this book is that of the little
known but vastly important inner development of the Negro American."[2] In practice, this means placing Brown in the context of the slave
experience and giving attention to his relationships with various black

groups and individuals. It means, for example, comparing Brown with Frederick Douglass in terms of strategies for ending slavery.

It does not mean, significantly, identifying and examining new materials in order to articulate this perspective. "After the work of Sanborn, Hinton, Connalley, and Redpath, the only excuse for another life of John Brown is an opportunity to lay new emphasis upon the material which they have so carefully collected, and to treat these facts from a different point of view" (*John Brown*, 7). In fact, Du Bois is convinced that new evidence does not exist: "Unfortunately, however, few written records of these friendships and this long continued intimacy [between Brown and blacks] exist, so that little new material along these lines can be adduced" (7). Thus, what Du Bois undertakes is not so much a new historiographic project as a new reading of the existing narrative. In this sense, he is less a historian than a literary critic, interpreting the story of Brown's life in the context of existing interpretations.

From the very beginning, then, this biography is designed to be unique. Only those elements of Brown's life that have some bearing on black experience are considered relevant. But this emphasis could lead to a factual, "objective" study that would stress information that had previously been obscured. Precisely such a study was carried out later by Benjamin Quarles. As already noted, however, Du Bois is willing to accept the facts given in secondary sources. The history that he writes is designed very differently: he intends to provide a historical example of the black ideal he articulated in *The Souls of Black Folk*. By choosing a white subject, he can demonstrate the universality of that ideal. He is not primarily interested in Brown the man who lived and acted in a specific historical context; rather, he discusses Brown as the symbol of a system of values. The Brown who touched black souls is vastly more important than the one who affected black lives. The abolitionist martyr is taken over for black history. He is one of the first of many saints canonized by Du Bois's interpretations of American history. It might well be said that hagiography has replaced historiography in this work.

How is it that a white man in a racist society can acquire such importance for blacks? For one thing, according to Du Bois, he must be very much like them in attitudes and experiences. Several traits Du Bois uses to characterize Brown he earlier, in "The Conservation of Races," attributed to blacks. One such trait is a life of hard, unremitting labor:

The gloom and horror of life settled early on John Brown. His childhood had had little formal pleasure, his young manhood had been serious and filled with responsibility, and almost before he himself knew the full meaning of life, he was trying to teach it to his children. The iron of bitterness entered his soul with the coming of death, and a deep religious fear and foreboding bore him down as it took away member after member of his family. (41–42)

Of course, Brown's experience was of the frontier rather than slavery; nonetheless he knew the meaning of hard labor and loss of family.

One effect of such an existence was, for Brown and for blacks, a religious sensibility that was both visionary and fatalistic: "Such a nature was in its very essence religious, even mystical, but never superstitious nor blindly trustful in half-known creeds and formulas" (23). Like those discussed in the "Sorrow Songs" chapter of *The Souls of Black Folk,* Brown's visions are described as closely related to nature: "It was the mystic, awful voice of the mountains that lured him to liberty, death, and martyrdom within their wildest fastness, and in their bosom he sleeps his last sleep" (48). Like the most religious slaves, Brown hears voices and has intense religious experiences.

The vision was a dark one; this John tends to brood the way the fictional John of *Souls* did. "Into John Brown's religious life entered two strong elements; the senses of overruling inexorable fate, and the mystery and promise of death" (40). These two elements came together in the deaths of family members. In a twelve-year period, Brown lost a wife and six children. This was only the beginning of a lifetime of premature deaths, concluding with his own. These early cases he felt were his personal responsibility: "Then there rose grimly, as life went on in its humdrum round of failure and trouble, the thought that in some way his own sin and shortcomings were bringing upon him the vengeful punishment of God" (43). This version of fatalism distinguishes Brown from slaves. They too felt that the world was controlled by outside forces, but most often those forces were clearly embodied in the slave trader and owner. Slaves did not carry such a strong sense of personal guilt.[3] Rather, Brown's perspective seems closer to that of the Africans Du Bois described in "Of the Faith of the Fathers" as feeling that there were forces in nature which, if not appeased, would exact terrible punishments.

But like the slaves, Brown had, according to Du Bois, a fundamental optimism that made the fatalism and suffering worthwhile. Despite all the troubles, "there wells up surging spiritual life out of great unfathomed depths—the intellectual longing to see, the moral wistfulness of the hesitating groping doer. This was the deeper, truer man, although it was not the whole man" (*John Brown*, 47). The ideal toward which this man strives is the same ideal articulated in "The Conservation of Races": human brotherhood.

By identifying Brown with blacks in such a way, Du Bois attempts to overcome an obvious difficulty: the limited contact Brown actually had with blacks, especially in the years when he was defining his relationship to them. By showing a spiritual connection, the issue of a historical connection can be avoided. Brown understood the souls of black folk and therefore his grasp of their physical reality is irrelevant.

Beyond specifying characteristics common to John Brown and blacks in general, Du Bois at least implicitly suggests a more specific parallel: Brown and himself. They share the same attitudes toward slavery, the same "critical" concern for black development, the same belief that knowledge must lead to action, the same ideas about leadership, the same (according to Du Bois) economic progressivism, and, most important, the same prophetic role. The statement above about intellectual longing and moral groping in fact more clearly defines the author of *The Souls of Black Folk* than it does either Brown or the mass of slaves.

Slavery is shown to be the obsession of Brown's life. At first only a vaguely understood principle was involved. "From his earliest he had dimly conceived, and the conception grew with his growing, that the cost of liberty was less than the price of repression" (75–76). This principle is a refrain in the book connecting it with the moral economics of *The Suppression of the Slave-Trade* and *The Philadelphia Negro*. Oppression is costly to everyone—the oppressor and the oppressed—and in a moral universe those costs must be paid. Concrete expenses are involved, but for Du Bois and his John Brown, the more important costs are psychological and spiritual. Blacks are degraded because of their victimization, but the victimizers and their collaborators are equally, though not identically, degraded.

But this statement of moral economy is also a political slogan that Du Bois can use elsewhere to attack segregation and imperialism. It is another aspect of the higher pragmatism described in *The Suppression of the Slave-Trade* and at work in the writings of the end of his career. He is not content to demonstrate that evil is abstractly opposed to good; he also wants to show that good is ultimately more practical. A concrete justification for resisting evil is designed to offer tough-minded, this-worldly men an alternative to self-interest and oppression. Du Bois wants to show that following the rules of a moral order can provide greater benefits and fewer costs than acting in the arbitrary manner of the old patriarchy. A secondary effect of such evidence, of course, is to show the author to be a tough-minded man himself.

The immediate emphasis, however, is on the spiritual effect of moral economy on John Brown:

> This marks a turning point in John Brown's life: in his boyhood he had disliked slavery and his antipathy toward it grew with his years; yet of necessity it occupied but little of a life busy with breadwinning. Gradually, however, he saw the gathering of the mighty struggle about him; the news of the skirmish battles of the greatest moral war of the century aroused and quickened him, and all the more when they struck the tender chords of his acquaintanceships and sympathies. He saw his friends hurt and imposed on until at last, gradually, then suddenly, it dawned upon him that he must fight this monster slavery. He did not now plan physical warfare—he was yet a non-resistant, hating war, and did not dream of Harper's Ferry; but he set his face toward the goal and whithersoever the Lord led, he was ready to follow. (92–93)

The designation "monster slavery" reflects Du Bois's own attitude toward the peculiar institution. "But when all is said and granted, the awful fact remains congealed in law and indisputable record that American slavery was the foulest and filthiest blot on nineteenth century civilization" (76). Brown's story is often forgotten in the biographer's desire to express his own historical disgust:

> It [slavery] took millions upon millions of men—human men and lovable, light and liberty-loving children of the sun, and threw them with no sparing of brutality into one rigid mold: humble, servile, dog-like devotion, surrender of body, mind and soul, and unaspiring animal content—toward this ideal the slave might strive, and did. . . . All were crushed to this mold and of them that did not fit, the sullen were cowed, the careless brutalized and the rebellious killed. (76–77)

One objective of this pattern of authorial intrusion is to define the black perspective mentioned in the preface. Since Du Bois has claimed this as the primary contribution of his text, he must articulate it. But given the description of the slave experience, the perspective is more logically that of the author than of the mass of Brown's black contemporaries. Du Bois in effect assigns his own views to Brown, thereby creating a transcendent slavery-hating brotherhood. For example, after extensively developing his theory of the devastating impact of enslavement on blacks, including a form of the emasculation idea mentioned in *The Souls of Black Folk*, as well as a version of the safety-valve theory of the Underground Railroad, Du Bois indicates that Brown understood matters in the same way: "Thus it was that John Brown even as a child, saw the puzzling anomalies and contradictions in human right and liberty all about him" (82). Such statements reveal much about the writer. Brown is important, not because he acted in a certain way, but because he justifes Du Bois's own interpretation of American and black history. A case is built, not for Brown, but for his biographer.

Similarly, the examination of Brown's thought leads back to the man doing the examining. In trying to explain the development of Brown's abolitionist ideology, Du Bois ponders, as he often does, the workings of the human mind. He is always uneasy with something so indefinite: "Human purposes grow slowly and in curious ways; thought by thought they build themselves until in their full panoplied vigor and definite outline not even the thinker can tell the exact process of the growing, or say that here was the beginning or there the ending. Nor does this slow growth and gathering make the end less wonderful or the motive less praiseworthy" (93). While his immediate focus is on Brown's gradual shift to violence, he is also describing and justifying the major changes in his own perspective that were already becoming the pattern of his career. Both his shifts from racial moderate to "radical" (in Kelly Miller's sense[4]) and from academic to "master of propaganda" are validated by this meditation. Thoughtful change is not cowardly but "wonderful" and the motive can easily be "praiseworthy."

But neither the complexity of motive nor the intensity of belief blinds either man to the real faults of blacks. If anything, the depth of belief in black potential makes the criticisms more acute. An essay written by Brown, entitled "Sambo's Mistakes," is made to sound much like the criticisms Du Bois made from *The Philadelphia Negro* on: "He found them 'intensely human,' but with their human frailties weakened by slavery and caste; and with their perfect faith in their ability to rise above their faults, he criticized and inspired them" (*John Brown*, 99). The faults found are virtually identical to those found by Du Bois: lack of education, lack of organizational skills, tendency to waste time and money, lack of occupational ambition, and religious sectarianism. Du Bois reiterates that it is bondage that causes these defects. "No one knew better than John Brown how slavery had contributed to these faults: for how many slaves could read anything, or when had they been taught the use of money or the A.B.C. of organization?" (100) Thus belief, not disbelief, inspires these two men to look critically at the social and historical development of the race.

"Not only did John Brown thus criticize, but he led these black folk" (101). Leadership is presented as a central factor for both the abolitionist and his biographer. In both cases, a talented tenth of the race is essential. One element of this group for Brown was the fugitive slaves, "the restless, the criminal, the unconquered—the natural leaders of the more timid mass" (82). Frederick Douglass, the most famous of these, is described as Brown's closest black confidant.[5] These men joined with the free blacks of the North to form a "black phalanx that worked and schemed and paid and finally fought for the freedom of black men in America" (82). Brown's belief in these men was long-standing and sincere: "From his earliest interest in Negroes, John Brown sought to know individuals among them intimately and personally. He talked to them, and listened to the history of their trials, advised them and took advice from them. His dream was to enlist the boldest and most daring spirits among them in his great plan" (247).

The elites described in *John Brown* and in *The Souls of Black Folk* and "The Talented Tenth" are very much alike despite differences in time and historical circumstances. Each group is the pinnacle of the race, a courageous, knowledgeable, self-sacrificing cadre dedicated to the advancement of blacks. Beyond personal identification, Du Bois manages here to provide a tradition for the Niagara movement, the black civil rights organization he had established shortly before undertaking the biography. A usable past can have very specific functions as well as more general racial ones.

Radical leadership is implicitly problematized here even as it is praised. Each man found it difficult to get significant support, even from the elite, for his program. Only twenty-nine men attended the first meeting of the Niagara movement, at which an uncompromising demand for equality was made. And even counting the temporarily freed slaves, twenty blacks at most were involved in the Harper's Ferry raid. The radicalism of Brown and Du Bois was simply, it would appear, too great for traditional black leadership. Du Bois's explanation of the attitude of Douglass and others comes close to a justification for the reluctance of men like Booker T. Washington to become activists, though Du Bois certainly would not recognize it as such:

> Both hated it [slavery] with all their strength, but one knew its physical degradation, its tremendous power and the strong sympathies and interests that buttressed it the world over; the other felt its moral evil and knowing simply that it was wrong, concluded that John Brown and God could overthrow it. That was all—a plain straightforward path; but to the subtler darker man, more worldly-wise and less religious, the arm of the Lord was not revealed, while the evil of this world had seared his vitals. . . . And this attitude of Douglass was in various degrees and strides the attitude of the leading Negroes of his day. They believed in John Brown but not in his plan. They knew he was right, but they knew that for any failure in his project they, the black men, would probably pay the cost. And the horror of that cost none knew as they. (109–10)

This division between moderation and absolutism makes it possible for the limited appeals of both the abolitionist and the biographer to be rationalized. Without calling into question the validity of their stances, explanations can be offered for their relative failures. Each was a visionary, willing to sacrifice himself,[6] but found that others, even if virtuous, could not meet such stringent standards. Du Bois and his John Brown, secure in their grasps of truth, can be tolerant of those less confident.

The level of security is indicated by the fact that this John Brown has virtually no faults. His only defect is an excess of saintly innocence: "In this English venture John Brown showed one weakness of his character: he did not know or recognize the subtler twistings of human nature. He judged it ever from his own simple, clear standpoint and so had a sort of prophetic vision of the vaster and the eternal aspects of the human soul. But of its kinks and prejudices, its little selfishnesses and jealousies and dishonesties, he knew nothing" (68–69). Brown's nature is too pure to be tainted by the pettiness of the world. And his naïveté with regard to psychology is very much like Du Bois's own discomfiture over mental processes. This uncertainty here is given the sanctity of moral innocence. It is not insignificant that when Du Bois spells out the "subtler twistings of human nature," they constitute a catalogue of defects rather than of complexities and ambiguities. This essentially premodern conception of the self remains consistent throughout his writings and especially his autobiographical work. No matter how complicated the story, there remains this subtext of absolute, transcendent virtue that can remain intact regardless of the forces aligned against it.

But in the narrative of John Brown, such purity does not lead to an inability to act responsibly in the world. Brown is another incarnation of Du Bois's ideal of higher practicality. Everything that this white man does is seen as eminently reasonable in the moral scheme of things. His rationality is especially seen in the military and economic spheres, two areas where other biographers have had serious misgivings. The murders at Pottawatomie, for example, are usually seen as terrorism.[7] Du Bois chooses to justify the act by pointing first to the criminal character of the victims and then by stressing its necessary function in making Kansas a free state: "To this day men differ as to the effect of John Brown's blow. Some say it freed Kansas, while others say it plunged the land back into civil war. Truth lies in both statements. The blow freed Kansas by plunging it into civil war, and compelling men to fight for freedom which they had vainly hoped to gain by political diplomacy" (*John Brown*, 157). Like the leaders of the Israelites, with whom he is metaphorically compared, Brown is justified in his killing because he is on the side of God. He refuses compromise and accommodation and thereby defends the higher reason of the "higher law."

Even the debacle of Harper's Ferry is seen by Du Bois as a potential victory. The failure lay in the weaknesses of Brown's lieutenants, not in the conception or immediate execution of the plan. Great pains are taken to demonstrate that the plan was militarily sound: "Brown knew guerrilla warfare, and the failure of the Harper's Ferry raid does not prove it a blunder from the start. The raid was not a foray *from* the mountains, which failed because its retreat was cut off; but it was a foray *to* the mountains with the village and the arsenal on the way, which was defeated apparently because the arms and ammunition train failed to join the advance guard" (276). The defect was not in Brown but in the lassitude of his subordinates.

Moreover, Du Bois believes that the raid did in fact achieve success; it caused the Civil War. It was Pottawatomie writ nationally. Du Bois cites with approval the opinion of Douglass: "Until this blow was struck, the prospect for freedom was dim, shadowy, and uncertain. The irrepressible conflict was one of words, votes, and compromises. When John Brown stretched forth his arm the sky was cleared,—the armed hosts of freedom stood face to face over the chasm of a broken Union, and the clash of arms was at hand" (353). Brown "aroused and directed the conscience of the nation" (355). Just as in Kansas, he forced the issue by an act of violence; he made the nation face the abomination of slavery. Furthermore, his trial was a condemnation of that institution: "Virginia attempted to hold scales of even justice between mob violence and the worldwide sympathy of all good men. To defend its domestic institutions, it must try a man for murder when that very man, sitting as self-appointed judge of those very institutions, had convicted them before a jury of mankind" (358). The mini-narrative Du Bois generates here symbolizes his own basic perspective: he desires, not the end of hierarchical structures, but the displacement of the existing ones, based on self-interest and compromise, and their replacement by those built on the moral order he spends his career defining. Through his writing, he takes the position of Brown here, the judge of judges, the critic of those who have presumed to name and organize the world.

A moral contradiction is evident in the interpretation of Brown and implicitly in Du Bois's own vision that is not addressed here or elsewhere. One argument consistently made is that self-interested actions lead to decay, death, and violence. Yet the claim made here is that it was Brown's self-sacrificing, violent gesture that led to the Civil War, that same war that, in *The Suppression of the Slave-Trade*, was attributed to the moral cowardice of the Founding Fathers. Du Bois's claim seems to be that the armies of God are not morally responsible in the same way as their opponents; once they are on the Lord's side, the ends justify the means. Even murder and mass destruction are justified as the sacrifices necessary for the realization of truth. Making such assumptions requires supreme confidence in one's moral system. It also suggests the fundamentally authoritarian nature of that system, despite its author's sincerely held democratic views. Du Bois, though generally pacifistic, repeatedly generates apocalyptic visions and seeks to legitimate violence on just such grounds.

Virtue is more clear-cut with regard to Brown's economic ideas. Du Bois sees financial failure as a measure of moral character. He attributes Brown's bankruptcies and other legal difficulties to his refusal to play according to the rules of self-interest. The beliefs he assigns to Brown are identical to ones expressed in his own earlier writings. Economics, according to these principles, ought to be subordinated to the moral good: "To him business was a philanthropy. We have not even to-day reached this idea, but, urged on by the Socialists, we are faintly perceiving it" (61). He ignored the idea of free enterprise: "Such a policy of financial free-booting never occurred to him, and he would have repelled it indignantly if it had" (64). He supplanted capitalism in his own dealings with the idea of the just price. Du Bois found this notion more attractive because it coincided with the progressivist socialism he was beginning to advocate, though the source of Brown's thinking, if in fact he had economic theories, was most likely Puritan New England, where the fair-price concept was a short-lived business principle.[8]

Du Bois's real object here is the elucidation, not of economic theory, but of Brown's character. He was willing to sacrifice personal wealth for the advancement of justice. "On the other hand, to offer no opposition to organized economic aggression is to depend on the simple justice of your cause in an industrial world that recognizes no justice. It means industrial death and that was what it meant to John Brown" (*John Brown*, 65). His belief in principle was economically costly, but his integrity remained intact; his pursuit of the interests of God was not compromised by self-interest. If we change "God" to "truth" or "justice," then the statement becomes a leitmotiv of Du Bois's autobiographies.

The theme of Brown as divine emissary is announced early in the book and repeated throughout. "To the unraveling of human tangles we would gladly believe that God sends especial men—chosen vessels which come to the world's deliverance" (19). Du Bois asserts that Brown saw himself in the same terms: "To him the world was a mighty drama. God was an actor and so was John Brown. But just what his part was to be his soul in the long agony of years tried to know, and ever and again the chilling doubt assailed him lest he be unworthy of his place or had missed the call" (46).

Every opportunity is taken to suggest associations with Old Testament prophets. Brown is called a patriarch and is seen as willing to sacrifice his family in pursuit of divine will. A humble man of the mountains, he feels an initial doubt about being God's messenger:

> The slough of despond through which John Brown passed in the succeeding years, from 1842 to 1846, was never fully betrayed by this stern, self-repressing Puritan. Yet the loss of a fortune and the shattering of a dream, the bankruptcy and imprisonment, and the death of five children, while around him whirled the struggle of the churches with slavery and Abolition mobs, all dropped a sombre brooding veil of stern inexorable fate over his spirit—a veil which never lifted. The dark mysterious tragedy of life gripped him with awful intensity—the iron entered his soul. He became sterner and more silent. He brooded and listened for the voice of the avenging God, and girded up his loins in readiness. (96)

After this voice is heard, Brown's role is dual. He is the spokesman of God, warning of the wrath to come; when he is ignored, he becomes the avenging angel carrying out the threat. He spoke and then he acted; he never debated or compromised. As Du Bois comments: "He did not use argument, he was himself an argument" (341). He had the divine message; he could not do otherwise than deliver it:

> Such a light was the soul of John Brown. He was simple, exasperatingly simple; unlettered, plain, and homely. No casuistry of culture or of learning, of well-being or tradition moved him in the slightest degree: "Slavery is wrong," he said,—"kill it." Destroy it—uproot it, stem, blossom, and branch; give it no quarter, exterminate it and do it now. Was he wrong? No. The forcible staying of human uplift by barriers of law, and might, and tradition is the most wicked thing on earth. It is wrong, eternally wrong. It is wrong, by whatever name it is called, or in whatever guise it lurks, and whenever it appears. But it is especially heinous, black, and cruel when it

masquerades in the robes of law and justice and patriotism. So was American slavery clothed in 1859, and it had to die by revolution, not by milder means. (340–41)

The extent to which Brown is mythologized in this work can be indicated by a brief comparison with Robert Penn Warren's biography published twenty years later. The two works are similar in that they are intended as interpretive rather than documentary studies. They rely largely on the same sources and present basically the same facts. But those sources and facts are put to very different ends. Where Du Bois finds proto-socialism in business, Warren finds embezzlement and incompetence. What the former portrays as saintly religious intensity, the latter depicts as egotistical, self-dramatizing tyranny. And most important, the higher law becomes in Warren's reading inhuman monomaniacal criminality. Brown is granted courage and charisma, but the uses to which these are put are vigorously denounced.

What this suggests is that Brown is important to each of his interpreters as a validation of an ideological position. For Warren, such a man exemplifies the Northern abstractions of liberty, equality, and the higher law that destroyed the repressive but organic and humane civilization of the South. For Du Bois, the same man is evidence of the value and validity of those same principles. Brown both speaks for and acts out the ideals of his black biographer.

This combined role of messenger and message that Brown fills is important for Du Bois's purposes in this book. By making the abolitionist a hero, a saint, and a prophet, and then by identifying Brown's message with his own, Du Bois creates a noble and useful past for himself, his race, and his beliefs. He seeks to perform for modern America the function of Brown in the antebellum nation. Taking his cue from the Hebrew prophets, he dons the mantle of the visionary Brown:

> Yet there are some great principles to guide us. That there are in this world matters of vast human import which are eternally right or eternally wrong, all men believe. Whether that great right comes, as the simpler, clearer minded think, from the spoken word of God, or whether it is simply another way of saying: this deed makes for the good of mankind, or that, for the ill—however it may be, all men know that there are in this world here and there and again and again great partings of the ways—the one

way wrong, the other right, in some vast and eternal sense. This is certainly true at times—in the mighty crises of lives and nations. (339)

Brown, as portrayed here, is one of "the simpler, clearer minded"; Du Bois, though he does not hear the voice of God directly, represents, in his narrative voice, himself as certain of what "makes for the good of mankind."

In the last chapter of the biography, entitled "The Legacy of John Brown," Du Bois reveals the true meaning of the man. Brown is no mere man and his meaning is manifold:

> Was John Brown simply an episode, or was he an eternal truth? And if a truth, how speaks that truth today? John Brown loved his neighbor as himself. He could not endure therefore to see his neighbor, poor, unfortunate or oppressed. This natural sympathy was strengthened by a saturation in Hebrew religion which stressed the personal responsibility of every human soul to a just God. To this religion of equality and sympathy with misfortune, was added the strong influence of the social doctrines of the French Revolution with its emphasis on freedom and power in political life. And on all this was built John Brown's own inchoate but growing belief in a more just and a more equal distribution of property. (374–75)

Having established the meaning of the past, Du Bois proceeds to speak its truths to a new age. That they must be spoken is clear: "Since that day tremendous scientific and economic advance has been accompanied by distinct signs of moral retrogression in social philosophy. Strong arguments have been made for the fostering of war, the utility of human degradation and disease, and the inevitable and known inferiority of certain classes and races of men" (375). The declension has advanced so far that even science is being twisted into a defense of race hatred. And Du Bois, unlike Brown, chooses to present rather than be an argument in this cultural conflict. According to the scientific racists, blacks are doomed by the laws of evolution to eternal inferiority. But unfortunately for the theory, the race has shown signs of achievement, with its businessmen, workers, and intellectuals. Therefore the theory is invalidated by a basic scientific rule: a law cannot be a law if there are exceptions. "If the doomed races of men are going to develop exceptions to the rule of inferiority, then no rule, scientific or moral, should or can proscribe the race as such" (377). The true interpretation of Darwinian selection is democracy. All people, given freedom and opportunity, will aid the upward evolution of humanity: "So, too, the doctrine of human equality passes through the fire of scientific inquiry, not obliterated but transfigured: not equality of present attainment but equality of opportunity, for unbounded future attainment is the rightful demand of mankind" (379).

In an ironic twist, Du Bois suggests that it is racist whites who are threatened with extinction by evolution. Their artificial barriers encourage the survival, not of the fittest, but of the weak and degenerate. "New reservoirs of ability and strength" are not being developed. Repression is becoming more and more costly economically, politically, and intellectually; progress cannot occur without new sources of human talent.

The shift from a scriptural to an evolutionary discourse in this last chapter allows Du Bois to counter the dominant culture of his time on its own ground. It cannot be subverted in the terms that Brown used because the age is different. Modern society listens to science, not to revelation. But in that new language, Du Bois can make fundamentally the same case as Brown: "Such a state of affairs is not simply disgraceful; it is deeply and increasingly dangerous. Not only does the whole nation feel already the loosening of joints which these vicious blows on human liberty have caused—lynching, lawlessness, lying and stealing, bribery and divorce—but it can look for darker deeds to come" (388). Both the modes of oppression and the terms by which the critique is made have changed, but the essential state of affairs has not: the country faces dire consequences unless it begins to behave more humanely, especially toward blacks.

But like all prophets, Du Bois offers his nation a way out of its troubles. The country can be saved by accepting the oft-repeated Brownian principle: the cost of liberty is less than the price of repression. This axiom of moral economy can be immediately applied to the race problem. Blacks ought be recognized for what they have already done. "They have given America music, inspired art and literature, made its bread, dug its ditches, fought its battles, and suffered its misfortunes" (389). For both scientific and moral reasons, they must not be artificially kept from contributing even more.

With this recognition must go a reconsideration of economic exploitation of blacks specifically but also of labor in general. The nation must set aside the argument that repression is essential for progress. It must believe more in quality than quantity. "Better smaller production and more equitable distribution; better fewer miles of railway and more honor, truth, and liberty; better fewer millionaires and more contentment" (394).

The two discourses are joined in Du Bois's concluding remarks, thus bringing together narrator and narrative: "The cost of liberty is less than the price of repression, even though that cost be blood. Freedom of development and equality of opportunity is the demand of Darwinism and this calls for the abolition of hard and fast lines between races, just as it called for the breaking down of the barriers between classes" (395). The old and the new abolitionisms are joined, as are their antagonists, in a cycle of moral conflict that Du Bois defines here and elsewhere as the nature of American history.

What Du Bois undertakes in his revision of John Brown's story is a subversion of existing forms of domination in the name of an eternal moral order. He rejects existing definitions of history and black identity as founded on self-interested and exploitative principles; in their place he puts principles of democracy, justice, and righteousness. These he clearly believes are the true values of the nation, and those that practice them the true Americans. He simultaneously validates his assertion by finding historical precedent and making John Brown a central actor in American history. In the process he redefines the mainstream of that history as flowing, not through the politically and economically powerful, but through the marginalized and outcast. The best self is the one that adheres to the nation's ideals regardless of the costs. The only economics that count are moral.

A complex set of metaphors serves to make this case. John Brown is variously equated to Christ, the prophets, a special kind of *homo economicus*, the true American, blacks, and Du Bois himself, with the implication that all of these are equated to each other. In addition, slave holders, Northern businessmen, social Darwinists, politicians, and even some abolitionists play virtually identical roles as the enemy in this melodrama. These connections make the narrative problematic in that it is difficult to determine whose story is being told.

Moreover, blacks are at times actors and at others essentially the passive site of the grand struggle; they are both heroes and the maiden being saved from the villain. *John Brown* becomes a palimpsest in which are inscribed endless versions of a self being created and then engaging in deadly combat with immoral antagonists.

In an appropriate completion of the pattern of discursive struggle, *John Brown* was reviewed by Oswald Garrison Villard, one of the founding fathers of the NAACP and one who enjoyed, according to histories of the organization, playing the patriarchal role. He was also the grandson of William Lloyd Garrison, along with Brown one of the white patriarchs of abolitionism. Villard's review was largely negative, giving special emphasis to what he saw as Du Bois's taking undue liberties with historical materials and his lack of research into primary materials.[9] Further complicating the situation was the fact that Villard was the owner of *The Nation,* in which the review appeared anonymously, and the author of a soon-to-appear biography of Brown.

Du Bois wrote to the editor, Paul Elmer More, asking that he be permitted to reply to the review, which he considered unfair. More's response was a condescending letter that first refused to publish Du Bois's comments and then presumed to instruct him on the nature of historical materials. Du Bois follows with an assertion that More's comments are "little short of insulting," and, consistent with the discourse of polite society he uses, insists that "courtesy among gentlemen" requires the printing of his letter. More then flatly refuses, prompting Du Bois to raise the question of Villard's motives for the review. To this accusation, Villard himself replies, expressing shock that Du Bois would believe him capable of self-interest, declaring that he is "quite indifferent" to the possible success of his own work. Du Bois answers by arguing that it is not praise or blame but justice that is at stake in his effort to publish a reply to the review.[10]

What is revealed here is a struggle over the control of discourse. Du Bois, as historian of John Brown, takes on the same role as his subject, battling for justice in a world in which the powerful manipulate the systems they control for their own advantage. Though the times and modes of conflict are different, the principles remain the same. The struggle for the black world that was Brown's story becomes the struggle for a black word in Du Bois's experience.

The Propaganda of Life

Darkwater and *Dusk of Dawn*

Autobiography has been one of the principal forms of black expression in America since the late eighteenth century. Beginning with slave narratives and spiritual autobiographies, the genre has developed over the years to include some of the best-known modern works: *Black Boy, Notes of a Native Son, The Autobiography of Malcolm X, I Know Why the Caged Bird Sings,* and *The Autobiography of LeRoi Jones.* The theme running through this tradition is the quest for freedom in the context of a society that has denied validity to the African-American self. Linked to this theme, as Robert Stepto and William Andrews have noted in different contexts, is the effort to control language, to be empowered through literacy.[1] The narrator seeks to define the self, its blackness, and its relationship to the dominant society in ways, as Andrews points out, that often run counter to the cultural assumptions of that society.[2] This leads, as Joanne Braxton has contended, to a particular kind of narrative: "Like the blues, most autobiographies by black Americans, male and female, tend to have a dominant internal strategy of action rather than contemplation."[3]

Clearly Du Bois's narratives fall into these thematic patterns. He is very much concerned with showing the relationship of his identity to the larger environment of American and world culture, politics, and racial assumptions. This relationship is generally one of struggle, in which the self finds itself fighting for respect and recognition in a world that is either indifferent or hostile to it. There is little introspection, as William Cain has observed: "Du Bois's concern for 'work,' for visible achievement that ratifies the worth and rightness of life, possibly accounts for the reticence about personal feelings. . . . Deeds matter more than feelings, in Du Bois's calculation. The self knows how it feels by looking back upon and confidently reckoning what it has done."[4] In the posthumously published *The Autobiography of W. E. B. Du Bois* (1968), he goes so far as to create a separate chapter entitled "My Character" when he wishes to discuss private matters.

The self that he generates through all his personal narratives, from essays in *The Souls of Black Folk* to *The Autobiography*, is active, public, resistant, and heroic. It is one proud of its racial identity, though sensitive to the problems for the self caused by the prejudices of the larger society. In its assertiveness and opposition, Du Bois's created self (or selves) seems to fall into the mold of the quest for black individuality that Andrews argues is part of the development of the genre.

But what is curious about Du Bois's narratives is an impulse to claim simultaneously difference and identity. From the versions of his childhood in which he emerges from innocence when forced to face the reality that his blackness meant otherness, to the end of his career when he embraces communism in conscious repudiation of contemporary American society, he makes active difference into one of his principal virtues. His critical, outsider perspective is central to his identity. At the same time, he positions himself at the center of the culture he is opposing. From the genteel style of *The Souls of Black Folk* to the identification of Soviet values with those of his New England birthplace, he offers himself as a representative man of Western culture and American society. He is the one upholding principles of equality, democracy, reason, and decency against those who proclaim such values but in fact defile them. Individuality is often lost in his construction of self as the symbol of all that is good and true in the modern world.

Every narrative shows him in conflict with some figure (always male) of power and authority who seeks to suppress Du Bois's reasonable and honest voice. One way to view this stance is in psychocultural terms. As Freud suggested in *Civilization and Its Discontents*, the sons justify their challenge to the arbitrary father by claiming their defense of law, which prohibits such abuse of power. Thus, resistance becomes a means of affirmation; the rebellious son creates the lawful father. Each autobiography, then, is a heroic tale in which the racial and/or political outsider fights the powerful insiders in order to defend the very culture that has defined him as an outsider. This dialectic of the self is perhaps the ultimate meaning of "double consciousness."

Darkwater (1921), like all of Du Bois's autobiographical works, constantly shifts between the experiences of the self and the representation of certain ideas. But his approaches to the ideas, rather than their content, change, thus making the works intellectual as well as personal life histories. In each case, Du Bois sees as a major part of his story the means by which he has arrived at his current attitudes toward education, economics, racial relations, and the nature of racial identity. Running through all the discussions is the dramatization of heroic struggle against forces of domination, unreason, and repression, the same struggle apparent in *John Brown* and *The Souls of Black Folk*. The principal distinction, then, in each book is neither the underlying pattern nor the overt subject matter, both of which remain much the same; rather it is the particular metaphoric pattern he devises for each narrative, which reveals both the play of history in his thinking and the strategies he uses to validate his heroic role. He must always make the story new without changing the essential plot. Thus, the autobiographies are best read as a continuing revision of a basic story.

In this sense, *Darkwater* may be seen as a post–World War I, Progressive Era version of *The Souls of Black Folk*. It involves the same shifting of styles from exposition and polemic to poetry and allegory; it contains historical and sociological discourses on education, race, economics, and politics; it includes a short story and expands the earlier work's epigraph-text format by interweaving poetry and parables between the essays; and finally it calls attention to its own intertextuality through a chapter entitled "The Souls of White Folk," which implicitly completes a binary opposition by describing the demonic character of white racism in contrast to black spirituality.

The key revision comes in the nature of the discourse. While *Souls* reads in many ways as a struggle for belief in the midst of quiet despair, *Darkwater* asserts simultaneously the primacy of reason and the expectation of apocalypse. The language of progressive reform competes with that of myth and violence for control of the text. The pattern is evident not only in the division between expository and "literary" passages but also within the essays themselves. In fact, it can be argued that the formal division is a means of disguising the internal tensions: "Between the sterner flights of logic, I have set some little alightings of what may be poetry. They are tributes to Beauty, unworthy to stand alone; yet perversely, in my mind, now at the end, I know not whether I mean the Thought for the Fancy—or the Fancy for the Thought, or why the book trails off to playing, rather than standing strong on unanswering fact."[5] The reader is called upon to accept the divisions between logic and beauty, fancy and thought, and though Du Bois claims uncertainty about which has primacy, the distinction itself is assumed to be absolute. But each chapter depends for its effect on the blurring of discursive distinctions. In each essay Du Bois's voice is that of the man of reason capable of imagining horrific consequences if his reason is ignored. While, as we will see, he shares with Jane Addams, Charlotte Perkins Gilman, John Dewey, and others a belief in rational reform, he also shares, as Robert Wiebe and Christopher Lasch have suggested about the progressives and intellectuals of the time, an anxiety that irrational forces are barely under control.[6]

For Du Bois, whose particular focus is race, such forces can be devastating. The discrimination against blacks in the military, the violent attacks on black soldiers returning from the war, antiblack riots in several Northern cities, and the resurgence of lynching indicate that reason and reform could well be inadequate in the face of white supremacy. Moreover, World War I itself exposed the thin veneer of European civilization; behind the claims of advanced culture and science lay jingoism and imperialistic greed. The role of Germany in the violence was especially significant for Du Bois, since it was on German principles that he built his scholarly career; his very sense of science came out of his training in Berlin. And finally, there was the betrayal of blacks by Woodrow Wilson, the progressive intellectual whom Du Bois controversially supported in 1912, precisely because he represented idealism and reason in the realms of power.[7] Instead, like so many other patriarchal figures in Du Bois's life, Wilson betrayed his principles by yielding to personal and general white prejudice and actually encouraging racial discrimination.

In such a historical context, Du Bois had to find a means of claiming the validity of reason and reform, because without these there was no hope for himself or blacks; at the same time, he was aware of the fragility of his claim. Moreover, he had to shape a self that could be effective and meaningful in such a complex world. Given the situation, it is not surprising that the self he re-creates in "The Shadow of Years" contains elements of myth. He was "born by a golden river and in the shadow of two great hills" (*Darkwater*, 5). Such a place is outside of history, appropriate for a hero. His ancestry is also distinguished in its own way: his mother's relations, he says, were "part of a great clan" (5). The men were warriors: Tom Burghardt, for example, earned his freedom fighting in the American Revolution. The women were fertile and strong, producing many children and providing for them and their husbands. Du Bois's own mother, Mary, "gave the impression of infinite patience, but a curious determination was concealed in her softness" (6). Because of changing economic circumstances, she raised her son in humble surroundings though not in deprivation. Thus, from this side of the family came quiet strength and determined character.

The paternal lineage, in contrast, emphasized pride and elegance. The Du Bois family was descended from wealthy French Huguenots and was cosmopolitan where the Burghardts were provincial. Du Bois's grandfather was disinherited because of his race, but he refused to be submissive: "He was not a 'Negro'; he was a man!" (8) He even wrote poetry, "stilted, pleading things from a soul astray" (8–9). He preferred not to identify with the black community but joined it in fighting discrimination. "So when the white Episcopalians of Trinity Parish, New Haven, showed plainly that they no longer wanted black folk as fellow Christians, he led the revolt which resulted in St. Luke's Parish, and was for years its senior warden" (8). Thus, Du Bois's career as a champion of black rights is, in a sense, a family tradition.

The curious figure in this lineage of strong male figures is Du Bois's own father: "Alfred, my father, must have seemed a splendid vision in that little valley under the shelter of those mighty hills. He was small and beautiful of face and feature, just tinted with the sun, his curly hair chiefly revealing his kinship to Africa. In nature he was a dreamer,— romantic, indolent, kind, unreliable. He had in him the making of a poet, an adventurer, or a Beloved Vagabond" (7). He is the antithesis of the solid Burghardts and very little like his own father, a man of passionate principle. The image itself is romantic, making a virtue of his restlessness and inability to hold a job.

The portrait is significant in that Du Bois largely defines himself against it. He becomes the proper son of his grandfather Du Bois—proud, principled, stable. Immediately after noting that during his childhood, Alfred "soon faded out of our lives into silence" (10), Du Bois points out that he himself went to school in the same place for twelve years. He is the one who remained with his mother until her death, and he is the one who assumes a leadership role in school. In this version of the story, even difference suggests his high character: "Very gradually,—I cannot now distinguish the steps, though here and there I remember a jump or a jolt—but very gradually I found myself assuming quite placidly that I was different from other children. At first I think I connected the difference with a manifest ability to get my lessons rather better than most and to recite with a certain happy, almost taunting, glibness, which brought frowns here and there" (11). In contrast to the version of difference in *The Souls of Black Folk*, here it is his intellectual superiority rather than imputed racial inferiority that marks him. When the question of race does impinge on his childhood, he inverts its usual implications: "At times I almost pitied my pale companions, who were not of the Lord's anointed and who saw in their dreams no splendid quests of golden fleeces" (12). Whenever he experiences intolerance, he uses it to spur him to greater heights. Thus, unlike the silent, invisible father, the son stays, fights, and makes himself seen and heard.

Such a remarkable childhood is consistent with the pattern of a heroic career. The rest of his life is allegorized into the Ages of Man: the Age of Miracles, the Days of Disillusion, the Discipline of Work and Play, and the Second Age of Miracles. This structure allows him to organize his experience on the theme of fate; the overriding question of the career is the extent to which Du Bois is "master" of his life. The generation of a retrospective structure itself makes apparent such mastery, even if the historical events raise doubts about his control. To make the life allegorical, moreover, allows him to present it as evidence of a master plan, reinforcing the image of the heroic self.

The first age was his education, for which he willed and received immersion in his race at Fisk, his dream of Harvard, and the cosmopolitan experience of Germany. All are presented as a kind of intellectual adolescent's fantasy: everything was achieved magically, without struggle. The days of disillusion are precisely an age of struggle, made more intense by the previous success. This was the beginning of his academic career, and it featured disappointments at Wilberforce and the University of Pennsylvania. The days of discipline come at Atlanta University, with fulfillment in rewarding work. Like many other progressives, he retrospectively discovers selfhood in productive labor. Not only does he do his research, with its implications for social reform, but he also finds, like Jane Addams and Frederic Howe,[8] that he must engage himself directly in the effort for change:

> At last, forbear and waver as I would, I faced the great Decision. My life's last and greatest door stood ajar. What with all my dreaming, studying, and teaching was I going to *do* in this fierce fight? Despite all my youthful conceit and bumptiousness, I found developed beneath it all a reticence and new fear of forwardness, which sprang from searching criticisms of motive and high ideals of efficiency; but contrary to my dream of racial solidarity and notwithstanding my deep desire to serve and follow and think, rather than lead and inspire and decide, I found myself suddenly the leader of a great wing of people fighting against another and greater wing. (*Darkwater*, 21–22)

Here he is the reluctant leader, the Achilles preferring to stay behind the lines. But fate and his own ideals will not permit nonengagement. Like so many reform intellectuals of the time, he finds the academic realm an uncomfortable one in which to dwell. Thinking and writing are not *doing*. The times require suppression of what he has seen as self-fulfillment in order to pursue what he sees as the greater good. But such self-sacrifice is right, because it produces the second age of miracles, his work with the NAACP.

The linkage of fate and will in this narrative permits Du Bois to present his career as inevitable and his role in the world as active. He acts out his destiny rather than merely accepts it. By doing so in the name of moral principles, he in effect revises the Christian allegory of sainthood and joins it to the Greek heroic tradition. He becomes Everyman as Jason, a leader in bringing heaven to earth.

Such a larger-than-life self is needed to encounter the antagonist. *Darkwater* can be read as an essayistic drama in which the first two chapters establish the protagonist and antagonist and the remaining essays define the fields of struggle, with the culminating short story as a vision of triumph for the hero. "The Souls of White Folk" works as a demonography in contrast to the near-hagiography of *The Souls of Black Folk*. The emphasis is consistently on white greed, corruption, violence, and racism. If the autobiographical chapter shared the progressivist view that the self must be engaged with the world, this one shares the corollary that engagement is necessary because civilization is in an advanced state of decline. For Du Bois, the progressive appeals to democratic reform, reason, and human decency are initially inadequate because racism is the heart of irrationality. Whereas in *The Souls of Black Folk* he made use of magical discourse to spiritualize the black experience, here he uses the language of demonism to attack those who have exploited racial differences.

Though the pattern of imagery is demonic, the position Du Bois himself takes is one of high-toned reason. He places himself initially in the tower, "above the loud complaining of the human sea" (29), from which he observes the world. But this intellectually aloof position, suggesting his role as disinterested observer, is necessarily joined with his racial role, which is that of personal servant: "I see these souls undressed and from the back and side" (29). This version of double consciousness gives him an advantage with his subject. He can at once speak with the wisdom of distance and with the knowledge of intimacy. Thus, he again validates his own voice. Moreover, he speaks what others cannot: most blacks do not have the training or the opportunity for objectivity, and whites do not have the perspective on themselves (and others) that blacks must develop.

The white evil is widespread. This chapter only suggests the range of attitudes and actions that will be detailed in other chapters. A key criticism here is the white presumption to define race as a fundamental human difference that "proves" their own superiority:

> The discovery of personal whiteness among the world's people is a very modern thing,—a nineteenth and twentieth century matter, indeed. The ancient world would have laughed at such a distinction. The Middle Age

regarded skin color with mild curiosity; and even into the eighteenth century we were hammering our national manikins into one, great, Universal Man, with fine frenzy which ignored color and race even more than birth. Today we have changed all that, and the world in a sudden, emotional conversion has discovered that it is white and by that token, wonderful! (30)

But this new-found meaning of human order is not a mark of progress, as whites claim; it produces violence and disorder instead. The Other rejects the self-evidence of white superiority, and so the "truth" must be beaten in. Racism inverts all moral values: greed overwhelms generosity, cruelty supercedes gentlemanliness, war destroys peace, exploitation supplants honor and decency. While whites may be deluded by their self-definition, those at the "back and side" both see the lie in that naming and bear the brunt of its violent consequences. Du Bois points to lynchings and riots in America and the European abuse of colonized people as counterevidence to the claims of white civilization.

But he goes further by arguing that the original act of naming was itself false: "Europe has never produced and never will in our day bring forth a single human soul who cannot be matched and over-matched in every line of human endeavor by Asia and Africa" (39). White superiority has required the suppression of nonwhite reality: "Run the gamut, if you will, and let us have the Europeans who in sober truth over-match Nefertari [sic], Mohammed, Ramses and Askia, Confucius, Buddha, and Jesus Christ. If we could scan the calendar of thousands of lesser men, in like comparison, the result would be the same; but we cannot do this because of the deliberately educated ignorance of white schools by which they remember Napoleon and forget Sonni Ali [king of the fifteenth-century Songhai Empire]" (39–40).

The discourse of whiteness begins in the denial of alternative discourses. It is not a universal truth but an exercise of power that suppresses certain knowledge in order to justify itself. This original violation then becomes the justification for all subsequent verbal, physical, moral, economic, political, and psychological violations:

> This theory of human culture and its aims has worked itself through warp and woof of our daily thought with a thoroughness that few realize. Everything great, good, efficient, fair, and honorable is "white"; everything mean, bad, blundering, cheating, and dishonorable is "yellow"; a bad

taste is "brown"; and the devil is "black." The changes of this theme are continually rung in picture and story, in newspaper heading and moving-picture, in sermon and school book, until, of course, the King can do no wrong,—a White Man is always right and a Black Man has no rights which a white man is bound to respect. (44)

The patriarchal trope of the kingdom is not accidental here. Precisely what Du Bois is describing is the claim of a divine right to order the universe according to the dictates of those who assert dominion. The kingdom is what the king says it is. The purpose of Du Bois's discourse is to expose the nakedness of this king with his false history and hypocrisy. The divine right is revealed as demonic, the order as chaos, and the language of "truth" as a system of lies. White superiority has produced murder, global thievery, rape, and nearly perpetual war. Instead of the kingdom of light, it is bringing the apocalypse: "Eastward and westward storms are breaking,—great, ugly whirlwinds of hatred and blood and cruelty" (51).

The only salvation Du Bois sees is in a return to the principles of human dignity he originally presented in *The Souls of Black Folk.* Here again blacks are the standard: "A belief in humanity is a belief in colored men. If the uplift of mankind must be done by men, then the destinies of this world will rest ultimately in the hands of darker nations" (49). The task of the hero of the book's first chapter becomes nothing less than the salvation of the world. He must challenge the law of the erratic and violent great white father and replace it with the rational and moral order of the black son. Such a new order is the only hope for the son, the father, and the "darker nations" (including black Americans), which are consistently in this book figured as maternal. Thus, in this version of the family romance, the father must be overthrown for his own good as well as that of the society as a whole.

The persona Du Bois creates in the remaining essays of *Darkwater* reinforces this image of the thoughtful son doing his moral duty. The essays demonstrate his awareness of and participation in the progressive intellectual community. John Dewey and Ralph Waldo Emerson inform his appeal for a child-centered system of education, one in which "we aim to develop human souls" (208). He argues, in concert with Margaret Sanger and Charlotte Perkins Gilman, that the new role of women in industrialized society requires more rational and professional approaches to motherhood and domestic labor. His arguments for governmental reform are consistent with those of Frederic Howe, Jane Addams, and others. His positions on the interactions of labor and race and on imperialism reveal careful reading of Marx and Lenin.

What Du Bois does in effect is add his voice to the chorus of those challenging the existing order of corruption and domination and demanding the emergence of true democracy and the authority of reason. This critical expression is itself a microcosm of the world it wishes to create, since each voice claims its own rationality and its right to be heard. Du Bois's contribution is to give a nonwhite voicing to issues considered by others. In each case—education, women's rights, labor, imperialism, politics—he reveals an awareness of the most current liberal and radical thought and then applies it to the experiences of nonwhite people. He takes into account not only black Americans, but also Africans and Asians. For example, imperialism is important primarily because of its effects on its victims:

> The indictment of Africa against Europe is grave. For four hundred years white Europe was the chief support of that trade in human beings which first and last robbed black Africa of a hundred million human beings, transformed the face of her social life, overthrew organized government, distorted ancient industry, and snuffed out the lights of cultural development. Today instead of removing laborers from Africa to distant slavery, industry built on a new slavery approaches Africa to deprive the natives of their land, to force them to toil, and to reap all the profit for the white world. (57–58)

In a similar fashion, each of the subjects under consideration is turned to its relationship to nonwhite life. And, in almost every case, Du Bois uses personal experience to make the matter concrete. For example, his chapter on women begins with remembrances of four women from his childhood. Their experiences form the grounds for a theoretical discussion of women in society. He then turns to black history to find other examples that help him demonstrate both the legitimacy of his own views and the absurdity of conventional thinking on the subject. He concludes by relating himself to them: "I have known the women of many lands and nations,—I have known and seen and lived beside them, but none have I known more sweetly feminine, more unswervingly loyal, more desperately earnest, and more instinctively pure in body and in soul than the daughters of my black mothers" (186). This tribute comes after a carefully logical, historical, and even statistical analysis of the situation of women. All the essays follow this form; any moral or reformist conclusions must be based on solid evidence. In this sense, Du Bois uses the techniques of his historical and sociological studies.

Such is not the case with the pieces inserted between the essays. In these poems and parables Du Bois gives vent to intense literary emotions, providing a sharp counterpoint to the expository writings. He suggests in these brief pieces the spiritual and emotional underpinnings of the book's various themes. Several of them are spoken by first-person narrators, making them even more subjective and affective.

These narrators, however, are not identical; the voices vary according to the subject matter. Thus, the poem "Children of the Moon," which comes between the essays "The Damnation of Women" and "The Immortal Child," is spoken by a female voice. She tells of a journey to the moon, on which she finds black men suffering and dying under the assaults of a monster: "Some wingèd thing of wings, filling all heaven,/ Folding and unfolding, and folding yet again,/Tore out their blood and entrails" (189). She urges them to build a tower that will rise to the sun of freedom in defiance of the monster. "Yet did we build of iron, bricks, and blood;/We built a day, a year, a thousand years,/Blood was the mortar . . ." (190). And in the end, they triumph:

> I rose upon the Mountain of the Moon,—
> I felt the blazing glory of the Sun;
> I heard the Song of Children crying, "Free!"
> I saw the face of Freedom—
> And I died. (192)

The woman is a black Moses, leading her people to a promised land she cannot enter. Refusing to accept their fatalism, she is an allegorical talented tenth whose idealism, skill, and persistence overcome the most terrible of obstacles. The poem is an object lesson in the virtue of vision. But it seeks not to persuade through logic but to implicate the reader in the vision. It appeals to terror and pity and hope rather than reason or morality.

A very different voice, that of a white man, is heard in "The Prayers of God." At first, the poem resembles others in the book. The voice denounces war and ponders the silence of God in the midst of such barbarity. God breaks his silence, not to answer vast questions but to interrogate the individual white man. He asks the source of the gold and blood in the man's hands and about another war:

> War? Not so; not war—
> Dominion, Lord, and over black, not white;
> Black, brown, and fawn,
> And not Thy Chosen Brood, O God,
> We murdered. (251)

He goes on to concede his complicity in a lynching. Then the divine message is revealed: *"Thou? / Thee? / I lynched Thee?"* (251):

> Is this Thy Crucifixion, God,
> And not that funny, little cross,
> With vinegar and thorns?
> Is this Thy kingdom here, not there,
> This stone and stucco drift of dreams? (252)

This realization leads to action: *"Courage, God, I come!"* (252)

What Du Bois attempts here is another exposure of the souls of white folk, both as they are and as they could be. As racial beings, whites may well be demons; but as souls, they have the same humanity as blacks, a humanity that can be taught to respond to all people sympathetically. But the division between expository and poetic discourses implies that the spiritual truth is fundamentally different from the social and historical reality. A deep pessimism is implicit in such discursive differences; white virtue must be recorded in the language of the imagination because, unlike black spirituality, it is not evident in Du Bois's reading of history.

Nonetheless, he concludes *Darkwater* with two efforts at resolution. The short story "The Comet" is a tale of aborted apocalypse. The tail of a comet sweeps across the face of the earth, apparently killing everyone except a poor, exploited, laboring black man and a wealthy young white woman. The scenes of death and destruction are presented with horrifying realism: "In the great stone doorway a hundred men and women and children lay crushed and twisted and jammed, forced into that great, gaping doorway like refuse in a can—as if in one wild, frantic rush to safety, they had crushed and ground themselves to death" (256–57).

The story line traces the growth of mutual understanding between the two survivors in the context of total devastation. They gradually come to accept their shared aloneness: "He did not look like men, as she had always pictured men; but he acted like one and she was content" (263). Even the prospect of sexual intimacy, at first as horrifying to her as the devastation, becomes acceptable and even desirable:

> A vision of the world had risen before her. Slowly the mighty prophecy of her destiny overwhelmed her. Above the dead past hovered the Angel of Annunciation. She was no mere woman. She was neither high nor low, white or black, rich or poor. She was primal woman; mighty mother of all men to come and Bride of Life. She looked upon the man beside her and forgot all else but his manhood, his strong, vigorous manhood—his sorrow and sacrifice. She saw him glorified. He was no longer a thing apart, a creature below, a strange outcast of another clime and blood, but her Brother Humanity incarnate, Son of God and great All-Father of the race to be. (269)

At the moment they embrace, car horns sound nearby; the world is not dead—only New York City. The woman's father and fiancé return and take her away, thanking the black man (after suspicions of his motives) and leaving him a roll of money. The story ends with his going off with his wife and the corpse of their baby.

The tale is fully immersed in history: the black man survives because he was in a deep basement performing menial labor, and the conclusion reasserts white patriarchal domination. But the vision of the story moves outside history. The resolutions of class, race, and sexual differences can only take place by a return to beginnings; the central characters come together, not through and because of human history, but only by its annihilation. The reinscription of history destroys the vision. Not even a black son of God can reinvent the world in competition with the white fathers.

In the last piece in the book, "A Hymn to the Peoples," Du Bois attempts resolution once again. The opening stanzas portray a meeting of the diverse peoples of the world, a meeting in which the full variety of human existence is recognized but in which there is also hope for unity. The reader also talks of human fallibility:

We are but weak and wayward men,
Distraught alike with hatred and vainglory;
Prone to despise the Soul that breathes within—
High visioned hordes that lie and steal and kill,
Sinning the sin each separate heart disclaims,
Clambering upon our riven, writhing selves,
Beseiging Heaven by trampling men to Hell! (275–76)

Du Bois does not here accuse only whites: "No one may blame the other in this sin!" (276) Hope and a new future can only be built upon the recognition of historical reality, because the "soul" that is now despised is part of that reality. Only by knowing and accepting all the truth can the future be made good:

Save us, World-Spirit, from our lesser selves!
Grant us that war and hatred cease,
Reveal our souls in every race and hue!
Help us, O Human God, in this Thy Truce,
To make Humanity divine! (276)

The future is to be gained by bringing God into history, not by taking humanity out of it. The future is found by going back to Emerson and the slaves. The Concord Sage insisted upon the divinity within, and the slaves sang about the brotherhood without. The souls of black folk become the world-soul. In the new world, spirituality must be grounded in history, and human history must rely on a soulful vision. But this unity is achieved through prophetic rhetoric, not through historical or cultural analysis. Du Bois verbally compels into being a world that the logic of his exposition and narration denies.

Like *Darkwater, Dusk of Dawn* (1940) joins an apocalyptic sensibility with the discourse of reason. But in the later work there is no effort to separate the two ways of speaking. No poems or short stories interrupt the flow of exposition. This results in part from the historical moment of writing. In Du Bois's view, the Depression has brought about the end of the dominant economic order; he has every confidence that capitalism will be replaced by some form of socialism. At this crucial moment, he wants to present an outline of what the racial as well as economic future can be. To this extent, the book is not designed as an autobiography in the usual sense. The subtitle, *An Essay toward an Autobiography of a Race Concept*, reflects a desire to examine an idea rather than a person:

> But in my experience, autobiographies have had little lure; repeatedly they assume too much or too little: too much in dreaming that one's own life has greatly influenced the world; too little in the reticences, repressions and distortions which come because men do not dare to be absolutely frank. My life has had its significance because it was part of a Problem; but that problem was, as I continue to think, the central problem of the greatest of the world's democracies and so the Problem of the future world. The problem of the future world is the charting, by means of intelligent reason, of a path not simply through the resistances of physical force, but through the vaster and far more intricate jungle of ideas conditioned on unconscious and subconscious reflexes of living things; on blind unreason and often irresistible urges of sensitive matter; of which the concept of race is today one of the most unyielding and threatening. I seem to see a way of elucidating the inner meaning and significance of that race problem by explaining it in terms of the one human life that I know best.[9]

The self here is symbol, drawing its meaning from the concept of race. But what in fact happens in the book is self-exposure that is significant in and of itself. The narrative requirements of a life story are such that the self cannot be kept within the boundaries of theory.

He defines his place in the world initially as one of the "rejected parts" of European civilization, thus establishing immediately his own double consciousness. This placement means that his contribution to history is minor: "Crucified on the vast wheel of time, I flow round and round with the Zeitgeist, waving my pen and lifting faint voices to explain, expound and exhort; to see, foresee and prophesy, to the few who could or would listen. Thus very evidently to me and to others I did little to create my day or greatly change it; but I did exemplify it and thus for all time my life is significant for all lives of men" (*Dusk*, 3–4).

The passive role of the self implicit in this statement is at odds with the recorded history that follows it, a history in which Du Bois engages in some of the most important intellectual and political activity on the issue of race that occurred during the period. But the assertion of such a claim would contradict the self-sacrificing, principled self he wishes to project. It would also put that self in conflict with the theory the book espouses, which assumes that individuals do not act independently of their economic and racial condition. Social determinism frees him of the task of introspection, since as a product of historical forces he can consider private motives irrelevant to his self-definition.

But precisely such motives are at issue in the conflicts he records throughout the text. He repeatedly argues that others act in self-interested ways in dealing with him; he, however, always acts according to established moral principle. His flaws are consistently those of ignorance, not venality or selfishness. The existence of such flaws revises the heroic drama of *Darkwater*. Whereas in that story he was the mythic hero in battle against demonism, here he is the gradually enlightened champion of reason, morality, and democracy. He slowly learns the ways of the world and devises strategies for meeting its challenges. Throughout, however, he is guided by moral principles Lacan would call the Law of the Father. Thus, whether Du Bois acts wisely or effectively at any point in the narrative is secondary to his need to act rightly.

His representation of self and its experience in such a way could obviously be both priggish and self-serving. He prevents such an interpretation by historicizing the experience as thoroughly as possible. Thus, the limits on his understanding at any given point are shown to be the product of the cultural conditions of that moment; the actions of his antagonists are similarly shown to result from their acceptance of cultural hegemony. What is not historicized is Du Bois's ability to surmount such conditioning and to act according to transcendent rules.

This ahistorical aspect of self can be explained as a desire to validate the ideological stance that is the justification for this autobiography. In order to lay claim to the truth value of his program of self-segregation and cultural nationalism, Du Bois has to establish his own credibility. Doing so is especially important since his position is a radical one, diametrically opposed to the reformist efforts of the NAACP, the group with which he had long been identified. To claim new ground and re-assert himself as the intellectual leader of blacks, he must demonstrate his own record of integrity and insight. He cannot concede that he was wrong before, since that might imply that he could be wrong now. What he points to instead is a long personal history of enlightenment and principled behavior. Unlike him, his foes have stood for that which was advantageous to them at the moment, with little regard for truth and goodness.

This history of conflict shows Du Bois in the position of the wronged son resisting arbitrary or self-aggrandizing father figures. And in the abstract, these individuals are shown to be products of a patriarchal culture. The latter is established in the childhood and college chapters of the narrative. Great Barrington is depicted as a largely typical nineteenth-century town, with clear but flexible class lines and a toleration for difference within hegemonic guidelines. Thus, established black families working as small farmers and laborers are easily accepted, while recently arrived Irish and German mill workers are despised by all the older families, black and white. The economic, political, and religious structure of the community was taken as the natural order of things. Similarly, education at Fisk and Harvard uncritically encouraged acceptance of a Eurocentric worldview. Capitalism, American democracy, and the superiority of European civilization were the beliefs inculcated in Du Bois and all others. He notes, for example, that Bismarck was the subject of his Fisk graduation address: "This choice in itself showed the abyss between my education and the truth in the world. Bismarck was my hero" (32). The only thing that saved him from total identification with this worldview was race. This critical disruption of the ideological structure was largely based on personal experience rather than academic study. Reading of lynchings and teaching in rural Tennessee brought to him an awareness that the widely accepted values had not yet triumphed in the world. Part of his evidence of his own ignorance is that this did not lead him to deeper criticism: "What the white world was doing, its goals and its ideals, I had not doubted were quite right. What was wrong was that I and people like me and thousands of others who might have my ability and aspiration, were refused permission to be a part of this world" (27).

It is precisely an inability to see beyond the existing order that is the basis of Du Bois's attacks on his antagonists. In each case that blindness combined with a willingness to compromise on principles produces a problem for the protagonist. As the initial example of Rutherford B. Hayes and the Slater Fund suggests, these antagonists are themselves at the heart of the dominant culture. The fund, headed by Hayes, indicated that it was willing to support advanced education for blacks in Europe. When Du Bois applied, Hayes denied that such a program existed, though Du Bois cited a newspaper story to the contrary. He then "deluges" the ex-president with recommendations and protests, "intimating that his change of plan did not seem fair or honest" (43). He persists until the fund offers him a fellowship. What is significant here is not merely that Du Bois at age twenty-two assumes his own moral as well as legal rightness vis-à-vis such a figure of authority, but also that the seventy-year-old autobiographer obviously approves of such presumption. What is also evident is the importance of language in sustaining such a position. Du Bois not only uses Hayes's own words against him (and provides an exact citation fifty years after the fact), but he also cites his own exact words to indicate his own worthiness for the award. In effect, documentation and narration come together to authenticate a self that is rational and moral. The fact that it also serves Du Bois's self-interest is elided into the representation of himself as the symbol of the race.

The much more important and complex conflict was with Booker T. Washington. It is recorded in a chapter significantly titled "Science and Empire." The overt referent for "empire" is the imperialist expansion of the late nineteenth and early twentieth centuries. Of these global developments Du Bois claims to have been largely ignorant, again carrying through the theme of education. But the subtext of the chapter is Washington as imperialist, with Du Bois correlatively as scientist. If Hayes was the somewhat dishonest father, Washington is the maliciously self-serving one. (It is important in this context to keep in mind that Du Bois is writing twenty-five years after Washington's death.)

Du Bois presents himself early in the chapter as the accomplished social scientist his training had prepared him to be. In this role, he has served the race by uncovering the truth about it. He talks in considerable detail about the research for *The Philadelphia Negro* and the Atlanta studies. He extensively cites his statements from that period about his methods. He also declares the importance of that work to the advancement of scientific knowledge. At the same time, he again casts himself in a heroic mold: "Yet, I made a study of the Philadelphia Negro so thorough that it has withstood the criticism of forty years. It was as complete a scientific study and answer as could have then been given, with defective facts and statistics, one lone worker and little money" (58–59). He is the stalwart champion of scholarship in the face of indifference and ignorance.

Defining himself as successful and heroic is essential, because it indicates what he gave up in order to engage in a different kind of struggle. He did not move into racial politics because of any lack in himself or his work; he did so out of moral necessity and at the sacrifice of an ongoing distinguished career.[10] This self-interpretation, as shall be seen, differentiates his character from those of his antagonists. The beginning of the change comes in a personal experience; he almost, but not quite, encounters a gruesome display of the body parts of a lynched black man. The "almost" is important. Du Bois's response is not to the physical reality; it is to the idea of the display. This distinction removes his reaction from the realm of emotionalism to that of moral revulsion. It causes for him a professional crisis: "Two considerations thereafter broke in upon my work and eventually disrupted it: first, one could not be a calm, cool, and detached scientist while Negroes were lynched, murdered and starved; and secondly, there was no such definite demand for scientific work of the sort that I was doing, as I had confidently assumed would be easily forthcoming" (Dusk, 67–68). It is noteworthy that this crisis occurs around 1901; blacks had been being lynched for many years; the 1890s was one of the worst decades in history. Yet, that period is the very time when Du Bois is becoming the "calm, cool, and detached scientist." Thus, it would seem that the near-direct confrontation with violent reality is the triggering mechanism. Like other progressives, such as Jane Addams, Du Bois finds that intellectual effort, even when heroic, is inadequate. Threatened at the moment of success with irrelevance, he is compelled to enter the lists more directly.

But he does so precisely in terms congruent with the intellectual sensibility he has just questioned. He defines his disagreement with

Washington initially in terms of divergent views of higher education for blacks. Washington's encouragement of industrial training to prepare blacks to be efficient workers is countered by Du Bois's view that university education was essential for an elite that could then "guide the American Negro into a higher civilization" (70). While on the surface this would appear to be a clearly delineated conflict that could be resolved, beneath is a deeper, essentially political issue. It is found in a statement appended and seemingly tangential to the discussion on education: "Moreover, it is characteristic of the Washington statesmanship that whatever he or anybody believed or wanted must be subordinated to dominant public opinion and that opinion deferred to and cajoled until it allowed a deviation toward better ways. This is no new thing in the world, but it is always dangerous" (70–71). The real issue is power and leadership. Washington uses his power, not to achieve meaningful and moral change, but to reaffirm the dominant ideology, even when that ideology violates the moral order. Truth and goodness are secondary to status within the existing structure. To talk of "deviation toward better ways," moreover, suggests that the usual direction of society is wrong. Washington here not only submits to the power of others but compromises his integrity by actively paying obeisance to that power.

The Tuskegean inverts the power relationship when it comes to blacks. As a second-rank patriarchal figure, he demands submissiveness from those politically weaker than himself. Du Bois describes the development of the Tuskegee machine, using the latter word in full recognition of its connotations of chicanery and corruption. He shows how Washington achieved standing as the father of the race, at least in the eyes of whites, and then used that status to compel black agreement with his views. For Du Bois, the crucial issue is not money or even political maneuvering; it is voice. Washington presumed to define both the public and private experience of blacks: "It did not seem fair, for instance, that on the one hand Mr. Washington should *decry* political activities among Negroes, and on the other hand *dictate* Negro political objectives from Tuskegee" (72, emphasis added). Washington claims the right, in effect, to designate what behavior and speech are acceptable. It is this denial of alternative voices that most arouses Du Bois:

Contrary to most opinion, the controversy as it developed was not entirely against Mr. Washington's ideas, but became the insistence upon the right of other Negroes to have and express their ideas. Things came to such a pass that when any Negro complained or advocated a course of action, he was silenced with the remark that Mr. Washington did not agree with this. Naturally the bumptious, irritated, young black intelligentsia of the day declared, "I don't care a damn what Booker Washington thinks! This is what I think, and *I have a right to think.*" (75)

Du Bois reshapes the conflict as an issue of intellectual freedom rather than power politics. In these terms, Washington's efforts at suppression become violations of basic American principles. Du Bois wants a marketplace of ideas, a version of the town meeting of his Great Barrington childhood and a version of the intellectual interaction that is the scientific method. In both democracy and science, truth is arrived at by authentic communication. When this is denied, a distortion like the Tuskegee machine results.

Du Bois develops this theme by showing how his various efforts at communication were thwarted and ultimately even his scientific undertakings were frustrated by the machine. Atlanta University, because Du Bois is associated with it, finds it increasingly difficult to get funding from private white sources, who turn to Washington for advice. Thus, even knowledge itself is subordinated to ideological conformity.

As the hero of the story, Du Bois responds forcefully, though fatally for his academic career. He challenges Washington's principles in *The Souls of Black Folk* and then sets up the Niagara movement as a counter organization. The principles and demands of this new group—civil rights, voting rights, education—are identical with those expressed in "Of Mr. Booker T. Washington and Others." Anxiety over Washington's control of black expression leads Du Bois to establish a series of publications, culminating in the NAACP's *The Crisis.* Such actions of course aggravate the situation and lead to the sacrifice of his academic career: "My career as a scientist was to be swallowed up in my role as master of propaganda. This was not wholly to my liking. I was no natural leader of men. I could not slap people on the back and make friends of strangers. I could not easily break down an inherited reserve; or at all times curb a biting, critical tongue. Nevertheless, having put my hand to the plow, I had to go on" (94). The change of roles is presented as a binary opposition: the "scientist" is fundamentally different from the "master of propaganda" in terms not only of different discourses but also different purposes and even different personality types. One is Du Bois's natural role; the other requires a strenuous effort not only in terms of work but also sensibility. It demands that he engage in behavior personally distasteful to him. What he gives up, in other words, is not merely a career but also a way of being that was his own. It is a true *self*-sacrifice. But that is what the struggle requires: "Here was an opportunity to enter the lists in a desperate fight aimed straight at the real difficulty: the question as to how far educated Negro opinion in the United States was going to have the right and opportunity to guide the Negro group. I did not hesitate because I could not. It was the voice without reply" (95).

This statement collapses the personal, political, ideological, and moral issues involved in the conflict. The "real" difficulty is not racial violence or civil rights; it is a problem of leadership: Whose position will the race follow? And since "the voice without reply" is the request for Du Bois to work for the NAACP by editing its journal, the question is finally whether *he* will be the leader of the race. In this context, it is significant that he designates his new role as "master of propaganda." It implies control of discourse rather than power politics. Leadership by "educated Negro opinion" will be through persuasion, not intimidation or deceit. To call it "propaganda," given the international situation in 1940 when *Dusk of Dawn* is published, raises questions about the kind of mastery Du Bois intends. The term carried at the time connotations of manipulation and verbal coercion that suggest underlying motives of personal and ideological power. Du Bois, though lacking the financial and political resources of the Tuskegee machine, could use his own resources—intellect and verbal facility—to create a counterforce. But the existence of such motives must be concealed if the self and the ideology of the autobiography are to be validated. Thus, the heroic drama of 1900 to 1910 serves to authorize the political position of 1940.

The theoretical and autobiographical elements are brought together in the story of his struggle within the NAACP. The theory has established the intellectual basis for an argument that race is an aspect of culture and economics rather than an autonomous category. This allows Du Bois to defend some form of racial solidarity and identity without falling into a position of racial essentialism.[11] Historical and social conditions, not biology, have put blacks in the situation they are in and are likely to keep them there. The self of the book has been shown to possess absolute integrity, sufficient intellectual flexibility to realize his occasional ignorance and to know that his perspective must be adapted to reality, and the strength to struggle against antagonists lacking his vision and moral character.

He sees, as others in the NAACP do not, two factors that fundamentally alter the prospects for blacks in the United States. The first is economics. A 1928 trip to the Soviet Union serves as a narrative turning point: "Mentally I came to know Karl Marx and Lenin, their critics and defenders. Since that trip my mental outlook and the aspect of the world will never be the same" (*Dusk*, 287). Such a perspective means that the old liberalism on which the NAACP was founded is not sufficient to change the underlying problems of blacks. Even if civil rights were achieved, they would only afford blacks a slightly better place in "the tyranny which now dominate[s] industrial life" (289). Meaningful freedom and justice can be gained only through a total restructuring of the economic order. Du Bois's colleagues in the organization, black and white, lacked the vision and courage to adapt policies to this new situation.

The second, related factor was Du Bois's increasing belief that racial oppression arose not from conscious evil or ignorance, but from deeply embedded irrationality: "We were facing age-long complexes sunk now largely to unconscious habit and irrational urge, which demanded on our part not only the patience to wait, but the power to entrench ourselves for a long seige against the strongholds of color caste" (296). Given this point of view, not only Du Bois's own earlier scholarly works but also court decisions and even legislation would do little to change underlying white attitudes and behavior. He here abandons in one sense his older optimism about the prospects for racial justice; to make the battle a psychological one is to make it much more difficult to win. At the same time, the demonism of *Darkwater* has been revised to a form of social pathology, which, given the references to Freud, Du Bois believes can be identified and treated in a rational manner. Only an approach that assumed the persistence of a racist unconscious could adequately counteract it.

Du Bois's response to the problems of economics and racism is black economic self-help to provide group strength for a long-term program of advancement and antiracist propaganda. This plan, which he provocatively calls self-segregation, is resisted by the NAACP. According to Du Bois, the resistance of blacks within the organization is based on self-interest: "I realized in later years the Association had attracted the higher income group of colored people, who regarded it as a weapon to attack the sort of social discrimination which especially irked them; rather than as an organization to improve the status and power of the whole Negro group" (297). Those whom he once touted as the talented tenth have, unlike him, lost a vision of uplift for the race. Instead, they seek personal and class advantage. The white members of the organization were themselves wealthy liberals who could not be expected to support a radical approach to the problems Du Bois defined.

The battle ensues because, in addition to the inability of others to see beyond their own interests, the organization itself had become a version of the Tuskegee machine. Over time, the secretary (Walter White at the time of the conflict) had become the central authority not only for operations but also, in effect, for policy. When, during the Depression, *The Crisis* became financially dependent on the association, control was attempted over Du Bois's expression of his new ideas. His efforts to establish his position as both practical and consistent with a tradition of pragmatism within the organization were fruitless. When he criticized the secretary for what he considered a dogmatic reading of association history and policy, he was instructed to be silent: " 'No salaried officer of the Association shall criticize the policy, work or officers of the Association in the pages of *The Crisis*' " (313). Given his moral imperative for self-expression—"and this conviction I had to express or spiritually die" (303)—he has no choice but to resign.

Repeatedly in this section, he describes his contributions to both the association and the race as a whole. Despite this work, he has again made a sacrifice to self-interest and power politics. Moreover, his next move, a return to Atlanta University, is portrayed as additional sacrifice: "The South is not a place where a man of Negro descent would voluntarily and without good reason choose to live" (316). To be a man of unshakeable integrity in a world of compromise is to risk repeated displacement and suffering.

What is constant is not the political stance that challenges established order. In fact, there is a compulsion to always find a new position, as though ideological stability were itself a kind of compromise. What remains fixed in all the autobiographies is a set of absolutes about reason, truth, and moral order that compel the self to put itself at risk in voicing whatever conclusions about reality its principles lead it to. The life story becomes a patterned drama in which Du Bois most frequently loses the surface battle but in the process demonstrates his spiritual triumph: "Life has its pain and evil—its bitter disappointments; but I like a good novel and in healthful length of days, there is infinite joy in seeing the World, the most interesting of continued stories, unfold, even though one misses THE END" (326). So, at the end of *Dusk of Dawn*, he leaves his latest life's work, again driven away by forces of suppression, but he takes up the challenge of the South. He writes constantly, and he remains active in shaping black political principles. The desire of his enemies to silence him fails, because he cannot be silenced. In the "good novel" of autobiographical writing, he depicts himself as the very emblem and embodiment of "black truth" and as such must and always does speak.

10

· · · · · · · · ·

Seizing the Self

· · · · · · · ·

In Battle for Peace and
The Autobiography of
W. E. B. Du Bois

· · · · · · · · ·

Du Bois presents the deepest threat to his
speaking of truth in his last two autobiographical works, *In Battle for
Peace* (1952) and *The Autobiography of W. E. B. Du Bois* (1968). The
first of these is a work of occasional writing, designed to defend himself against government attack, and the second is written from the
same ideological position and, in fact, incorporates verbatim much of
In Battle for Peace. The ideological position is that of Soviet socialism,
though it is not until 1961 that Du Bois actually joins the Communist party. Ideology in part shapes both the narrative stances of these
works and the selves that are narrated. Du Bois is careful to make clear
his political values in each work, going so far in *The Autobiography*
as articulating a credo on communism. The experiencing selves of the
narratives are placed in their political, historical, and economic contexts, thus implying the influence of these factors on his identity. But
In Battle for Peace and *The Autobiography* cannot be read simply as
defenses of his ideology any more than *Dusk of Dawn* could. These life
studies continue the heroic adventures of the earlier works. In fact, *The
Autobiography* is largely an anthology of previous self-portraits, with
interesting implications for the very ideology it espouses.

In Battle for Peace, though clearly an apologia for Du Bois's views on American foreign policy in the late 1940s and early 1950s, calls attention to itself as an artful production. From the oxymoronic title to word plays to the sometimes serious, sometimes chatty commentary of Shirley Graham (Du Bois's second wife), the narrative qualifies its overt purposes in almost self-subversive ways. The effect is to join political tract with something like celebrity biography. Thus, though the central drama of the work is Du Bois's trial for not registering as a foreign agent, he subtitles the book "The Story of My 83rd Birthday," as though it were an extended society column. Consistent with this latter impulse, it engages in leftist name-dropping and, in Graham's portions, comments on aspects of their personal lives, such as wedding arrangements.

While much of this material is used for its ironic and politically symbolic value, it problematizes the narrative. For example, in the first chapter, Du Bois portrays a self that disdains celebrity status, seeing such activities as public birthday celebrations as embarrassments. Graham's commentary at the end of the chapter neutralizes this self-effacement by effusively describing Du Bois's importance to the nation and including citations from historians and friends on his contributions. These materials function to humanize the text, to save it from the appearance of a purely ideological gesture. Du Bois becomes a grandfather figure, both proud of his achievements and unwilling to boast of them, though others are permitted to do so. Such a characterization also carries with it the validation of his authority concerning his subject. The weight of years implies an accumulation of wisdom, certified by personal, political, and professional recognition.

Moreover, the figuration as wise old man accentuates the injustice and insensitivity of his antagonists. Those who threaten to imprison the body and impugn the character of an eighty-three-year-old world-renowned scholar and activist are not merely wrong in their views; they are contemptible. Given the complex politics of the time, such a self-presentation is essential. The House Un-American Activities Committee and others were defining various groups and activities as communist and therefore criminal and treasonous. Du Bois's vehement denunciations of American internal and foreign policies and his advocacy of positions identified with the Soviet Union would make him suspect in the eyes of much of his audience. Close examination of policies under such circumstances would be less effective than dramatization of the essential integrity of himself and his associates and of the fundamental unfairness—and thus un-Americanness—of his opposition. The differing political perspectives in fact are shown to be the products of character. Belligerent, self-interested, morally compromised men have produced current American policy and attacked those who disagree with them. These fathers of the Cold War and anticommunist hysteria become, in Du Bois's narrative, the ones subversive of American values, while the protagonist and his friends are the true patriots in their upholding of democracy and moral order. The story, then, as always in the autobiographical writings, is a tale of good and evil, of false and true authority. Here it is the struggle, not just for the souls of black folk, but for the soul of America.

The hysteria of the time, according to Du Bois, made real democracy impossible:

> But here in America lately we have had seemingly sane citizens, statesmen and thinkers, who loudly and angrily refuse now the support of Communists, Socialists, or Progressives; now of Negroes, Catholics, Jews and the foreign-born; and because they do not believe in everything that these groups do believe in, although these do agree in some matters. Some men therefore apparently demand complete unity of belief and object as a prerequisite to any co-operation at all. This attitude thwarts democracy and stops progress.[1]

The problem is not Du Bois's politics; rather the nation itself has become un-American. It has turned its back on democratic ideals and become, in a sense, a totalitarian state, precisely what it accuses the Soviet Union of being. It becomes the duty of radicals to call it back to its first principles. And, as always, performing this duty brings with it suffering.

Du Bois insists repeatedly on the legitimacy and patriotism of his own actions and views:

> We know and the saner nation knows that we are not traitors nor conspirators; and far from plotting force and violence it is precisely force and violence that we bitterly oppose. This conference was not called to defend communism nor socialism nor the American way of life. It was called to promote peace! It was called to say again and again that no matter how

right or wrong differing systems of beliefs in religion, industry or government may be, war is not the method by which their differences can successfully be settled for the good of mankind. (*Battle*, 27–28)

The position articulated is depicted as perfectly rational. He even rejects the implication that his actions are ideological in the same sense as his opponents'. Instead he simply wants to present the moral premise that peace is better than war. Peace, for him, is ideologically neutral; like all of Du Bois's essential values, it is seen as transcending particular systems. It is an ideal with which all "sane" people can agree.

The difficulty for him then was not the stand he took, but the historical circumstances in which he took it:

For fifty years I have been in touch with social currents in the United States. Never before has organized reaction wielded the power it does today: by ownership of press and radio, by curtailment of free speech, by imprisonment of liberal thinkers and writers. It has become almost impossible today in my country even to hold a public rally for peace. This has been accomplished by inducing Americans to believe that America is in imminent danger of aggression from communism, socialism and liberalism, and that the peace movement cloaks this threat. (41)

The enemy Du Bois faces is the same as always: a powerful conspiratorial group antagonistic to his different ideas and willing to subvert democracy in order to prevent their expression.

The result for him is his trial. But he interrupts the legal story to describe his venture into the 1950 New York senatorial campaign as the candidate of the Progressive Party. This is not a digression but an exemplification of the corruption of American ideals in the current environment. He shows the interactions of intimidation, money, and propaganda that created the possibility of his indictment. Dramatically, the campaign foreshadows the trial by revealing various character types that appear in both events.

In conventional political terms, the campaign is an exercise in futility, a fact that Du Bois claims to understand from the beginning. The point was never to win but to publicize the peace movement. The opportunity was important, for he felt increasingly isolated:

Because of my support of the Progressive Party in 1948, my acceptance of an honorary and unpaid office with Paul Robeson in the Council on African Affairs, and my activity in Peace Congresses in New York, Paris and Moscow, I found myself increasingly proscribed in pulpit, school and platform. My opportunity to write for publication was becoming narrower and narrower, even in the Negro Press. I wondered if a series of plain talks in a political campaign would not be my last and only chance to tell the truth as I saw it. (44)

The sense of alienation so evident in this passage is not remarked upon, though it is faced in *The Autobiography*. Nonetheless, it does help to explain why he repeatedly insists that an audience of believers can be found if only he has the means of reaching them. His hostility toward those in power is based on his claim that a majority of Americans would support his views if they had the opportunity of hearing them. The isolation he expresses exists, not because of anything foreign in his beliefs, but because democracy and freedom are not permitted to function. Like the heroes (including himself) in earlier works, the fault lies not in himself or in "the people" but in the self-interested, powerful group that comes between them.

Du Bois insists that his campaign for the U.S. Senate did not succeed largely because of the vast expenditures by his opponents: "It just did not make sense. But dollars did it—just plain cash to purchase the election of as reactionary and characterless a nonentity as ever sat in Congress" (50). The moral dynamic articulated in other works is also apparent here: morality is effective for most people only when it is supported by self-interest: "Lehman was different. He was an honest man and wealthy; he had behind him a fairly good record of public service. Yet he ought not to sit in the United States Senate because he represented finance and foreign investment, and because of this was frantically backing Truman in the Korean crime which Big Business precipitated" (48).

The same does not hold for Du Bois himself. He enters the campaign, not for money or power, but to articulate an ideal. He was old, ill, and politically inexperienced. "I went into the campaign for Senator knowing well from the first that I did not have a ghost of a chance for election, and that my efforts would bring me ridicule at best and jail at worst" (46). He offers himself as a sacrifice for truth, hoping that at some future time his ideal will be realized. Even the relatively small vote for him is heartening: "I was astonished by a vote of 205,729, a vote from men and women of courage, without the prejudice against color which I always expect and usually experience. This meant that these faced poverty and jail to stand and be counted for Peace and Civil Rights" (50). A "talented twenty-fifth" (his proportion of the vote) had been created to replace the talented tenth. If so many could be found in New York in such critical times, then there was hope for America: "Yet there is a sense in which no sound effort is in vain, least of all a struggle with high ideal and personal integrity. One feels that, in the end, all of this can never be lost; that somehow, somewhere, whatever was fine and noble in this campaign will triumph" (50). Though economics is the prime mover for most people, for the heroic few moral order shapes the universe, meaning that the failure of the good is only apparent and that Du Bois is guaranteed victory over his opponents.

In contrast to the clear-cut good and evil competing in the senatorial campaign, another figure makes an appearance in the political drama. This is the Failed Hero, here represented by Henry Wallace. He had been the hero of the 1948 presidential campaign, displaying the courage and idealism Du Bois felt should always motivate leaders. He suffered, however, from moral hesitancy: "But as I came to know Henry Wallace, I realized the uncertainty of his intellectual orientation, and the strong forces close to him which wanted respectability and feared too close association with unpopular causes. In a sense Wallace lacked guts and had small stomach for martyrdom; and all this despite his facing of Southern rotten eggs in 1948" (46). Unlike Alexander Crummell, John Brown, and of course Du Bois himself, Wallace is not willing to go beyond correct politics into the realm of self-sacrifice. When he realizes Wallace's limitations, Du Bois offers to become a leader of the leader, in the mold of Harry Hopkins of *The Black Flame* trilogy. He calls for courage and idealism rather than conventional political wisdom. When he is ignored, his judgment is stern: "I received no reply, and on July 15, 1950, Wallace deserted the Progressive movement. Thereafter, and perhaps ungenerously both to him and the slender little animal who, after all, can fight, I thought of Wallace as no longer the crusader, but as Wallace the Weasel" (46).

As early as his book on the slave trade, Du Bois had a propensity to put the greatest burden of guilt on those who had sufficient character to conquer self-interest but who hesitated and thereby allowed immorality to triumph. These figures are consistently father figures who betrayed their responsibility to define and maintain the moral order. The Founding Fathers, Southern gentlemen, Woodrow Wilson, Booker T. Washington, and most bitterly in these two works, his own talented tenth, all saw the light of truth and goodness but turned away from it. The invective against Wallace demonstrates again the absoluteness of Du Bois's system of moral law. No middle ground exists between good and evil and, furthermore, recognition of the good requires positive action on its behalf, even to the point of self-annihilation.

The trial becomes the ritual drama by which Du Bois's own moral strength is tested and his truth validated. He portrays himself as a loyal, principled, freedom-loving American demanding that his country live up to its ideals. He observes that the officers of the Peace Information Center repeatedly sought to discuss the legality of its activities with the Justice Department. Their voices were ignored in the government's drive to discredit them. They refused to register the organization or themselves as foreign agents because, in their view, to do so would in fact be lying. They did begin, however, to disband the center. Despite such efforts, they were indicted. Du Bois can reach only one conclusion: "The Department of Justice thus assumed that our real crime was peace and not foreign agency" (56). No accusation of treason was ever overtly made; the real issue, as Du Bois sees it, is the nation's refusal to see the truth about itself.

The measure of the fear and desperation of the government was the flimsiness of its case. The Justice Department even tried to avoid a trial altogether by encouraging Du Bois to plead "no contest": "It was all naturally 'unofficial,' but if Du Bois would enter a plea of 'Nolo Contendere,' the procedure against him would undoubtedly be dropped. In other words, I only had to lie and the case against me would not be pressed. I immediately wrote my attorney and said flatly that before I would enter such a plea I would rot in jail" (89). He is tempted, but being one of the righteous, he has no doubts about his willingness to suffer for truth rather than submit to someone else's definition of himself. The same uncompromising nature that made him reject political accommodation (as Wallace did) in his senatorial campaign now leads him to risk imprisonment rather than act self-interestedly against his principles.

A sharp contrast is set up between such heroism and the actions of John Rogge, the government's chief witness. Rogge is portrayed as a moral coward, a once-principled man who, out of fear and self-interest, betrays his friends and their cause. He is the trial's equivalent of Henry Wallace. One of the founders of the Peace Information Center, he represented it at international conferences and helped to formulate its policies and activities. Du Bois, however, claims to have seen a much more mundane Rogge behind the idealist: "But he pushed ahead, believing that his Pot of Gold was still at the end of his rainbow, through popularity and political preferment. But it wasn't. Despite his crusade for peace and the promise of the progressive Wallace, Rogge realized that if he wanted to make money—and of course he did, for what else was there for a man to do?—he must make a right-about face" (117–18). He betrays his friends to save himself. "And so in my mind—I trust not unjustly—to Wallace the Weasel I now add, Rogge the Rat" (118).[2]

The wages of betrayal are apparent: "Rogge the witness was a caricature of Rogge the crusader for Peace and Reform. In place of the erect, self-confident if not arrogant leader, came a worn man, whose clothes hung loosely on him, and who in a courtroom where he had conducted many cases, had difficulty locating me in the defendants' chairs. I voluntarily stood up to help him out" (126). Though Rogge could become a traitor because he was already self-interested, association with idealistic behavior gave him the only real stature he ever had. Even those lacking the character of Du Bois are made better by engaging in virtuous activities.

Du Bois's lack of sympathy and indifference to possible complexities of motive in Wallace and Rogge follow from the sense he gives of deep personal insult at their actions. But more than this, they do violence to the very principles on which he has built his identity. All his writings, including the autobiographical works, insist that the life of moral courage and self-sacrifice is not only possible but actual. It is real because he has lived it. The fact that most people do not is of little account, since most people do not have moral vision. But when those who do nonetheless compromise with self-interest, then it raises the potential for it to happen to anyone, even perhaps Du Bois himself.

In the book, Rogge is not overtly important. In fact, the trial itself is almost an anticlimax. The government wants to imply but not prove that the Peace Information Center was a front for Soviet activities. But its case is so poor that it cannot even demonstrate that it was a front for another front, the Defenders of Peace. Rogge is the one who is supposed to make this connection, but even though he was a policy-making member of both groups, he cannot demonstrate that one acted for the other. His betrayal, in this sense, is for naught.

The prosecutor then tries to contend that he does not have to prove direct relationship; he argues that mere similarity of ideas and activities is punishable under the law. He seeks, in other words, to impose arbitrarily a meaning on the law that will serve the interests of those in power and, by extension, allow them to designate acceptable speech and behavior in defiance of American democratic traditions. The judge rejects the argument and dismisses the case.

The failure of the prosecution and the quick dismissal do not lead Du Bois to reassess either his ideology or American justice. In fact, the incident only validates his belief in the conspiratorial nature of capital-ist "democracy" and possible salvation under socialism. The trial was not the misguided effort of patriotic government officials, but a care-fully orchestrated attempt by the political-corporate-military complex to destroy its opponents:

> The nation was ruled by the National Association of Manufacturers, the United States Chamber of Commerce, and like affiliated organizations. That is, concentrated control of the whole industrial process coupled with direction of public opinion through nationally organized propaganda. This new concentration of economic power guided the rapidly accumu-lating profits of national enterprises, and planned to increase them by buying labor and using land in Asia, Africa, the Caribbean area, and South America at lower prices than they would have to pay in Europe or North America. Even in these latter lands their rate of profit was threatened by rising socialism among the organized labor vote which had now actually taken from exploitation the whole of Eastern Europe. It was necessary to fight or threaten to fight to stem this socialistic tide. . . . The public fright and hysteria consequent on this policy began to get out of control, and the nation was faced with "war or bust"; with continued concentration of capi-tal in unproductive enterprises or danger of a financial crisis brought on by inflation and unemployment. Warning or discussion of this was stopped by refusing publicity to criticism in education, art, or literature; by making it difficult for critics to earn a living, and by persecuting dissenters. (87–88)

Du Bois is far from simplistic in his conspiracy theory. The capitalists are everywhere, but they are not omnipotent. First, the policy of self-interest they pursue has, dialectically, generated its own opposition in the form of socialism. The threat of the proletariat is significant enough to require at least militaristic propaganda, and, as he notes at one point, conflicts such as the Korean War.

But this response creates a second difficulty. War (and rumors of war) does not provide a stable economic environment. The very act of fighting socialism threatens an economic crisis that can only encourage a socialist mentality in the populace. Self-interest, as always in Du Bois's moral universe, is not only immoral, it is also ultimately impractical. It involves so many contradictions and inconsistencies that no matter what dominant group uses it—slave owners, Southern racists, capitalists—they will inevitably find themselves in impossible circumstances. Morality, logic, and practicality are ultimately harmonious, but one must be able to transcend mundane reality to perceive this "fact."

Ironically, those caught in the tangled web understand the truth of the previous statement and for that very reason must deny it. Capitalists, Du Bois implies, are doomed and know it. Their only hope is in keeping the public from discovering the true state of affairs and thereby delaying to some future time their destiny. Propaganda and repression, with the attendant corrupting effects on the culture ("education, art, [and] literature") are the tools of this deception. That the media could be used for such purposes Du Bois has no doubts: "We [Americans] secured thought control in the United States by concentrating ownership of the press and news-gathering agencies in the hands of powerful, integrated agencies, while the periodical and book publishing business was also kept subservient" (87). Manipulation in his own case is equally clear: "Just as the newspapers suppressed foreign statements and petitions about me and about this case because of my connection with it, so consciously and according to specific orders from the High Command they suppressed, or their editors cut out, all news about the white defendants and the general aspects of the case" (85).

Such an interpretation of the role of the press is essential if Du Bois is to explain his isolation adequately. He must see the public, both black and white, as deceived if he is going to explain the neglect he endures. Since the isolation is real and his word is truth, the problem must be caused by some evil design to keep him and a putatively sympathetic public apart. The issue is not simply guilt or innocence; it is the integrity of the man Du Bois and the meaning of his existence. He refuses to accept the possibility that he is wrong ideologically. His life as scientist, social critic, writer, publicist, and racial spokesman has been premised on the assumption that truth is available to everyone and that he has only asserted what the better nature of every person would assert if properly educated. A prophet may be without honor in his own country, but that is because the country fears the truth; if the prophet himself ever loses sight of truth, then the meaning of his existence is lost. Du Bois cannot deny what he believes, nor even, as is evident in both *Dusk of Dawn* and *The Autobiography*, repudiate what he has believed in the past, even though it means separation from two groups with whom he has long identified.

The intelligentsia, whom Du Bois expected to penetrate the veil of deception, refused to come to his aid, even though he felt he was defending rationality in the face of hysteria:

This is the most astonishing and frightening result of this trial. We five are free but America is not. The absence of moral courage and intellectual integrity which our persecution revealed still stands to frighten our own nation and the better world. It is clear still today, that freedom of speech and of thinking can be attacked in the United States without the intellectual and moral leaders of this land raising a hand or saying a word of protest or defense, except in the case of the Saving Few. Their ranks did not include the heads of the great universities, the leaders of religion, or most of the great names in science. (151)

Intellectuals, especially black ones, always served for Du Bois a crucial function as transmitters of culture, educators of the young, defenders of truth, freedom, and morality, and, in his more elitist pronouncements, as civilizers of the masses. They are supposed to save civilization from the depradations and vulgarities of self-interest and irrationality. If they can be intimidated or become indifferent, then the nation is lost.

Similarly, blacks as a group have been a source of hope that disappoint him in this crisis: "The very loosening of outer racial discriminatory pressures has not, as I had once believed, left Negroes free to become a group cemented into a new cultural unity, capable of absorbing socialism, tolerance and democracy, and helping to lead America into a new heaven and a new earth. But rather, partial emancipation is freeing some of them to ape the worst of American and Anglo-Saxon chauvinism, luxury, showing-off and 'social climbing'" (155). The integration he spent a lifetime advocating has worked all too well. The "Negro-American" dichotomy has dissolved, at least for the black bourgeoisie, into rather undiluted Americanism. The result, of course, Du Bois considers a disaster.

But the black ideal is not dead. "In contrast to [the elite's] lethargy and fright, the mass support which I gained from the Negroes of the nation began slowly as soon as they could understand the facts, and then swelled in astonishing volume as the trial neared" (154). The support of the masses is demonstrated by reference to two groups, black members of "left-wing unions" and the black press. Though the first of these, given the small number of blacks in any unions, serves to suggest Du Bois's ideology more than his popularity, the second is significant. Defense of him by the black press he takes to imply approval of his politics, though the examples he gives point to his record of service to the race and not to his current views on international policy. By assuming what he does, however, he can maintain his claim to moral leadership of the race despite appearances to the contrary.

The uncertainties implicit in his definition of his role are not apparent on the surface of the text. If intellectuals and the black middle class reject him, he can still identify a talented tenth that believes in him:

> On the other hand, I am free from jail today, not only by the efforts of that smaller part of the Negro intelligentsia which has shared my vision, but also by the steadily increasing help of Negro masses and of whites who have risen above race prejudice not by philanthropy but by brotherly and sympathetic sharing of the Negro's burden and identification with it as part of their own. Without the help of the trade unionists, white and black, without the Progressives and radicals, without Socialists and Communists and lovers of peace all over the world, my voice would now be stilled forever. (155)

The alignment is new, but the principle is old. Black experience remains a touchstone for true idealism. The measure of sincerity is one's willingness to identify with blacks and their ideal, especially as these have been defined and enacted by Du Bois himself. It is not sufficient to express sympathy; one must, in a sense, will oneself black, just as Du Bois described himself doing in *Dusk of Dawn*. Conscious self-sacrifice remains the standard by which an elite is determined.

What he does in effect is engender a new America in the act of repudiating the father figures of the old. Those who accept his spiritual fatherhood are the new nation that will emerge from the ruins produced by those currently in power. But the new nation will work precisely because its principles are the old ones of democracy, morality, and reason. He is its father because he has stood for these when all around him have failed.

The personal meaning of his worldview is the subject of *The Autobiography of W. E. B. Du Bois*. On one level, the book is an experiment in Marxist self-analysis. History is shown to create consciousness. The events and economic conditions of the world make Du Bois the person he is. The connection is not an overly simple one. His middle-class (in terms of values, not family income) childhood in Great Barrington results in his early bourgeois thinking. But it is the entire cultural context that molds him: "The chief criterion of local social standing was property and ancestry; but the ancestors were never magnates like the patroons of the manors along the Hudson to the west. . . . They were usually ordinary folk of solid respectability, farm owners, or artisans merging into industry. Standing did not depend on what the ancestor did, or who he was, but rather that he existed, lived decently and thus linked the individual to the community."[3]

The fact of wealth was not overly obvious in such a town. Du Bois himself was from one of the old families and thus, despite poverty, was given access to the homes and lives of the well-to-do citizens. Class lines were not clearly drawn except against Irish laborers, a prejudice the young William shared (*Autobiography*, 82). In many ways, the Great Barrington of his childhood is shown to be outside the capitalist mainstream. The values learned there were not greed and self-interested individualism. Instead, a strong emphasis was placed on respectability, moral probity, tradition, and socially responsible individuality. Economic assumptions were also evident: "I grew up in the midst of definite ideas as to wealth and poverty, work and charity. Wealth was the result of work and saving and the rich rightly inherited the earth. The poor, on the whole, were themselves to be blamed. They were unfortunate and if so their fortunes could be mended with care. But chiefly, they were 'shiftless,' and 'shiftlessness' was unforgivable" (80).

The problem for Du Bois as narrator is how to separate the moral values from the economic ones. He has to demonstrate that the system of production created notions that had to be overcome so that later he might see the Marxist light. But Great Barrington would not easily lend itself to repudiation; it was simply too nice a place in which to grow up. He has to distinguish two sets of principles and in fact use the moral values to reject the economic ones.

This complex reading of his development is possible because he does not insist on a rigid Marxist perspective. It becomes the whole cultural experience rather than the economic order that determines his identity. Though he occasionally makes reductive assertions about economic determinism, the subtler point is that this particular time and place shaped him.[4] The town meeting, in which everyone had the opportunity to speak and be listened to, remained throughout his life the model of true democracy. The ideals of community and social responsibility at the heart of his concept of leadership grew out of life in this town of neighbors. His struggle for racial equality had as one of its sources the lack of discrimination he claims to have experienced as a child. Even his critique of capitalism can be seen as a response to the failure of that system to live up to the economic opportunities and fairness of Great Barrington. It was a place in which the moral order did not openly conflict with the economic one, and it thus created the expectation of harmony in the larger world. The quest for that harmony is one of the themes of Du Bois's life and writing. Consistent with this view, his opening description has more power than later criticisms of its factories:

> I was born by a golden river and in the shadow of two great hills, five
> years after the Emancipation Proclamation, which began the freeing of the
> American Negro slaves. The valley was wreathed in grass and trees and
> crowned to the eastward by the huge bulk of East Mountain, with crag and
> cave and dark forest. Westward the hill was gentler, rolling up to gorgeous
> sunsets and cloud-swept storms. The town of Great Barrington, which lay

between these mountains in Berkshire County, Western Massachusetts, had a broad Main Street, lined with maples and elms, with white picket fences before the homes. The climate was to our thought quite perfect. (*Autobiography*, 61)

It is a valley of dreams and ideals in which a child gains clear views of what constitutes goodness and truth, not merely from being told, but by living in such a place. The Du Bois who narrates this passage and who shortly after writing it renounced his American citizenship, obviously felt strongly about this all-American town. His characterization of it suggests what might be called a radicalism of nostalgia.[5] Great Barrington represents order, equality, democracy, community, virtue, and tranquility. At that moment of history in that place, utopia was achieved. Figuring it in such a way allows Du Bois to establish an American basis for what many readers would see as his alien politics and critique of America.

His comments on the writing of autobiography are significant in this regard: "What I think of myself, now and in the past, furnishes no certain document proving what I really am. Mostly my life today is a mass of memories with vast omissions, matters which are forgotten accidently or by deep design. . . . This book then is the soliloquy of an old man on what he dreams his life has been as he sees it slowly drifting away; and what he would like others to believe" (*Autobiography*, 12–13). The conjunction here of omission, dream, and design is important. This "soliloquy" is, after all, a waking, not a sleeping dream. The memory of Great Barrington is presented in such a way as to provide us with a key to the man doing the remembering. It is a lesson in how to read the town, the life, and the writer. The life story becomes the quest to remake the nation in the image of the remembered town. The experiencing self of that story becomes the protagonist, because he lived according to its values. And the writer becomes worthy of our attention, because his current values and beliefs further those principles. But the nation's corruption and recalcitrance have led him to a position of resistance and radicalism. The autobiography seeks then to fix the memory and its significance outside of the ravages of time and politics and to extend it even beyond the life of the man remembering.

The self that is formed by this memory is the subject of a chapter entitled "My Character." Separating one's character into a distinct section of the story of the self is a peculiar gesture; moreover, as the editors of the Library of America volume on Du Bois point out, this is the only wholly new chapter in the book, indicating that Du Bois felt it both possible and desirable to distinguish character from other aspects of identity.[6] But something particular is meant by "character": "When I was a young man, we talked much of character. At Fisk University character was discussed and emphasized more than scholarship. I knew what was meant and agreed that the sort of person a man was would in the long run prove more important than what he knew or how logically he could think. . . . I still retain an interest in what men are rather than what they do" (*Autobiography*, 277). Concern for "what men are" suggests an essence that precedes existence, a principle at odds with any sort of historical or cultural determinism. When Du Bois catalogues the specific elements of his own character, however, he makes it clear that he is speaking of learned values, not inherent ones, though the actual distinction is less clear than he implies. He talks about his honesty, his lack of interest in financial gain, his sexual prudence, his shyness, his nondogmatic Christianity, his reverence for life, and his sense of social responsibility. Most of these have been specifically mentioned in discussing the impact of Great Barrington on him.

He presents all of these, including sexuality, as behavior learned at particular times and in particular ways; he excludes the unconscious from his narrative. Behaviors and values are consciously taught and consciously accepted as good, leaving the impression that, in one sense, the autobiography teaches us nothing about its author that could not be learned from his other writings.

His discussion of his sexuality provides an instructive example: "Indeed the chief blame which I lay on my New England schooling was the inexcusable ignorance of sex which I had when I went south to Fisk at 17. I was precipitated into a region, with loose sex morals among black and white, while I actually did not know the physical difference between men and women" (279–80). This ignorance had the important effect of making him seek bad advice. "It began to turn one of the most beautiful of life's experiences into a thing of temptation and horror" (280). Sexuality needs to be taught, to be rationalized, so that one does not experience "horror." Mastery of the self, such an important value to him, can only be achieved if ambiguity and unconscious urges are brought into the realm of rational discourse.

The results of a lack of sexual education are shocking:

> Then, as a teacher in the rural districts of East Tennessee, I was literally raped by the unhappy wife who was my landlady. From that time through my college course at Harvard and my study in Europe, I went through a desperately recurring fight to keep the sex instinct in control. A brief trial with prostitution in Paris affronted my sense of decency. I lived more or less regularly with a shop girl in Berlin, but was ashamed. Then when I returned home to teach, I was faced with the connivance of certain fellow teachers at adultery with their wives. I was literally frightened into marriage before I was able to support a family. (280)

This recollection is an argument of sorts for sex education. Ignorance leads to rape, prostitution, adultery, and premature marriage. This detailing of sexual experiences appeared in none of the earlier autobiographical writings, in part because his first wife was still living when most of those works were written. He presents it in this work to demonstrate the problems of nineteenth-century education and culture.

But attention should be paid to the need to detail them at all. The fear of the unconscious that made the experiences so painful initially motivates him to rationalize them at this late date. By putting them into words, he controls and refines his memory of them. They demonstrate simultaneously his potency and his morality. His manhood is proven by both his experiences and his resistance to them. A natural impulse is brought by the autobiographer under the guidance of a system of rational ethics, which presupposes that a natural instinct is to be feared. Given the language of the narrative—"desperately," "ashamed," "connivance," "frightened"—seventy years after the events, the temptation to surrender must have been very powerful. Reason takes on heroic qualities in the face of such odds.

The struggle with sexuality symbolizes the narrative's theme of lifelong resistance to nonrational forces. Du Bois fights, singly or in combination, racism, self-interest, and war. In this last book, he confronts the ultimate unknown, death: "We know that Death is the End of Life. Even when we profess to deny this we know that this hope is mere wishful thinking, pretense broidered with abject and cowardly Fear. Our endless egotism cannot conceive a world without Us and yet we know that this will happen and the world will be happier for it" (412–13). Even this ultimate irrationality must be treated in a rational manner. Death is a fact of existence to be faced without emotion or self-interested religious delusion. "I have lived a good and full life. I have finished my course. I do not want to live this life again. I have tasted its delights and pleasures; I have known its pain, suffering and despair. I am tired, I am through" (413).

But the calmness with which he contemplates his physical demise does not hold when he considers the meaning of the life he has lived. He uneasily foresees the possibility that his physical death may mean his disappearance as a fact of history. The annihilation that was hinted at in *In Battle for Peace* now receives explicit comment. He comments on the effects of his trial:

> I lost my leadership of my race. It was a dilemma for the mass of Negroes;
> either they joined the current beliefs and actions of most whites or they
> could not make a living or hope for preferment. Preferment was possible.
> The color line was beginning to break. Negroes were getting recogni-
> tion as never before. Was not the sacrifice of one man small payment for
> this? Even those who disagreed with this judgment at least kept quiet. The
> colored children ceased to hear my name. (395)

The ironies in this statement are rich. The very integration that Du Bois spent his life fighting for becomes the basis of his martyrdom. The prophet of self-sacrifice is sacrificed so others may realize his vision. The great black historian is himself denied a place in history. The very visibility with which he pursued the truth has led to his invisibility.

But Du Bois refuses to go quietly. *The Autobiography* is filled with statements by others of his reality and significance. He notes the honors received from various universities and the attention given him by vari- ous governments. He cites in full the statement of the NAACP board upon accepting his resignation in 1934. He drops the names of dozens of individuals with whom he was acquainted and who had only good things to say about him.

What is demonstrated in this catalogue of recognition is not mere egotism. Instead, like the slave narrators who used the words of others to validate their characters and stories, Du Bois "proves" himself and his importance by a range of external references. Denied by others a role in history, he will invent one for himself and show its reality. If "the colored children" do not hear his name, it will not be because his name is unworthy.

But he does more than designate names and places that verify his existence. He replicates his authorial career by anthologizing his earlier writings. Most of *The Autobiography* is drawn directly from *The Souls of Black Folk, Darkwater, Dusk of Dawn,* and *In Battle for Peace.* In many cases, he does so even though the works quoted are ideologically at odds with his present position. But it is clear that surface ideological consistency is secondary to the necessity of generating a self that is unitary and whole. Du Bois reinscribes his personal narrative, bringing it into one text so that it cannot be lost. He both justifies and captures his life by taking over the past in such a way. He invests his earlier work with greater authority by recognizing it in his last book. His life thus has integrity in both senses of the term: it is a life of principle and a life of unity. By putting it all in one place, he proclaims a coherence that others may not see and makes it more difficult to be forgotten, to be silenced. He does the job that other historians, by ignorance or design, may fail to do. He resists invisibility by reproducing, not merely the events of his life, but the very words by which he made sense of it. The word gives substance to the flesh. He may be the sacrifice by which his people are saved, but his writings transubstantiate him. In making a text of texts of himself, he engenders a version of the self that transcends history.

The last lines of the book, addressed to the dead, complete his transcendence:

Reveal, Ancient of Days, the Present in the Past and prophesy the End in the Beginning. For this is a beautiful world; this is a wonderful America, which the founding fathers dreamed until their sons drowned it in the blood of slavery and devoured it in greed. Our children must rebuild it. Let then the Dreams of the Dead rebuke the Blind who think that what is will be forever and teach them that what was worth living for must live again and that which merited death must stay dead. Teach us, Forever Dead, there is no Dream but Deed, there is no deed but Memory. (422–23)

Du Bois does not leave the final validation of his life to the whims of fallible, corruptible humans. Instead he grounds it in the nature of the universe. As one who has devoted himself to deed and memory, his triumph is ultimately assured. In this final statement in his final book, he returns to the fathers of his first one and defines the nation's sins in terms of the order that they generated. A new and truer nation must be made by the generations he and those like him have produced. But such a new nation will be grounded in the ancient principles he has spent his life struggling for. He authors his life in such a way as to authorize his vision of the future. In the name of the father, he proclaims his fatherhood of America.

Notes

· · · · · · · · ·

Introduction: The Word and the Self

1. "Program for the Celebration of My Twenty-fifth Birthday." Ms., cover page. W. E. B. Du Bois Papers, University of Massachusetts Archives. Further references to this work will be cited in the text.

2. Allison Davis, in a brief psychological study, argues that Du Bois experienced anxiety in his life about the possibility of his own illegitimacy. See *Leadership, Love, and Aggression* (New York: Harcourt, Brace, Jovanovich, 1983), 106–8.

3. *The Gift of Black Folk: Negroes in the Making of America* (Boston: Stratford, 1924), 262–65.

4. See Davis, *Leadership*, 105–52.

5. See *Young Man Luther: A Study in Psychoanalysis and History* (New York: Norton, 1958), 63–67.

6. See *Young Man Luther*, 43.

7. See *Young Man Luther*, 47.

8. "Ideology" is used here in Erikson's sense of the effort "to create a world image convincing enough to support the collective and the individual sense of identity" (*Young Man Luther*, 22).

9. "Talented tenth" is the name Du Bois used for educated, sophisticated African Americans he believed should lead the race.

10. The "Law of the Father" is Lacan's term for the moral order created by civilization and which he argues has as a primary function the suppression of desire. See *Écrits: A Selection*, trans. Alan Sheriden (New York: Norton, 1978), 66, and Juliet Flower MacCannell, *Figuring Lacan: Criticism and the Cultural Unconscious* (Lincoln: University of Nebraska Press, 1986), 121–26.

1. Master and Man

1. See Houston Baker, "The Black Man of Culture: W. E. B. Du Bois and *The Souls of Black Folk*" in *Critical Essays on W. E. B. Du Bois*, ed. William Andrews (Boston: G. K. Hall, 1985), 129–38, for another reading of Du Bois as cultural figure.

2. For a detailed discussion of the rhetorical forms used in the book, see Arnold Rampersad, *The Art and Imagination of W. E. B. Du Bois* (Cambridge: Harvard University Press, 1976), 68–90.

3. *The Souls of Black Folk* (Chicago: A. C. McClurg, 1903), v. Further references to this work will be cited in the text.

4. "Signifying" is the black rhetorical device of indirect commentary, often implicitly critical. For a detailed discussion, see Gates, *The Signifying Monkey: A Theory of Afro-American Literary Criticism* (New York: Oxford University Press, 1988), especially 44–88.

5. Jacques Lacan argues that the "gaze" creates the sense of otherness. See *Four Fundamental Concepts of Psycho-Analysis*, trans. Alan Sheridan (New York: Norton, 1978), 214.

6. Anthony Appiah has extensively examined the meaning of "race" in Du Bois's thought. See "The Uncompleted Argument: Du Bois and the Illusion of Race" in *"Race," Writing, and Difference*, ed. Henry Louis Gates, Jr. (New York: Oxford University Press, 1988), 21–37.

7. See *Principles of Psychology* (New York: Holt, 1890), 1: 399.

8. James Baldwin perceives precisely such a problem in Richard Wright's *Native Son*. See "Everybody's Protest Novel" in *Notes of a Native Son* (New York: Bantam, 1964), 9–17.

9. See William J. Scheick, *The Half-Blood: A Cultural Symbol in 19th Century American Fiction* (Lexington: University of Kentucky Press, 1979) and Judith R. Berzon, *Neither White nor Black: The Mulatto Character in American Fiction* (New York: New York University Press, 1978) on the representations of mulattoes in American culture.

10. See, among other works, Ann Douglas's *The Feminization of American Culture* (New York: Knopf, 1977).

11. In addition to nineteenth-century critics of industrialism and capitalism such as Emerson, Thoreau, Arnold, and Ruskin, see also T. J. Jackson Lears, *No Place of Grace: Antimodernism and the Transformation of American Culture, 1880–1920* (New York: Pantheon, 1981), on the ideological implications of anticapitalist thought.

12. Du Bois consistently identifies the strong figures of the race as mascu-

line. In contrast, the masses are represented in much of his work in traditionally feminine terms.

13. See Lacan on the Name of the Father, the symbolic mode by which patriarchy maintains its hegemony over all its members, male and female. *Écrits: A Selection*, trans. Alan Sheridan (New York: Norton, 1977), 67.

14. See the review in *The Dial*, 16 July 1901: 53–55; reprinted in Du Bois, *Book Reviews*, ed. Herbert Aptheker (White Plains: Kraus-Thomson, 1985), 3–5.

15. Du Bois's Harvard commencement address was on Davis, describing him as "a typical Teutonic hero" who had an "overweening sense of the I and the consequent forgetting of the Thou" (*Writings*, 811–12).

16. On this essay as elegy, see Rampersad, *Art and Imagination*, 72–73.

17. See "Criteria of Negro Art," *The Crisis* 32 (October 1926): 290, 292, 294, 296–97. Though written several years after *The Souls of Black Folk*, this essay clearly reflects principles Du Bois held throughout his career.

18. See *From behind the Veil: A Study of Afro-American Narrative* (Urbana: University of Illinois Press, 1979), 52–91.

2. "Cold-Blooded Science"

1. See Thorpe, *Black Historians: A Critique* (New York: William Morrow, 1971), 9–10.

2. See *Metahistory: The Historical Imagination in Nineteenth-Century Europe* (Baltimore: Johns Hopkins University Press, 1973), x–xi.

3. See Broderick, *W. E. B. Du Bois: Negro Leader in a Time of Crisis* (Stanford: Stanford University Press, 1959), 27–28, and Rampersad, *Art and Imagination*, 19–67.

4. *The Suppression of the Slave-Trade to the United States, 1638–1870* (1896; New York: Dover, 1970), x. All further references to this work appear in the text.

5. In addition to Broderick and Rampersad, see Harry Elmer Barnes, ed., *The History and Prospects of the Social Sciences* (New York: Knopf, 1925); L. L. and Jessie Bernard, *Origins of American Sociology: The Social Science Movement in the United States* (New York: Crowell, 1943); Jurgen Herbst, *The German Historical School in American Scholarship: A Study in the Transfer of Culture* (Ithaca: Cornell University Press, 1965); and John Higham, *History: The Development of Historical Studies in the United States* (Englewood Cliffs: Prentice-Hall, 1965).

6. Broderick, *W. E. B. Du Bois*, 17.

7. The moralistic reference to "whiskey-using" suggests that biography plays a part in the moral vision here. As a young man in Great Barrington, Du Bois belonged to an abstinence club. See *The Autobiography of W. E. B. Du Bois: A Soliloquy on Viewing My Life from the Last Decade of Its First Century* (New York: International Publishers, 1968), 81–82.

8. See Rampersad's discussion of the religious influence of Du Bois's early life, 1–18.

9. Julius Lester, ed., *The Seventh Son: The Thought and Writings of W. E. B. Du Bois* (New York: Random House, 1971), 1:187.

10. Herbst, *The German Historical School*, 143.

11. Elliott Rudwick, "W. E. B. Du Bois as Sociologist," in *Black Sociologists: Historical and Contemporary Perspectives*, ed. James E. Blackwell and Morris Janowitz (Chicago: University of Chicago Press, 1974), 26.

12. *The Philadelphia Negro: A Social Study* (1899; New York: Schocken Books, 1967), 3. All further references to this work appear in the text.

13. *The Black Bourgeoisie* (New York: Free Press, 1957).

14. "The Talented Tenth" was published in *The Negro Problem: A Series of Articles by Representative American Negroes of To-day* (New York: James Pott, 1903), 33–75; "The Conservation of Races" was presented to the Negro Academy in 1897 and is discussed in chapter 4 of this book.

3. The Propaganda of History

1. *Black Reconstruction in America: An Essay toward a History of the Part Which Black Folk Played in the Attempt to Reconstruct Democracy in America, 1860–1880* (1935; New York: World Publishing, 1964), 725. All further references to this work will be cited in the text.

2. *The Politics of History* (Boston: Beacon Press, 1970), 24.

3. See Abram Harris, "Reconstruction and the Negro," *New Republic* 7 (August 1935): 367–88; Ralph Bunche, "Reconstruction Reinterpreted," *Journal of Negro Education* 4 (October 1935): 568; Sterling Spero, "The Negro's Role," *The Nation*, 24 July 1935, 108–9; and James O. Young, *Black Writers of the Thirties* (Baton Rouge: Louisiana State University Press, 1973), 121–27.

4. The "American Assumption" is Du Bois's label for the belief that every person in America, with freedom and hard work, can become prosperous.

4. Inscribing the Race

1. See Appiah, "Uncompleted Argument," for a different reading of Du Bois. For discussions of various aspects of the discourse on race, see Donald P. DeNevi and Doris A. Holmes, *Racism at the Turn of the Century: Documentary Perspectives, 1870–1910* (San Rafael: Leswing, 1973); Thomas F. Gossett, *Race: The History of an Idea in America* (Dallas: Southern Methodist University Press, 1963); George W. Stocking, Jr., *Race, Culture, and Evolution: Essays in the History of Anthropology* (New York: Free Press, 1968); George M. Frederickson, *The Black Image in the White Mind: The Debate on Afro-American Character and Destiny, 1817–1914* (New York: Harper, 1971); R. Fred Wacker, *Ethnicity, Pluralism, and Race: Race Relations Theory in the United States before Myrdal* (Westport: Greenwood, 1983); Werner Sollors, *Beyond Ethnicity: Consent and Descent in American Culture* (New York: Oxford University Press, 1986); Berzon, *Neither Black nor White*; Scheick, *The Half-Blood*; and various essays in Gates, ed., *"Race," Writing, and Difference.*

2. See Stocking, *Race, Culture, and Evolution*, 110–32.

3. See Gossett, *Race*, 144–97.

4. Frederickson, *The Black Image*, 97–129.

5. See *Encyclopedia of Philosophy*.

6. *The Gift of Black Folk*, 1. Further references to this work will be cited in the text.

7. *The Opening Up of Africa* (New York: Henry Holt, n.d.), 25. Elsewhere in his work, Johnston indicates that virtually all aspects of culture found in Africa—agriculture, religion, even language itself—had Caucasian origins.

8. See Patrick Brantlinger, "Victorians and Africans: The Genealogy of the Myth of the Dark Continent" in Gates, ed., *"Race," Writing, and Difference*, 185–222; John Cullen Gruesser, *White on Black: Contemporary Literature about Africa* (Urbana: University of Illinois Press, 1992); Abdul JanMohamed, "The Economy of Manichean Allegory: The Function of Racial Difference in Colonialist Literature," in Gates, ed., *"Race," Writing, and Difference*, 78–106; and Christopher Miller, *Blank Darkness: Africanist Discourse in French* (Chicago: University of Chicago Press, 1985), for detailed discussions of European views of Africa. Both the term *Africanist discourse* and the image of blankness originated with Miller. Eric Sundquist's recent work on race in American literature argues persuasively that one overlooked source of Du Bois's views on Africa came out of Ethiopianism, a messianic and political perspective that linked nationalist impulses with African Christian church beliefs and activities. See *To Wake the Nations: Race in the Making of American Literature* (Cambridge: Harvard University Press, 1993), 540–81.

9. See Elliott P. Skinner, *African Americans and U.S. Policy toward Africa, 1850–1924* (Washington: Howard University Press, 1992) for a detailed discussion of the history and politics of the movement.

10. See Boas, *Race and Democratic Society* (New York: J. J. Augustin, 1945), 61–69.

11. See Royce, *Race Questions, Provincialism and Other American Problems* (New York: Macmillan, 1908).

5. The Propaganda of Art

1. Du Bois to Guggenheim Memorial Foundation (Henry Allen Moe), 16 November 1927. W. E. B. Du Bois Papers, University of Massachusetts Archives.

2. Review of Hughes, *Not without Laughter*, in Herbert Aptheker, ed., *Book Reviews* (White Plains: Kraus-Thomson, 1985), 149–50; review of McKay, *Home to Harlem*, *Book Reviews*, 113–14; review of Toomer, *Cane*, "Younger Literary Movement," *The Crisis* 27 (February 1924): 161–62.

3. See Addison Gayle, Jr., ed., *The Black Aesthetic* (New York: Doubleday, 1971), 175–81.

4. John Francis McDermott to Du Bois, 25 May 1930; Du Bois to McDermott, 3 June 1930. W. E. B. Du Bois Papers, University of Massachusetts Archives.

5. In *W. E. B. Du Bois: Writings*, Nathan Huggins, ed. (New York: Library of America, 1986), 1000. Further references to this work will be cited in the text.

6. See Houston A. Baker, Jr., *Modernism and the Harlem Renaissance* (Chicago: University of Chicago Press, 1987), 71–107, for a discussion of modernism in early twentieth-century writing.

7. *The Crisis* 31 (January 1926): 141. Further references to this work will be cited in the text.

8. All further references to this work will be cited in the text.

9. See M. M. Bakhtin, *The Dialogic Imagination: Four Essays*, ed. Michael Holquist, trans. Caryl Emerson and Michael Holquist (Austin: University of Texas Press, 1981), esp. 41–83.

6. Race and Romance

1. Thomas Nelson Page was only the most prominent of a large group of "plantation school" writers. See Lucinda MacKethan, "Plantation Fiction, 1865–1900" in *The History of Southern Literature*, ed. Louis D. Rubin, Jr. et al. (Baton Rouge: Louisiana State University Press, 1985), 209–18.

2. *The Quest of the Silver Fleece* (1911; Miami: Mnemosyne, 1969), xi. Further references to this work will be cited in the text.

3. "Up from servility" echoes Booker T. Washington's *Up from Slavery* and thus suggests in context a covert attack on Du Bois's political nemesis.

4. While studying in Germany, he prepared a thesis on the economics of Southern agriculture.

5. See Herbert Ross Brown, *The Sentimental Novel in America, 1789–1860* (Durham: Duke University Press, 1940), 34.

6. For another interpretation of Zora, see Nellie McKay, "W. E. B. Du Bois: The Black Women in His Writings—Selected Fictional and Autobiographical Portraits" in Andrews, *W. E. B. Du Bois*, 230–52.

7. *Allegory: The Theory of a Symbolic Mode* (Ithaca: Cornell University Press, 1964), 22–23.

8. *Dark Princess: A Romance* (1928; Millwood, N.Y.: Kraus-Thomson, 1974), 18. Further references to this work will be cited in the text.

7. Revisions and Visions

1. *The Ordeal of Mansart* (New York: Mainstream, 1957), 315. Further references to this work will be cited in the text.

2. See White, *Metahistory*, 1–42.

3. For Du Bois's attitude on Garvey, see "Marcus Garvey," *The Crisis* 21 (December 1920 and January 1921): 58, 60, 112–15; "The Black Star Line," *The Crisis* 24 (September 1922): 210–14; and "A Lunatic or a Traitor," *The Crisis* 28 (May 1924): 8–9.

4. *Mansart Builds a School* (New York: Mainstream, 1959), 35. Further references will be to *School* and cited in the text.

5. *Worlds of Color* (New York: Mainstream, 1961), 174–75. Further references will be cited in the text.

6. See *The Art and Imagination of W. E. B. Du Bois*, 274–75.

7. Compare Rampersad, *Art and Imagination*, 281–82.

8. Rampersad, *Art and Imagination*, 282.

9. The two cases appear in *Worlds*, 262–66; and *In Battle for Peace: The Story of My 83rd Birthday* (1952; Millwood, N.Y.: Kraus-Thomson, 1976), discussed here in chapter 10.

10. See *Dusk of Dawn: An Essay toward an Autobiography of a Race Concept* (1940; New York: Schocken, 1968), chapter 2.

11. Rampersad, *Art and Imagination*, 284.

8. History as Hagiography

1. Letters between Du Bois and Ellis Oberholtzer of the George W. Jacobs Co. are collected in Herbert Aptheker, ed., *The Correspondence of W. E. B. Du Bois* (Amherst: University of Massachusetts Press, 1973–78), 1:60–65.

2. *John Brown* (1909; New York: International Publishers, 1962), 7. Further references to this work will be cited in the text.

3. See Lawrence Levine, *Black Culture and Black Consciousness: Afro-American Folk Thought from Slavery to Freedom* (Oxford: Oxford University Press, 1977), passim, for the worldview of slaves.

4. See *Radicals and Conservatives: And Other Essays on the Negro in America* (1908; New York: Schocken, 1968).

5. This may be Du Bois's effort to radically revise Washington's contribution, published in 1906, to the series.

6. See the following chapters on Du Bois's autobiographies for this view of himself.

7. See Richard O. Boyer, *The Legend of John Brown: A Biography and a History* (New York: Knopf, 1973); Stephen Oates, *To Purge This Land with Blood: A Biography of John Brown* (New York: Harper, 1970); Oswald Garrison Villard, *John Brown, 1800–1859* (1910; New York: Knopf, 1943) and Robert Penn Warren, *John Brown: The Making of a Martyr* (New York: Payson and Clark, 1929).

8. See Larzar Ziff, *Puritanism in America: New Culture in a New World* (New York: Viking, 1973), 149–50, for a discussion of the fair-price principle.

9. See the full review in *The Nation*, 28 October 1909, 405.

10. See *Correspondence* 1:153–64.

9. The Propaganda of Life

1. Stepto, *From Behind the Veil*, and Andrews, *To Tell a Free Story: The First Century of Afro-American Autobiography* (Urbana: University of Illinois Press, 1986).

2. Andrews, *To Tell a Free Story*, 1–2.

3. Joanne M. Braxton, *Black Women Writing Autobiography: A Tradition within a Tradition* (Philadelphia: Temple University Press, 1989), 5.

4. "W. E. B. Du Bois's *Autobiography* and the Politics of Literature," *Black American Forum* 24 (1990): 308.

5. *Darkwater: Voices from within the Veil* (1921; New York: Schocken, 1969), vii. Further references to this work will be cited in the text.

6. See Christopher Lasch, *The New Radicalism in America, 1889–1963: The Intellectual as Social Type* (New York: Vintage, 1965); and Robert Wiebe, *The Search for Order, 1877–1920* (New York: Hill and Wang, 1967).

7. Three essays in *The Crisis* argued for Wilson's election in 1912: "Politics," vol. 4 (August 1912): 180; "The Last Word in Politics," vol. 5 (November 1912): 29; and "The Election," vol. 5 (December 1912): 75–76.

8. See Addams, *Twelve Years at Hull House* (1910; New York: New American Library, 1960); and Frederic Howe, *Confessions of a Reformer* (1925; Chicago: Quadrangle, 1967).

9. *Dusk of Dawn: An Essay toward an Autobiography of a Race Concept* (1940; New York: Schocken, 1968), 1–2. Further references to this work will be cited in the text.

10. Du Bois's own interpretation here is at odds with the readings of his life offered by Francis Broderick, *W. E. B. Du Bois;* Elliott Rudwick, *W. E. B. Du Bois: Voice of the Black Protest Movement* (Urbana: University of Illinois Press, 1982); and August Meier, *Negro Thought in America, 1880–1915* (Ann Arbor: University of Michigan Press, 1963), who see him reaching a dead end at this point in his career and being saved by the NAACP.

11. See Anthony Appiah's contention in "The Uncompleted Argument" that Du Bois's earlier work depended on such a position.

10. Seizing the Self

1. *In Battle for Peace*, 161. Further references to this work will be cited in the text.

2. The insults against Wallace and Rogge, with their flagrantly insincere qualifications, suggest the pleasure Du Bois seems to take in his verbal aggres-

siveness. This is reinforced with the pun on Oetje John Rogge's name in the title of chapter 11: "Oh! John Rogge." In this way, Du Bois takes control not merely of the characters of traitors but also the very names by which they will be known to history.

3. *The Autobiography of W. E. B. Du Bois*, 80. Further references to this work will be cited in the text.

4. See Frederic Woodard, "W. E. B. Du Bois: The Native Impulse: Notes Toward an Ideological Biography, 1868–1897" (Ph.D. dissertation, University of Iowa, 1976), for an argument that Great Barrington is the source of Du Bois's politics.

5. See Wiebe and Lasch, among others, for discussions of American radicalism and its ties to views of an earlier America.

6. See *Writings*, 1308.

Bibliography

. . . .

Works by W. E. B. Du Bois

The Autobiography of W. E. B. Du Bois: A Soliloquy on Viewing My Life from the Last Decade of Its First Century. New York: International Publishers, 1968.

In Battle for Peace: The Story of My 83rd Birthday. 1952. Reprint. Millwood, N.Y.: Kraus-Thomson, 1976.

Black Folk, Then and Now: An Essay in the History and Sociology of the Negro People. New York: Henry Holt, 1939.

Black Reconstruction in America: An Essay toward a History of the Part Which Black Folk Played in the Attempt to Reconstruct Democracy in America, 1860–1880. New York: Harcourt, Brace, 1935.

Book Reviews. Edited by Herbert Aptheker. White Plains: Kraus-Thomson, 1985.

"The Conservation of Races." American Negro Academy Occasional Paper, no. 2. Washington, D.C.: American Negro Academy, 1897. Reprinted in *Writings*, 815–26.

The Correspondence of W. E. B. Du Bois. 3 vols. Edited by Herbert Aptheker. Amherst: University of Massachusetts Press, 1973–78.

Creative Writings. Edited by Herbert Aptheker. White Plains: Kraus-Thomson, 1985.

"The Criteria of Negro Art." *The Crisis* 32 (October 1926): 292.

Dark Princess: A Romance. 1928. Reprint. Millwood, N.Y.: Kraus-Thomson, 1974.

Darkwater: Voices from within the Veil. 1921. Reprint. New York: Schocken, 1969.

Dusk of Dawn: An Essay toward an Autobiography of a Race Concept. 1940. Reprint. New York: Schocken, 1968.

The Gift of Black Folk: Negroes in the Making of America. Boston: Stratford, 1924.

John Brown. 1909. Reprint. New York: International Publishers, 1962.

Mansart Builds a School. (Vol. 2 of *The Black Flame.*) New York: Mainstream, 1959.

The Negro. New York: Henry Holt, 1915.

The Ordeal of Mansart. (Vol. 1 of *The Black Flame.*) New York: Mainstream, 1957.

The Philadelphia Negro: A Social Study. 1899. Reprint. New York: Schocken, 1967.

"Program for the Celebration of My Twenty-fifth Birthday." MS. W. E. B. Du Bois Papers, University of Massachusetts Archives, Amherst, Mass.

The Quest of the Silver Fleece. 1911. Reprint. Miami: Mnemosyne, 1969.

Review of Alain Locke, *The New Negro. The Crisis* 31 (January 1926): 140–41.

Review of Langston Hughes, *Not Without Laughter. The Crisis* 37 (September 1930): 313, 321.

The Souls of Black Folk. Chicago: A. C. McClurg, 1903.

"The Study of Negro Problems." *American Academy of Political and Social Sciences Annals* 11 (1898): 1–23.

The Suppression of the African Slave-Trade to the United States, 1638–1870. 1896. Reprint. New York: Dover, 1970.

W. E. B. Du Bois: Writings. Edited by Nathan Huggins. New York: Library of America, 1986.

The World and Africa. 1946. Rev. ed. New York: International Publishers, 1965.

Worlds of Color. (Vol. 3 of *The Black Flame.*) New York: Mainstream, 1961.

"The Younger Literary Movement." *The Crisis* 27 (February 1924): 161–62.

Other Sources

Addams, Jane. *Twenty Years at Hull House.* 1910. Reprint. New York: New American Library, 1960.

Andrews, William L. *To Tell a Free Story: The First Century of Afro-American Autobiography.* Urbana: University of Illinois Press, 1986.

———, ed. *Critical Essays on W. E. B. Du Bois.* Boston: G. K. Hall, 1985.

Appiah, Anthony. "The Uncompleted Argument: Du Bois and the Illusion of Race." In *"Race," Writing, and Difference,* edited by Henry Louis Gates, Jr., 21–37. New York: Oxford University Press, 1988.

Aptheker, Herbert, ed. *Annotated Bibliography of the Published Writings of W. E. B. Du Bois.* Millwood, N.Y.: Kraus-Thomson, 1973.

Auerbach, Erich. *Mimesis: The Representation of Reality in Western Literature*, translated by Willard R. Trask. Princeton: Princeton University Press, 1953.

Baker, Houston A., Jr. "The Black Man of Culture: W. E. B. Du Bois and *The Souls of Black Folk*." In *Critical Essays on W. E. B. Du Bois*, edited by William Andrews, 129–38. Boston: G. K. Hall, 1985.

———. *Long Black Song: Essays in Black American Literature and Culture*. Charlottesville: University Press of Virginia, 1972.

———. *Modernism and the Harlem Renaissance*. Chicago: University of Chicago Press, 1987.

Bakhtin, M. M. *The Dialogic Imagination: Four Essays*. Edited by Michael Holquist, translated by Caryl Emerson and Michael Holquist. Austin: University of Texas Press, 1981.

Baldwin, James. *Notes of a Native Son*. Boston: Beacon Press, 1955.

Barnard, F. M., ed. *J. G. Herder on Social and Political Culture*. Cambridge: Cambridge University Press, 1969.

Barnes, Harry Elmer, ed. *The History and Prospects of the Social Sciences*. New York: Knopf, 1925.

Bernard, Jessie, and L. L. Bernard. *Origins of American Sociology: The Social Science Movement in the United States*. New York: Crowell, 1943.

Berzon, Judith R. *Neither White nor Black: The Mulatto Character in American Fiction*. New York: New York University Press, 1978.

Blackwell, James E., and Morris Janowitz, eds. *Black Sociologists: Historical and Contemporary Perspectives*. Chicago: University of Chicago Press, 1974.

Blasing, Mutlu Konuk. *The Art of Life: Studies in American Autobiographical Literature*. Austin: University of Texas Press, 1977.

Boas, Franz. *Race and Democratic Society*. New York: J. J. Augustin, 1945.

Bone, Robert. *The Negro Novel in America*. New Haven: Yale University Press, 1958.

Bowers, Claude G. *The Tragic Era: The Revolution after Lincoln*. Boston: Houghton Mifflin, 1929.

Boyer, Richard O. *The Legend of John Brown: A Biography and a History*. New York: Knopf, 1973.

Bracey, John, August Meier, and Elliott Rudwick. *Black Nationalism in America*. Indianapolis: Bobbs-Merrill, 1970.

Brantlinger, Patrick. "Victorians and Africans: The Genealogy of the Myth of the Dark Continent." In *"Race," Writing, and Difference*, edited by Henry Louis Gates, Jr., 185–222. Chicago: University of Chicago Press, 1986.

Braxton, Joanne M. *Black Women Writing Autobiography: A Tradition within a Tradition*. Philadelphia: Temple University Press, 1989.

Broderick, Francis. *W. E. B. Du Bois: Negro Leader in a Time of Crisis.* Stanford: Stanford University Press, 1959.

Brown, Herbert Ross. *The Sentimental Novel in America, 1789–1860.* Durham: Duke University Press, 1940.

Bruss, Elizabeth W. *Autobiographical Acts: The Changing Situation of a Literary Genre.* Baltimore: Johns Hopkins University Press, 1976.

Bunche, Ralph. "Reconstruction Reinterpreted." *Journal of Negro Education* 4 (October 1935): 568.

Butterfield, Stephen. *Black Autobiography in America.* Amherst: University of Massachusetts Press, 1974.

Byerman, Keith E. "Hearts of Darkness: Narrative Voices in *The Souls of Black Folk.*" *American Literary Realism* 14 (1981): 43–51.

Cain, William E. "W. E. B. Du Bois's *Autobiography* and the Politics of Literature." *Black American Literature Forum* 24 (1990): 299–313.

Cooley, Thomas. *Educated Lives: The Rise of Modern Autobiography in America.* Columbus: Ohio State University Press, 1976.

Couser, G. Thomas. *American Autobiography: The Prophetic Mode.* Amherst: University of Massachusetts Press, 1979.

Cruse, Harold. *The Crisis of the Negro Intellectual.* New York: William Morrow, 1967.

Davis, Allison. *Leadership, Love, and Aggression.* New York: Harcourt, Brace, Jovanovich, 1983.

DeNevi, Donald P., and Doris A. Holmes. *Racism at the Turn of the Century: Documentary Perspectives, 1870–1910.* San Rafael: Leswing, 1973.

de Rougemont, Denis. *Love in the Western World.* Translated by Montgomery Belgion. New York: Harcourt, Brace, 1940.

Douglas, Ann. *The Feminization of American Culture.* New York: Knopf, 1977.

Drake, Willie Avon. "From Reform to Communism: The Intellectual Development of W. E. B. Du Bois." Ph.D. diss., Cornell University, 1985.

Du Bois, Shirley Graham. *His Day Is Marching On: A Memoir of W. E. B. Du Bois.* Philadelphia: Lippincott, 1971.

Earle, William. *The Autobiographical Consciousness.* Chicago: Quadrangle, 1972.

Egan, Susanna. *Patterns of Experience in Autobiography.* Chapel Hill: University of North Carolina Press, 1984.

Erikson, Erik H. *Childhood and Society.* 2d ed. New York: Norton, 1963.

———. *Life History and the Historical Moment: Diverse Presentations.* New York: Norton, 1975.

———. *Young Man Luther: A Study in Psychoanalysis and History.* New York: Norton, 1958.

Fletcher, Angus. *Allegory: The Theory of Symbolic Mode.* Ithaca: Cornell University Press, 1964.

Foucault, Michel. *The Archeology of Knowledge.* Translated by A. M. Sheridan Smith. New York: Pantheon, 1972.

————. *Language, Counter-Memory, Practice: Selected Essays and Interviews.* Edited by Donald F. Bouchard, translated by Donald F. Bouchard and Sherry Simon. Ithaca: Cornell University Press, 1977.

Frazier, E. Franklin. *Black Bourgeoisie.* New York: Macmillan, 1962.

Fredrickson, George M. *The Black Image in the White Mind: The Debate on Afro-American Character and Destiny, 1817–1914.* New York: Harper, 1971.

Gates, Henry Louis, Jr. *The Signifying Monkey: A Theory of Afro-American Literary Criticism.* New York: Oxford University Press, 1988.

————, ed. *Black Literature and Literary Theory.* New York: Metheun, 1984.

————, ed. *"Race," Writing, and Difference.* Chicago: University of Chicago Press, 1986.

Gayle, Addison, Jr., ed. *The Black Aesthetic.* Garden City: Doubleday, 1971.

Gornick, Vivian. *The Romance of American Communism.* New York: Basic, 1977.

Gossett, Thomas F. *Race: The History of an Idea in America.* Dallas: Southern Methodist University Press, 1963.

Gruesser, John Cullen. *White on Black: Contemporary Literature about Africa.* Urbana: University of Illinois Press, 1992.

Gunn, Giles. *The Culture of Criticism and the Criticism of Culture.* New York: Oxford University Press, 1987.

Gunn, Janet Varner. *Autobiography: Toward a Poetics of Experience.* Philadelphia: University of Pennsylvania Press, 1982.

Harris, Abram. "Reconstruction and the Negro." *New Republic* 7 (August 1935): 367–88.

Herbst, Jurgen. *The German Historical School in American Scholarship: A Study in the Transfer of Culture.* Ithaca: Cornell University Press, 1965.

"Herder, Johann Gottfried." *The Encyclopedia of Philosophy.* 1967.

Higham, John. *History: The Development of Historical Studies in the United States.* Englewood Cliffs: Prentice-Hall, 1965.

Horne, Gerald. *Black and Red: W. E. B. Du Bois and the Afro-American Response to the Cold War, 1944–1963.* Albany: State University of New York Press, 1986.

Howe, Frederic C. *Confessions of a Reformer.* 1925. Reprint. Chicago: Quadrangle, 1967.

Howe, Irving. *Politics and the Novel.* New York: Fawcett, 1967.

Howe, Irving, and Lewis Coser. *The American Communist Party: A Critical History*. Boston: Beacon Press, 1957.

Huggins, Nathan. *Harlem Renaissance*. New York: Oxford University Press, 1971.

James, William. *The Principles of Psychology*. 2 vols. New York: Holt, 1890.

Jameson, Frederic. *Marxism and Form: Twentieth-Century Dialectical Theories of Literature*. Princeton: Princeton University Press, 1974.

———. *The Political Unconscious: Narrative as a Socially Symbolic Act*. Ithaca: Cornell University Press, 1981.

———. *The Prison-House of Language: A Critical Account of Structuralism and Russian Formalism*. Princeton: Princeton University Press, 1972.

JanMohamed, Abdul. "The Economy of Manichean Allegory: The Function of Racial Difference in Colonialist Literature." In *"Race," Writing, and Difference*, edited by Henry Louis Gates, Jr., 78–106. Chicago: University of Chicago Press, 1986.

Johnson, James Weldon. *Along This Way: The Autobiography of James Weldon Johnson*. 1933. Reprint. New York: Viking, 1963.

———. *Black Manhattan*. 1930. Reprint. New York: Atheneum, 1969.

Johnston, Harry. *The Opening Up of Africa*. New York: Henry Holt, n.d.

Kirby, John B. *Black Americans in the Roosevelt Era: Liberalism and Race*. Knoxville: University of Tennessee Press, 1980.

Klehr, Harvey. *The Heyday of American Communism: The Depression Era*. New York: Basic, 1984.

Kostelanetz, Richard. *Politics in the African-American Novel: James Weldon Johnson, W. E. B. Du Bois, Richard Wright, and Ralph Ellison*. Westport: Greenwood, 1991.

Lacan, Jacques. *Écrits: A Selection*. Translated by Alan Sheridan. New York: Norton, 1977.

———. *Four Fundamental Concepts of Psycho-Analysis*. Translated by Alan Sheridan. New York: Norton, 1978.

Lasch, Christopher. *The Agony of the American Left*. New York: Vintage, 1969.

———. *The New Radicalism in America, 1889–1963: The Intellectual as Social Type*. New York: Vintage, 1965.

Lears, T. J. Jackson. *No Place of Grace: Antimodernism and the Transformation of American Culture, 1880–1920*. New York: Pantheon, 1981.

Lester, Julius, ed. *The Seventh Son: The Thought and Writings of W. E. B. Du Bois*. New York: Random House, 1971.

Levine, Lawrence. *Black Culture and Black Consciousness: Afro-American Folk Thought from Slavery to Freedom*. Oxford: Oxford University Press, 1977.

Lewald, H. Ernest. *The Cry of Home: Cultural Nationalism and the Modern Writer.* Knoxville: University of Tennessee Press, 1972.

MacCannell, Juliet Flower. *Figuring Lacan: Criticism and the Cultural Unconscious.* Lincoln: University of Nebraska Press, 1986.

MacKethan, Lucinda. "Plantation Fiction, 1865–1900." In *The History of Southern Literature,* edited by Louis D. Rubin, Jr., et al., 209–18. Baton Rouge: Louisiana State University Press, 1985.

Marable, Manning. *W. E. B. Du Bois: Black Radical Democrat.* Boston: Twayne, 1986.

Meier, August. *Negro Thought in America, 1880–1915.* Ann Arbor: University of Michigan Press, 1963.

Meier, August, and Elliott Rudwick. *Black History and the Historical Profession, 1915–1980.* Urbana: University of Illinois Press, 1986.

Miller, Christopher. *Blank Darkness: Africanist Discourse in French.* Chicago: University of Chicago Press, 1985.

Miller, Kelly. *Radicals and Conservatives: And Other Essays on the Negro in America.* 1908. Reprint. New York: Schocken, 1968.

Milligan, Nancy Muller. "W. E. B. Du Bois' American Pragmatism." *Journal of American Culture* 8.2 (1985): 31–37.

Moore, Jack B. *W. E. B. Du Bois.* Boston: Twayne, 1981.

Morison, Samuel Eliot. *Three Centuries of Harvard, 1636–1936.* Cambridge: Harvard University Press, 1936.

Oates, Stephen B. *To Purge This Land with Blood: A Biography of John Brown.* New York: Harper, 1970.

Oliver, Roland. *Sir Harry Johnston and the Scramble for Africa.* London: Chatto and Windus, 1964.

Olney, James. *Metaphors of Self: The Meaning of Autobiography.* Princeton: Princeton University Press, 1972.

————, ed. *Autobiography: Essays Theoretical and Critical.* Princeton: Princeton University Press, 1980.

Ovington, Mary White. *The Walls Come Tumbling Down.* New York: Harcourt, Brace and World, 1947.

Partington, Paul G., ed. *W. E. B. Du Bois: A Bibliography of His Published Writings.* Whittier, Calif.: Partington, 1977.

Pascal, Roy. *Design and Truth in Autobiography.* Cambridge: Harvard University Press, 1960.

Pocock, J. G. A. *Politics, Language and Time.* New York: Atheneum, 1973.

Quarles, Benjamin. *Black Abolitionists.* London: Oxford University Press, 1969.

Rampersad, Arnold. *The Art and Imagination of W. E. B. Du Bois.* Cambridge: Harvard University Press, 1976.

Record, Wilson. *The Negro and the Communist Party*. Chapel Hill: University of North Carolina Press, 1951.

―――. *Race and Radicalism: The NAACP and the Communist Party*. Ithaca: Cornell University Press, 1964.

Robinson, Cedric J. *Black Marxism: The Making of the Black Radical Tradition*. London: Zed, 1983.

Ross, B. Joyce. *J. E. Spingarn and the Rise of the NAACP, 1911–1939*. New York: Atheneum, 1972.

Royce, Josiah. *Race Questions, Provincialism and Other American Problems*. New York: Macmillan, 1908.

Rudwick, Elliott. *W. E. B. Du Bois: Voice of the Black Protest Movement*. Urbana: University of Illinois Press, 1982.

Ryan, Michael. *Marxism and Deconstruction: A Critical Articulation*. Baltimore: Johns Hopkins University Press, 1982.

Santayana, George. *The Genteel Tradition: Nine Essays*. Edited by Douglas L. Wilson. Cambridge: Harvard University Press, 1967.

Scheick, William J. *The Half-Blood: A Cultural Symbol in 19th Century American Fiction*. Lexington: University of Kentucky Press, 1979.

Scholes, Robert, and Robert Kellogg. *The Nature of Narrative*. New York: Oxford University Press, 1966.

Skinner, Elliott P. *African Americans and U.S. Policy toward Africa, 1850–1924*. Washington: Howard University Press, 1992.

Sollors, Werner. *Beyond Ethnicity: Consent and Descent in American Culture*. New York: Oxford University Press, 1986.

Spengeman, William C. *The Forms of Autobiography: Episodes in the History of a Literary Genre*. New Haven: Yale University Press, 1980.

Spero, Sterling. "The Negro's Role." *The Nation*, 24 July 1935, 108–9.

Stepto, Robert B. *From behind the Veil: A Study of Afro-American Narrative*. Urbana: University of Illinois Press, 1979.

Stewart, James B. "The Psychic Duality of Afro-Americans in the Novels of W. E. B. Du Bois." *Phylon* 44.2 (Summer 1983): 93–107.

Stocking, George W., Jr. *Race, Culture, and Evolution: Essays in the History of Anthropology*. New York: Free Press, 1968.

Stone, Albert E. *Autobiographical Occasions and Original Acts: Versions of American Identity from Henry Adams to Nate Shaw*. Philadelphia: University of Pennsylvania Press, 1982.

Sundquist, Eric. *To Wake the Nations: Race in the Making of American Literature*. Cambridge: Harvard University Press, 1993.

Taylor, Gordon O. "Voices from the Veil: Black American Autobiography." *Georgia Review* 35 (1981): 341–61.

Thorpe, Earl E. *Black Historians: A Critique*. New York: William Morrow, 1971.

Turner, Darwin W. "W. E. B. Du Bois and the Theory of a Black Aesthetic." *Studies in the Literary Imagination* 7 (Fall 1974): 1–21.

Tuttle, William M., ed. *W. E. B. Du Bois*. Englewood Cliffs: Prentice-Hall, 1973. Boston: Beacon Press. 1957.

Villard, Oswald Garrison. *John Brown, 1800–1859*. 1910. Reprint. New York: Knopf, 1943.

Wacker, R. Fred. *Ethnicity, Pluralism, and Race: Race Relations Theory in the United States before Myrdal*. Westport: Greenwood, 1983.

Walden, Daniel. "W. E. B. Du Bois: A Renaissance Man in the Harlem Renaissance." *Minority Voices* 2.1 (1977): 11–20.

Warren, Robert Penn. *John Brown: The Making of a Martyr*. New York: Payson and Clark, 1929.

Washington, Booker T. *Up from Slavery*. 1901. Reprint. New York: Bantam, 1959.

White, Hayden. *Metahistory: The Historical Imagination in Nineteenth Century Europe*. Baltimore: Johns Hopkins University Press, 1973.

———. *Tropics of Discourse: Essays in Cultural Criticism*. Baltimore: Johns Hopkins University Press, 1978.

White, Morton. *Social Thought in America: The Revolt against Formalism*. Boston: Beacon, 1957.

White, Walter. *A Man Called White*. 1948. Reprint. Bloomington: Indiana University Press, 1970.

Wiebe, Robert. *The Search for Order, 1877–1920*. New York: Hill and Wang, 1967.

Williams, Raymond. *Culture and Society, 1780–1950*. New York: Columbia University Press, 1958.

Woodard, Frederic. "W. E. B. Du Bois: The Native Impulse: Notes toward an Ideological Biography, 1868–1897." Ph.D. diss., University of Iowa, 1976.

Wright, William D. "The Socialist Analysis of W. E. B. Du Bois." Ph.D. diss., State University of New York at Buffalo, 1985.

Young, James O. *Black Writers of the Thirties*. Baton Rouge: Louisiana State University Press, 1973.

Ziff, Larzer. *Puritanism in America: New Culture in a New World*. New York: Viking, 1973.

Zinn, Howard. *The Politics of History*. Boston: Beacon Press, 1970.

Index

Broderick, Francis, 38
Brown, John, 5, 29, 151, 162–78,
210; Du Bois's identification with,
165–70; idealization of, 169–74
Burghardt, Idelbert (half-brother), 2
Burghardt, Tom (ancestor), 183

Cain, William, 179
"The Case," 112–14
"The Coming of John," 3; discussed,
31–34
"The Conservation of Races," 54, 93,
94, 163; discussed, 82–84
Creative Writings: themes in, 108;
poetic devices in, 108–9; discussed,
108–14; Christ imagery in, 110;
attitude toward beauty in, 113–
14
The Crisis, 100, 110, 154, 200, 203
"Criteria of Negro Art," 107, 108,
110, 114; discussed, 101–6; beauty
as abstract in, 102–3; role of
history in, 103–4; role of
propaganda in, 104
Crummell, Alexander, 27–29,
33, 210

Dark Princess, 115, 139, 145; as
allegory, 129, 132; discussed, 129–
37; realism in, 130; black middle
class in, 131; as bourgeois fantasy,
134–35
Darkwater, 7, 195, 202, 223; related
to *The Souls of Black Folk*, 181–82,
184, 186; discussed, 181–93; as
progressivist work, 182, 188–89; as
heroic narrative, 183–85; allegory
in, 184–85; dramatic structure of,
186; demonic whites in, 186–88;
literary aspects of, 190–93
Dewey, John, 188

discourse, 8, 18, 38, 52, 71, 81, 97,
201; deconstruction of, 79; of
historiography, 79–80, 95, 106; in
Gift of Black Folk, 84–86; on
Africa, 89–90; and art, 110, 115; in
John Brown, 176–77, 178; in
Darkwater, 181–82, 186–87,
188, 191
dominant culture, 10, 11, 13, 16, 35,
53, 161; discourse of, 81, 88, 99;
racism of, 98; and art, 103–4, 105
double consciousness, 15, 28, 37, 181
Douglas, Georgia, 100
Douglass, Frederick, 158, 162, 168,
169, 171
Du Bois, Alfred (father), 2, 3, 183–84
Du Bois, Burghardt (son), 29–31
Du Bois, Mary Burghardt (mother),
2–3, 183–84
Du Bois, William Edward Burghardt:
twenty-fifth birthday ceremony,
1–2; relationship with parents,
2–3; conflict with father figures,
3–4, 6, 8, 11; pattern of self-
marginalization, 5–6; academic
training, 38–39; conflict with
Oswald Garrison Villard and Paul
Elmer More, 178
Dunbar, Paul Laurence, 109
Dusk of Dawn, 7, 155, 205, 215, 217,
223; discussed, 193–204; self as
symbol in, 194–95, 204; self-
representation in, 195–96; theme
of education in, 195–97; heroic self
in, 198; importance of voice in,
199–200; conflict with Booker T.
Washington, 199–201; conflict
with NAACP, 201–3

Emerson, Ralph Waldo, 188, 193
Erikson, Erik, 3, 4, 6

master text, 10; discussed, 10–35; black identity in, 14–16; black masses as feminine in, 18; role of father figures, 18; Gospel of Pay in, 19–21, 25; discussion of Booker T. Washington in, 24–27, 200; Du Bois as father in, 29; death of son discussed, 29–31; discussion of spirituals, 34–35; and *John Brown*, 163–66, 167, 168; and *Darkwater*, 186, 188

"Spanish Fandango," 111–12

Stepto, Robert, 34

Stevens, Thaddeus, 65–66

Sumner, Charles, 65–66

The Suppression of the Slave-Trade, 7, 54, 56, 60, 62, 67, 68, 73, 98, 107, 140, 147, 165, 171; discussed, 38–50; economic argument in, 41–47; as moral drama, 44–47; lessons of, 48–50

talented tenth, 5, 23, 31, 131, 136, 145, 151, 153, 168, 190, 203, 210, 211, 216; defined, 225 (n. 9)

"The Talented Tenth," 54, 168

Thorpe, Earl, 36

Tillman, Ben, 143

Toomer, Jean, 100, 106, 107, 111

Truman, Harry, 3

Tubman, Harriet, 87

Turner, Henry, 90

University Negro Improvement Association, 142

Up from Slavery, 24

Villard, Oswald Garrison, 178

Wagner, Adolf, 39, 53

Walker, Madame C. J., 141, 142, 149, 150–51

Wallace, Henry, 210–11, 212

Walrond, Eric, 107

Washington, Booker T., 3, 4, 24–27, 50, 141, 142, 154, 162, 169, 198–99, 211

Watson, Tom, 143, 145

White, Hayden, 37

White, Walter, 203

Wiebe, Robert, 182

Wilson, Woodrow, 182, 211

Woodson, Carter G., 36

The World and Africa, 84, 89, 90, 93, 97, 98

Worlds of Color, 140

Wright, Richard, 106

"The Younger Literary Movement," 106

Zinn, Howard, 63